MY ACES, MY FAULTS

MY ACES,
MY FAULTS

NICK BOLLETTIERI
AND
DICK SCHAAP

AVON BOOKS ◆ NEW YORK

MY ACES, MY FAULTS is an original publication of Avon Books. This work has never before appeared in book form.

AVON BOOKS
A division of
The Hearst Corporation
1350 Avenue of the Americas
New York, New York 10019

Copyright © 1996 by Nick Bollettieri Tennis and Sports Academy, Inc., and Dick Schaap
Interior design by Rhea Braunstein
Photos courtesy of Jimmy Bollettieri except where otherwise noted.
Published by arrangement with Nick Bollettieri Tennis and Sports Academy, Inc., and Dick Schaap
Library of Congress Catalog Card Number: 96-22180
ISBN: 0-380-97306-5

Library of Congress Cataloging in Publication Data:

Bollettieri, Nick.
  My aces, my faults / by Nick Bollettieri and Dick Schaap.
    p.   cm.
1. Bollettieri, Nick. 2. Tennis coaches—United States—Biography. I. Schapp, Dick, 1934–   . II. Title.
GV994.B64A3 1996   96-22180
796.342'092—dc20   CIP

First Avon Books Hardcover Printing: September 1996

AVON TRADEMARK REG. U.S. PAT. OFF. AND IN OTHER COUNTRIES, MARCA REGISTRADA, HECHO EN U.S.A.

Printed in the U.S.A.

FIRST EDITION

QPM 10 9 8 7 6 5 4 3 2 1

I would like to dedicate this book to all tennis coaches, on the tour and in the schools, but especially to the memory of Tim Gullikson, who pushed himself to the limits of his ability as a player and then distinguished himself as the coach of Martina Navratilova and of Pete Sampras, arguably the two greatest players in the history of the game.

I would also like to dedicate this book to all tennis players, the pros and the hackers, but especially to the memory of Arthur Ashe, who was an athlete, a scholar and a gentleman, a champion in every sense of the word.

Tim and Arthur were my friends, and they remain my inspiration.

This book is for them, and also for my family: for my parents, who watched my struggles and my successes with great pride; and for my loving sister, Rita; and for my children, Jimmy, Danielle, Angel, Nicole and Alexandra, who fill me with love and pride.

And, of course, for Leah.

NICK BOLLETTIERI, PRO AND CON

Nick will always be the greatest tennis coach in the world.
—Carling Bassett Seguso

Nick is the ultimate motivator.
—Billie Jean King

Some people consider Nick Bollettieri to be nothing more than a hustler and a self-promoter. I see him as an inspiration. He overcame a severe tennis disability—not knowing a forehand from a backhand—to become one of the most famous coaches in the world.
—Mike Lupica
New York Daily News

Since I was thirteen years old, Nick has been there for me, through good times and bad. Without his influence, I'm not certain I would have become a professional player.
—Paul Annacone
Pete Sampras's coach

You could be dead tired, and Nick would get thirty minutes more out of you.
—Marianne Werdel Witmeyer
President, Women's Tennis Federation

NICK BOLLETTIERI, PRO AND CON

Nick puts his arm around you a lot more than he yells at you.
—Arthur Ashe

Nick loves adversity and never regrets a defeat.
—Ivo Barbic
Coach

The common thread among Nick's players is confidence. So much of winning in pro tennis is pure confidence. Nick understands how to instill confidence, how to make people believe in themselves.
—Tracy Austin

I like Nick Bollettieri as a person. I just can't stand what he has created in Bradenton—a boot camp for teenaged tennis players.
—John Feinstein
Hard Courts

The game is richer for having had Nick in it, and possibly Nick is, too.
—Gene Scott
Editor, *Tennis Week*

Arthur Ashe said to me, "If you want Venus and Serena to be great tennis players, take them to Nick."
—Richard Williams
Tennis parent

Nick can never remember names. For years, he called my daughter Tracey instead of Stacey.
—Bob Jellen
Tennis parent

NICK BOLLETTIERI, PRO AND CON

Bollettieri [is] a law-school dropout who never played competitive tennis.

—Peter de Jonge
New York Times Magazine

If Nick Bollettieri had been his coach, Portnoy would have used a two-fisted grip.

—Bill Conlin
Philadelphia Daily News

I've never seen Nick tired. He just keeps going and going and going.
—Mary Pierce

Nick Bollettieri is unique. Like him, love him, loathe him, he has stood the test of time.

—Neil Amdur
Sports editor, *New York Times*

Nick Bollettieri doesn't know anything about tennis.
—John McEnroe

Nick's passion for the game of tennis is unparalleled.
—Patrick McEnroe

Nick is inspiring—like Patton or Lombardi.
—Ron Simone
Tennis parent

NICK BOLLETTIERI, PRO AND CON

Nick is a believer—and he doesn't just believe in himself. He believes in his sport.

—Mary Carillo
Broadcaster

There is no one I would rather be in a fox hole with than Nick Bollettieri.

—Steve Contardi
Tennis coach

Nick Bollettieri has not only perfected the art of tanning, he has perfected the art of player development.
—Leif Shiras
All-American, Princeton University

Every mirror Dad walks by, he looks into.

—Angel Bollettieri

Nick's eccentric personality has aided him immensely.
—Phil Knight
Chairman of the board, Nike

Nick Bollettieri, in his own inimitable way, has contributed more to tennis than perhaps any other individual in the United States.
—Rolla Anderson
U.S. Tennis Association

Nick Bollettieri is the most charismatic person in tennis.
—Allen Fox
Pepperdine University coach

NICK BOLLETTIERI, PRO AND CON

When Nick teaches, he gives so much of himself that you try to improve as much for him as for yourself.

—Louis Marx Jr.

Nick motivates his students to be the best they can be. And he is also their caring friend.

—Donald Dell
Chairman and CEO, ProServ

Nick is a soft touch for a kid of any age who has a burning desire to excel at the game. He has the biggest heart in tennis.

—Dennis Emery
University of Kentucky

Headmaster Bollettieri gives invaluable tanning tips, marital counseling, pasta recipes, gurudimentary cosmology, kickbutt homilies—but never, never "No comment!" What more could you ask of a guy? Especially when you're looking for a column or sound bite.

—Bud Collins
Boston Globe/NBC

We are so lucky to have Nick in our game.

—Luke and Murphy Jensen

CONTENTS

CONTENTS

MY ACES,
MY FAULTS

INTRODUCTION:

EVERYTHING TO EXCESS

EVERYTHING TO EXCESS

I have collaborated on best-selling autobiographies with Joe Montana and Bo Jackson, Joe Namath and Jerry Kramer, and none of those muscular authors put nearly so much time and effort and thought into his story as Nick Bollettieri has put into his. Day after day, for more than a year, he bombarded me with tapes, notes, letters, documents, clippings, and telephone numbers. I think he wanted me to call everyone in the Western world to ask them what they thought of him.

Nick cared passionately about this book, just as he cares passionately about tennis, football, golf, his girlfriend, his children, his students, his assistants, his academy, his Sports Grille, his friends, his tan, his teeth, his waistline, his biceps, his sunglasses, his condo, and his cars, not necessarily in that order. Nick does nothing (that he enjoys) in moderation.

Nick Bollettieri is sixty-five years old, and in the past year, when he wasn't busy shooting golf in the low eighties or hanging ten in the Persian Gulf or stunt flying with the Blue Angels, he found time to take up in-line skating. He Rollerbladed with his seven-year-old daughter, who is his youngest child, and surfed with his forty-year-old son, who is his oldest.

When he was not traveling to Melbourne, Monte Carlo, or Dubai, Nick, a former U.S. Army paratrooper, journeyed to the gym at 6:30 every morning to work out for an hour with his personal trainer. Almost every day, he managed to steal some time in the sun, its rays ricocheting off a reflector and into his face, blackening his already bronzed skin. Once, when he was skiing the Alps with Rudi Sailer, the brother of the great Austrian Olympic champion Toni Sailer, a woman stared at Nick and said, "Aren't you a movie star?" Nick beamed, and the woman went on, "Aren't you Bill Cosby?" Nick could not have been more flattered.

Nick Bollettieri is not, however, the total Renaissance man. He does not love to do everything. He hates to go to museums. He hates to go to fancy restaurants. He hates to wear a tie. And he hates to go to sleep.

Nick has been accused of being compulsive, obsessive, brash, egotistical, dictatorial, ungrammatical, and vain, and he pleads guilty on all counts. One of his virtues, however, is that he can take both criticism and kidding without flinching and without bitterness. Nick is what he is, and what I love about him is that he doesn't pretend to be anything else.

To help prepare this book, Nick wrote to dozens of friends, rivals, students, and acquaintances, asking them to share their memories and their thoughts, good or bad, and an incredibly high percentage responded, almost all of them favorably. Even three of his five ex-wives gladly recalled their lives with Nick. "I wouldn't have missed it for the world," said Nancy, his second wife. "We're proud of the excellent work Nick's done," said Phyllis, his first wife. His third wife, Jeri, works for him at the Nick Bollettieri Tennis Academy

(NBTA) and occasionally goes out for dinner with him and their daughters and his girlfriend, Leah Rhodes, who also contributed her recollections. "Sometimes I wonder what it would be like to be with someone who has a normal schedule," Leah wrote, "whatever normal means these days. The thought passes quickly. I honestly cannot imagine my life with anyone else. How very boring it would be!"

Nick did not bother asking his fifth wife, Kellie, for comments; the wounds are still too fresh. Kellie is a very religious woman, and a couple of years ago, when an item appeared in a local newspaper mentioning an expensive antiqued crucifix she had purchased, I needled Nick, who was paying a sizable amount of alimony at the time. "Yeah, and you're on it."

Nick's college roommate, Jerry O'Leary, sat down and fired off a handwritten letter twenty pages long, recounting in detail episodes Nick had long forgotten. David Landow, a former student who had just run his first marathon, wrote, "I wanted you to know that my wearing a Bollettieri shirt for this event was a tribute to the many great experiences we have shared, as well as the inspiration that you have always provided. You always told me never to give up on my goals. I always wanted to run a marathon."

Julio Moros, who worked at Nick's side for fifteen years, then went off on his own in the late 1980s, scrawled a lengthy letter that concluded, "I love you, Nick." Fritz Nau, a coach who walked out on Nick to work for Andre Agassi in 1993, ended his note, "I love you, man." Fritz is still not going to get Nick's Bud Light.

All of Nick's children were anxious to talk about their

dad. Nicole and Alex, the youngest, agreed he could be grumpy at times, but they loved the gifts he lavished on them, loved the fact that they had a famous father. Angel, the middle child, a psychology major in college, remarked on Nick's insecurities and said she could never imagine being married to anyone like her father. Still she marveled at his energy and his ability to mesmerize people. "I have a hard time talking to my father," Angel admitted. "God knows why, he's leaned over backward. It's something that I've struggled with all my life. I get nervous any time we have a meal alone, just the two of us."

Jimmy, the oldest child, an accomplished tennis coach himself, but one who would rather be surfing or snapping photographs, lamented Nick's lack of appreciation of art and culture. Danielle, the oldest daughter, who chose to stay with her dad after her parents divorced and now works full-time for him, spoke of the frustration of always sharing her father, of his habit of including an entourage in all their plans. Danielle, incidentally, devoted countless hours to gathering material and checking facts for this book. None of his children was blind to Nick's flaws, but everyone was grateful he was their father.

This book examines all of Nick's remarkable life, his flaws and his virtues, but it does so within the dramatic framework of a seven-month period, starting at Wimbledon in July 1995, through the U.S. Open in August and September 1995, and concluding with the Australian Open in January 1996. During those seven months, in those three Grand Slam tournaments, so many of Nick's students, so many of the champions he helped forge—most notably Andre Agassi and Monica Seles,

EVERYTHING TO EXCESS

Boris Becker and Mary Pierce—achieved memorable victories, suffered devastating defeats, or both. Over the same period, two of Nick's teenaged prodigies—Mark Philippoussis and Anna Kournikova—began the pleasantly painful process of emerging as stars. Nick shared in all their triumphs and all their setbacks, and now he shares his aces and his faults with you.

—Dick Schaap
New York City
August 1, 1996

WIMBLEDON: THE WAR

The man I used to coach, Andre Agassi, was on one side of the net. The man I was now coaching, Boris Becker, was on the other. Becker used to be the No. 1 player in the world. Agassi was now the No. 1 player in the world. They were about to meet in the semifinals of the Wimbledon men's championship, the centerpiece of the most prestigious tennis tournament in the world. The winner would play Pete Sampras for the title.

I was sitting in the courtside box reserved for friends and family of the players. Of the four Grand Slam tournaments—the Australian, the French, and the U.S. Opens are the other three—Wimbledon is the only one that puts the friends and family of the opposing players in the same courtside box. This can create some interesting situations.

I was sitting right in between Barbara Becker, Boris's beautiful wife, and Brooke Shields, Andre's beautiful girlfriend, and through my Oakleys, my wraparound sunglasses, I could see my beautiful girlfriend, Leah Rhodes, sitting on the other side of the court, studying me through her binoculars. I was afraid to move. *Holy shit!* I thought. *What a day this is going to be!*

There are twelve seats in the players' box at Centre Court of the All England Lawn Tennis and Croquet Club, two rows of six. The Agassi camp had three seats in the top row and three in the bottom. So did the Becker team. I was in the top row on one side of Barbara, and Mike DePalmer Jr., Boris's traveling coach and hitting partner, sat on her other side.

I had known Mike since he was a child. His father had

helped me start the NBTA on the west coast of Florida in the late 1970s, and young Mike had been one of our earliest students. Both Mike and his father then went to the University of Tennessee, Mike Sr. to coach the tennis team, Mike Jr. to become an all-American. Young Mike spent the next several years on the pro tour, enjoying greater success in doubles than in singles.

Now Mike Jr. and Mike Sr. were both back at the academy, Mike Sr. directing our tennis program and Mike Jr. serving as one of our elite coaches. I had assigned young Mike, who was in his early thirties, to travel with Boris.

I had never met Brooke Shields before. When I stopped coaching Andre two years earlier, he was still seeing Barbra Streisand. Like most people, I never quite figured out that relationship, never knew whether it was primarily physical or spiritual. I could understand Streisand dating a man less than half her age; I'd always preferred to date younger women myself. (My Leah was thirty-two, exactly half my age, at the time of the Wimbledon semifinal.) And I could understand the star appeal of Streisand. I knew the relationship between Andre and Barbra was not a casual one. He used to call her from Japan and Australia and sometimes he'd stay on the phone with her for five and six hours at a time.

Andre met Brooke Shields late in 1993, five months after he and I parted. When she entered the box at Wimbledon, she said, "Hi," to me, and I said, "Hello, dear, I'm Nick Bollettieri," and she seemed very pleasant, very friendly.

On the other side of Brooke sat Brad Gilbert, Andre's current coach, and his wife, Kim. Brad, too, had attended the NBTA, never as a full-time live-in student going to one of the local high schools, but as a young touring professional who wanted to polish his strokes and his strategy. His sister, Dana, had also spent time at the academy and had tried the women's tour. The Gilberts came from the San Francisco Bay area, and Dana always used to bring us loaves of sourdough bread.

Brad never gave the academy even a crumb of credit for the considerable success he enjoyed as a professional. Brad was a very intelligent player, a shrewd strategist who was not above using gamesmanship to compensate for the physical skills he lacked. He wrote a book about his style of play, and he called it *Winning Ugly*. His game may not have been pretty—his serve bordered on the grotesque—but he earned almost $5 million in prize money during his playing career, and once, at the start of 1990, he ranked fourth in the world, his highest singles ranking, behind only Ivan Lendl, Stefan Edberg, and Boris Becker.

Brad had a history with Becker. He put Boris out of the U.S. Open in the fourth round in 1987, a rare five-set defeat for Becker, who had won the first two sets. Beating Boris lifted Brad into the quarterfinals, one of only two times he ever got that far in thirty-seven Grand Slam tournaments. It amazes me that Brad Gilbert never reached even one semifinal in a Grand Slam, but I'm sure Brad has a good explanation.

Brad started coaching Andre in March 1994, eight months after our separation, three months after Andre had surgery to remove scar tissue from his right wrist, one month after Andre won a tournament in Scottsdale, Arizona. Andre had dropped to No. 32 in the world before the Scottsdale victory reversed his fall. He was No. 24 when he joined up with Brad.

"When he came to me," Gilbert said of Agassi, "he was

a diamond that was uncut. He could play some great tennis, but there were flaws all over the place."

Brad did not mention that Andre, under my coaching, had by the age of twenty-two won Wimbledon and had reached the finals of the French championship twice and the U.S. Open once, not too bad for a flawed and uncut diamond.

Andre, who was clearly hurt by our split, joined Brad in sniping at me. "If Brad had been my coach earlier," he said, "I think I would have been No. 1 in the world when I was eighteen." I got him only as high as No. 3 in the world when he was eighteen.

Of course Brad deserves credit for the job he's done coaching Andre—Brad's smart and he's a serious student of the game—but sometimes I think he tries to take a little too much credit. I draw the line when Brad suggests that if he had had Andre at a younger age, he would have gotten him to the top sooner. I believe that if Brad had had Andre at a younger age, Andre would have been in trouble.

I don't think Brad, who is only nine years older than Andre, would have had the sensitivity and the mentality and the experience to deal with Andre when he was young, when he was a teenager, when the most important thing for him was survival. I think I helped Andre get through his most difficult years, get through them without giving up on himself or on tennis, and strangely perhaps, I think that my departure from Andre helped him, too, gave him a wake-up call, a jolt, a kick in the pants. I think it created in Andre the same sort of feeling it would have created in me: Sonuvabitch, I'm going to show you I don't need you. I'm gonna stick it up your ass.

Brad and I did not exchange pleasantries at courtside.

Boris's racquet stringer/bodyguard, Ulrich "Ulli" Kuhnel, and his road manager/masseur, Waldmar "Val" Kliesing, used two of the Becker seats in the front row; the other was empty. The Agassi team also used only two of its front-row seats, one for Ian Hamilton, the director of tennis marketing for Nike, an old friend of mine—I had helped bring Andre and Nike together, a very profitable match for both of them— and the other for Steve Miller, the director of all sports marketing for Nike.

Barbara on one side of me and Brooke on the other were both obviously very nervous, very much into the confrontation between my past and present pupils. Brooke kept saying things like, "Come on, sweet, come on, sweet, you can do it, sweet," and more than once, she volunteered, "I love Andre. I just love my Andre."

In my own way, I still loved Andre, even after his bitter words following our breakup. Andre lived at the NBTA through most of his teenage years. Part of that time, he lived in my home, with me and my wife Kellie and our children. I had a remarkably talented group of students at the time, including Jim Courier and David Wheaton, but Andre was my favorite. He was the chosen one. They knew it, and so did he.

In 1991, Kellie, who was my fifth wife, who had been incredibly patient in housing and feeding the army of young players who shared our home, told me she was very unhappy that I was spending so much time on the road, away from the family, working with Andre. She told me I had to make

WIMBLEDON: THE WAR

a choice: either her and the children or "that character," Andre. "It's us or him," she said.

I didn't hesitate. "I have to travel with Andre," I said.

"Then get your ass out of here," Kellie said.

"What do you mean?" I said.

"I'm kicking you out. You're not a member of this family anymore."

I packed up, and within half an hour, I was gone. I took $4,000 and some dirty clothes, nothing more. I left the house and everything else to Kellie.

I hated to leave my children, young Nicole and Alex, but I still think I made the right choice. Even though Andre and I also split up two years later.

Now, at Wimbledon, Andre was the enemy. Now I was on Boris Becker's team. I resented the way Andre had dealt with me financially, that despite promises and hints from both Andre and his father, suggestions that my years of commitment to them would be amply rewarded, I had never shared fairly in the millions and millions of dollars Andre had earned from tennis. Boris was paying me a handsome salary to be his coach, rewarding me with bonuses when he did well and seeing to it that I and my Leah and my assistants lived and traveled first class. Boris was the first player with whom I'd ever had a contract, and he had been more than fair, more than generous.

Naturally, I wanted him to win. More than that, I wanted Boris to kick Andre's butt. Andre had beaten Boris the last eight times they'd played, but in most of those matches, I was coaching Andre. I told him exactly what he had to do to beat Boris. Now I was telling Boris exactly what he had to do to beat Andre.

The first set began, and Boris, who had won the first of his three Wimbledon championships when he was only seventeen, opened with a big ace, a huge ace. Then Boris served again, and Andre just ripped it. He ripped the next return, too. Then Boris came in, fell down, and Andre passed him. Within seconds, it seemed, we were broken in the first game. The second game went to Agassi just as swiftly.

Andre was playing unbelievably well. He could've gotten a speeding ticket for how fast he was going through Boris. Barbara Becker could barely watch. She turned to Mike De-Palmer and said, "Mike, sit over here next to Nick. It might bring us better luck." Barbara was very superstitious. She switched places with Mike.

It didn't help. Andre won the first set, 6–2, then took a 4–1 lead in the second. He was up one set and two service breaks, and every shot he hit was crisp, accurate, intimidating. How well was Andre playing? He "used his ground strokes like flamethrowers," Robin Finn wrote in the *New York Times*, "and treated Becker like a cross between a target and a punching bag."

"I've never seen anyone hit the tennis ball the way he did," Boris said afterward.

"Don't you dare put your head down if Andre beats the crap out of you in the beginning of the match," I had told Boris that morning. "Don't you dare put your head down and let him think for one second that you've given up."

But the way the match started, it was all I could do to

WIMBLEDON: THE WAR

keep *my* head up. Everything I had told Boris to do was backfiring. I was almost ready to give up.

On one side of me, Barbara Becker was in agony. On the other, Brooke Shields was beaming.

This was July 7, 1995. I had by then known Andre Agassi for more than eleven years, which was almost half his life.

1

RAISING ANDRE

RAISING ANDRE

On January 1, 1984, the CBS television program *60 Minutes* ran a segment about the NBTA in Bradenton, Florida. The report was called "Tennis Boot Camp," and it began with me on the court, coaching:

> NICK BOLLETTIERI: *Don't tense up. Don't use so much body. Don't spin. Don't ...*
>
> MORLEY SAFER: *Nick Bollettieri is a professional coach—some would say a professional tyrant, a scold, a hard taskmaster.*
>
> NICK BOLLETTIERI: *No misses at all, again, up, hit under it. Come on! Pick it up! Come on, more aggressive, Donna. More aggressive, dear.*

Not long after the program was on the air, my phone rang. I picked it up and heard a raspy voice say, "Is this Mr. Bollettieri?"

"Yes, it is," I said.

"This is Mike Agassi, and I just watched you on television," the caller said. "I have a son, and I know that if he comes to you, you can make him a champion."

MY ACES, MY FAULTS

Mike Agassi, I later learned, had been a boxer on the Iranian Olympic team in 1948 and 1952. After his second Olympics, he had moved to the United States, to Chicago, tried professional boxing, gave it up quickly, decided he hated cold weather, and settled in Las Vegas. He had learned to play tennis in Iran, and he turned to the sport with a passion. He dreamed that one of his children would become a great player.

Mike and Elizabeth Agassi had four children, two boys and two girls, all of whom Mike taught and pushed to play the game. The oldest child, Rita, rebelled against her father and, to escape him, at a very young age married Pancho Gonzalez, who was, many years earlier, in the 1950s, the greatest tennis player in the world. She and her father stopped speaking to each other. Mike's other daughter, Tammi, was good enough to play college tennis at Texas A & M University. The older son, Phillip, played at the University of Nevada–Las Vegas and briefly gave the pro tour a try, but his confidence and his self-esteem had been shaken by years of harsh criticism and scant praise from his father. Andre, the youngest child, was Mike's great hope.

When Andre was an infant, Mike hung a tennis ball above his crib so that he would learn to follow it with his eyes. When Andre was big enough to sit in a high chair, Mike taped a cut-down Ping-Pong paddle to his hand and tossed him balloons to swat. As soon as he could stand, Andre was swinging a full-size racquet. His hand-and-eye coordination was already extraordinary.

At the age of three, Andre was invited to play an exhibition match in the Robert F. Kennedy Memorial Tennis Tournament at Forest Hills but was unable to participate because he had a ruptured appendix. (It was a real injury; he wasn't faking it.) At the age of four, he played an exhibition against the most talented of all tennis hustlers, Bobby Riggs, at the Tropicana Hotel in Las Vegas. By the time he was eight, Andre had met most of the major tennis stars in the world, from Björn Borg to Jimmy Connors to Ilie Nastase, and he had hit with many of them.

Mike had him on the tennis court four hours or more every day, facing a battery of ball machines specially designed to spit balls at him from every angle. Mike estimated that his older children hit seven to eight thousand balls a week and that Andre hit fourteen thousand.

"I taught him to hit and to hit and to hit," Mr. Agassi said when he called me the first time. "Now I can't do anything more. He doesn't listen to me. He doesn't want to play. And Las Vegas isn't the place for him. If he comes to you, I know he can make it."

Mr. Agassi told me that he wasn't a rich man, that he was a captain in a night club, the show room at the MGM Grand, but that he was willing to pay Andre's way at the academy. The *60 Minutes* segment had pointed out that the cost of the NBTA in 1984 was close to $1,500 a month, which did not include tuition at one of two local private high schools, Bradenton Academy or Saint Stephen's. "Whatever it takes," Mr. Agassi said, "I'm going to do it. I want him to be a champion."

MORLEY SAFER: Anyone who comes here thinking he's going to play a game is quickly disillusioned. This is work—child labor, if you like—of the most grueling, most exacting kind. But it is self-inflicted. Certain tennis parents notwithstanding, these kids are here because they want to be here, to make a perfect backhand more perfect, to make their overheads one hundred percent unreturnable . . .

I had heard of Andre Agassi but only vaguely, of his success in junior tournaments on the West Coast, competing against, among others, Pete Sampras and Michael Chang, who were both younger than he. "I'll tell you what, Mr. Agassi," I said. "I'll give you somewhat of a break. I'll give your son a partial scholarship."

I offered the Agassis almost a fifty percent discount, agreeing to take Andre on for $800 a month. Mr. Agassi sent me a check for $1,600 to cover the first two months, and Andre, at the age of thirteen, arrived in Bradenton.

For the first few weeks, I really didn't pay much attention to him. He was on the back courts, battling the other thirteen- and fourteen-year-olds, struggling to establish himself, to earn respect from his peers. I was busy on the front courts, concentrating on my rising stars, Aaron Krickstein and Carling Bassett.

They were both only sixteen, but the year before Aaron had become the youngest player to win a Grand Prix singles championship, and he had reached the round of sixteen in the U.S. Open. Carling already ranked among the top twenty women in the world, and later in 1984, a month before her seventeenth birthday, she would reach the semifinals of the U.S. Open. I had dreams that one of them might be the first student from the academy to win one of the Grand Slam championships.

RAISING ANDRE

But it was impossible to ignore Andre for long. He was too talented. He was a short, skinny kid who tried to kill every shot, who never held back. If the ball went in, fine. If it didn't, he would just hit it harder the next time. You could see the enormous power he had already developed in his forehand. You could also see that he was a scrapper, a street fighter, that he would bite and scratch and claw to win. I liked what I saw. I was a street fighter, too.

After the second month, I sent Mr. Agassi his money back. "Look," I told him, "I think you're right. Your boy has the potential to be an outstanding player someday." We put Andre on a full scholarship.

Andre remained on scholarship, one way or another, the rest of the time he was with me. In his early teens, he received several grants from the International Tennis and Educational Foundation, a fund established largely by wealthy friends of mine. On one application for financial aid, Andre wrote, "I, André Agassi [he liked to put an accent on the *e* in his name then], have been playing tennis since I was old enough to walk." On another, Andre predicted, "I can do quite well playing professional tennis."

In 1984, his first year at the academy, after he turned fourteen, Andre won the National Boys Indoor sixteen-and-under singles and doubles championships. Every time he played a match, he had to report the result to his father, but no matter how well Andre did, he never quite seemed to measure up to Mr. Agassi's expectations. If Andre called Las Vegas and said, "Dad, I won two and two," meaning 6–2 and 6–2, Mike would say, "Why wasn't it love and love?" Mike never congratulated Andre and often excoriated him.

MY ACES, MY FAULTS

If Andre's ability was unmistakable, so was his attitude. At the beginning, he made no secret of the fact that he didn't want to be at the academy. He wanted to be with his friends eating chicken fingers at the tennis club in Las Vegas, and even though he had battled fiercely with his father about his training regimen, he objected to the fact that his father had sent him away. He would call home and tell his father that I was changing his grip, I was changing his style, I was hurting his game, hoping that his father would panic and bring him home. I talked to Mr. Agassi; I reassured him. He was supportive. He wanted Andre to be in Bradenton.

I had never met a kid quite like Andre. Rules were made for him to break. Adults were made for him to test. Schedules were made for him to ignore. He didn't dress like anyone else. He didn't look like anyone else. He didn't practice like anyone else. He didn't even play matches like anyone else.

Start with his appearance. He walked different, with his pigeon-toed gait, and he looked different, with his big eyes accented by makeup and, after he went through a crew-cut stage, his frosted, tinted hair running down his back. Sometimes he dyed his hair red, sometimes orange, sometimes both. He let his nails grow long, too, and painted them with polish, and he pierced his ears and wore earrings. He even wore lipstick once in a while. I was told his look had something to do with heavy metal or punk rock or something like that. I preferred jazz. The girls at the academy thought Andre was sexy. I thought he was weird.

Practice? He slept through some sessions and cut others short. If he wasn't hitting the ball just the way he wanted to, he'd quit. Matches? Andre would go up against a strong opponent, someone who figured to be able to beat him, and Andre would wipe him out in the first set, annihilate him. Then the challenge would be gone, and Andre would be bored. He'd stop playing, literally or figuratively. He'd walk off in the middle of a point, or his mind would wander off.

Once, in Pensacola, Florida, playing in a tournament against a guy he didn't like, Andre showed his disdain by announcing he would beat the guy wearing jeans, high tops, and heavy makeup. He looked more like a rock musician, I suppose, than a tennis player, but he won the match.

Andre seemed to me to be a ticking time bomb, waiting to explode. With so many kids, you could read their future, see exactly where they were heading. Not Andre. He could skyrocket. He could tumble. He could dominate. He could self-destruct. The thin line between triumph and disaster was never thinner, and the potential for both was enormous.

He drove me crazy. I was used to intimidating kids. I was harsher then than I am now. I was also louder. And less flexible. Everything had to be my way. Andre flouted my rules, defied my discipline, violated the spirit of the NBTA and of Bradenton Academy. Dr. Murray Gerber, who ran the private school, threatened to kick Andre out almost every time his hair changed color. I pleaded for Andre. "Hey, Doc," I'd say, "I know you've got those rules, but you've got to give me a little leeway here." Dr. Gerber was, reluctantly, understanding.

So was I. I heard stories about drinking and drug abuse, about Andre and other students experimenting with marijuana and with psychedelic mushrooms that supposedly thrived in the cow pastures adjacent to the academy. Once, when he

MY ACES, MY FAULTS

was about fifteen, Andre built a pyramid in his room of miniature Jack Daniel's bottles, all of them empty. How did they get empty? None of my coaches could figure it out. They never saw the bottles full, only empty. Maybe Andre bought empty bottles. It's possible. I believe it. The pyramid kept growing. I also heard stories about Andre visiting the rooms of female students at the academy, but he was never caught in the wrong room at the wrong time. Maybe he just wanted to borrow nail polish, lipstick, or hair spray. It's possible.

We had strict rules against the use of drugs and alcohol and tobacco at the NBTA, and over the years more than one student was expelled for violating those rules, but nobody ever presented any proof that Andre drank or smoked pot or did whatever you do with mushrooms. What would I have done if I had seen proof? I'd like to think that I would've treated Andre just like any other student, that I would have kicked him out. But I don't know. I'm not sure. I could see his talent; I could sense his appeal, his presence, even his commercial potential—at junior tournaments, coaches and parents would wander away from their own kids' matches to watch Andre play—and, to be honest, I didn't always treat the stars at the academy the way I treated everyone else. They got more of my attention. Sometimes I was harder on them. Sometimes I was softer. I played favorites.

When we caught Andre breaking minor rules, skipping classes or practices, I punished him the same way I punished other kids. He had to pull weeds around my house, mow the lawn, trim the hedges, wash dishes, polish my cars.

In Andre's second year at the academy, when he was

fifteen, I decided that, as gifted as he was, I couldn't take any more of his antics. I was going to kick him out. I was going to make an example of him. We couldn't have one set of rules for Andre Agassi and one set for everyone else. It was over. I let all my top pros know that Andre was on the way out.

I summoned Andre to my office. I yelled at him. I scolded him. I lectured him. I told him, "Andre, you just can't go to school the way you want, in red hair, orange hair, lipstick, earrings, everything else."

Andre heard me out, then looked at me and said, "Do you ever listen?"

"Not very often," I admitted.

"Well, try it," he said, and then he opened up. He thanked me for what I'd done to try to help him, but he let me know exactly what he didn't like about the academy, what he thought of some of the coaches, what he thought of the food, what he thought of the rules and the curfew and the boot-camp atmosphere. He held nothing back. He stood up to me, which was very rare, and I was impressed. I actually listened.

He also told me about his life in Las Vegas, what his father had sacrificed for him and his brothers and sisters, what his mother had put up with, what they had all gone through, what they had all suffered. "If I didn't leave Las Vegas," Andre said, "either my dad was going to pop me or I was going to pop him, and I was probably going to quit tennis."

We talked about his attitude toward tennis, his love/hate relationship to the game, which very likely reflected his attitude toward his father and maybe toward the academy, too. He let me know that he believed he was special, he was going places, and that if I worked with him, concentrated on him, gambled on him, I would benefit, and so would the academy.

I began to recognize that I couldn't treat Andre Agassi the way I had treated other students, that he was like a wild horse, and I had to capitalize on his free spirit, not break it.

Sometimes I wonder what would have happened if Andre hadn't convinced me that he should stay at the academy. Suppose I had kicked him out. Would he have turned on tennis? Would he have walked away from the game? He might have. He might be dealing blackjack in Las Vegas today.

I told Andre I would keep him in the academy, and I would continue to fight to keep him in school, and as he was about to leave, he turned and smiled and said, "Hey, Coach, Dr. Gerber said I had to cut my hair. Would you take care of that?"

I did. I didn't think a person had to be measured by the length of his hair.

The next day, I found a huge teddy bear in my office, a toy Andre had won during a visit to Busch Gardens in Tampa. He had been planning to take it home to a girlfriend in Las Vegas. Instead, he explained in a note, he was leaving it for my young daughter, Nicole. "It wouldn't fit in the plane," Andre wrote.

My oldest child, my son Jimmy Boy, from my first marriage, befriended Andre. So did one of my coaches, Fritz Nau. Jimmy was more than fifteen years older than Andre, Fritz more than twenty, but they could relate to him. Jimmy was into rock music and photography; Fritz, who looked

RAISING ANDRE

much younger than he was, talked to the kids in their own language, called them Little Dudes. They called him Big Dude.

One of my jobs was to juggle Andre and his father, maintain peace, or at least a truce, between them. I had to give Andre the praise that his father withheld, and I had to give Mr. Agassi the credit that Andre withheld. I had to reassure both of them, pat both of them on the back. I was like a second father to Andre. I don't know what I was like to Mr. Agassi.

Andre wasn't much of a student—he liked to sit in class and ignore the teacher and write poetry, none of which he ever showed me—but he managed to stay in school and stay in the academy. He did stir up trouble. He liked to sit in the back of the cafeteria, and as his fellow students picked up their meals, he made loud comments about them. "Hey, how 'bout a little more cottage cheese?" he'd yell to a girl who was overweight. "Cut out those fried foods!"

Andre did get kicked off a junior team that was being sponsored by Nike. Ian Hamilton of Nike found out that Andre, always playing the angles, was selling the sneakers and the sweatsuits the company was giving him.

Late in 1985, after Andre had been at the academy for more than a year, his brother Phillip came to Bradenton to live with him. (His sister Tammi also came to Florida to train at the NBTA on a scholarship and to attend Bradenton Academy; she took school more seriously than Andre did.) At fifteen, Andre was already thinking about turning professional; Phillip, who was in his early twenties, was going to be his father, his mother, his traveling coach, his trainer, his manager, all in one. Who got Andre on track as a tennis player? Certainly, Mr. Agassi got him started, taught him the basic weapons. I helped polish those weapons, and so did Brad Gilbert. But the person who did the most for Andre, I think, was Phillip. He sacrificed a large part of his own life for his brother.

By 1985, Jim Courier was living at the academy, and so were David Wheaton, Martin Blackman, Mark Knowles, David Kass, John Falbo, and Chris Garner, all of them in their midteens, all of them talented, and all of them fiercely competitive. Everyone of them won at least one major junior tournament in singles or doubles. Andre at one time shared a dormitory suite with Falbo (the national sixteen-and-under singles champion in 1985) and Blackman (who won the same title the following year). Both Agassi and Courier eventually rose to No. 1 in the world, and Wheaton ranked as high as No. 12, but in the mid-1980s, Chris Garner, from Bay Shore, Long Island, a slender six-footer who was a year older than Agassi and Courier, was clearly the best of them all, the most accomplished.

Why didn't Garner ever make it into the top one hundred in the world? Maybe because he didn't have the kind of huge weapon you need in the modern power game; maybe he needed a killer serve. Maybe he was just too nice a kid; maybe he needed a killer instinct. Or maybe, as he told people, he got to a certain point, and when he tried to lift himself to another level, he couldn't quite break through, he got frustrated, and his confidence suffered. In 1994, when Andre rose to No. 2, Chris was ranked 474th in the world. It's not bad to be one of the five hundred best in the world at anything, but Chris had dreamed of being much more.

RAISING ANDRE

These gifted juniors fought some ferocious battles on the backcourts of the academy, and every three or four weeks, when we had what we called our Grand Prix tournaments, our intra-academy championships, with stereos for prizes, they played for blood. "You went to war," Jim Courier said. Most of them had a grudging respect for each other, but there was real animosity, too. Some of the kids resented David Wheaton, felt that he was pampered by his parents, that he was a little too good to be true.

> *There was a camaraderie based on mutual respect and survival.*
> *Mutual respect because we were good and knew it and made sure everybody else knew it. There were two kinds of bragging rights at Nick's: one for breaking the rules and getting away with it and one for winning/being a player. Andre and I had both.*
> *Survival because the academy was tough, Nick was a tough SOB, tough but fair, and it came down the line. The pros who supervised us at night were tough, and sometimes mean, and we the kids were for the most part rebellious smart-asses. The key was never getting caught breaking the rules, and never letting "them," the pros, know when they got to you.*
> —Martin Blackman

> *Andre and I got along well. I always let him be the king.*
> —John Falbo

Monica Seles came to the academy early in 1986, only twelve years old, and even though Andre was three and a half years older, they had some unbelievable contests, seeing who could hit the sharpest angles and playing the box game: testing their accuracy and their speed by aiming forehands and backhands at a corner of the court marked off by rubber cones. Monica would win her share of the contests, but in a match, of course, Andre would have been too strong for her. Once, when they were rallying and Andre put the ball away, Monica got very upset. "Dear," I reminded her, "that's Andre Agassi. You have to be reasonable with your expectations." She turned to me with tears in her eyes and said, "I can beat him." Courier went on the court once to rally with her, and before he even loosened up, Monica hit two winners—boom! boom!—and Jim marched off, fuming. "I'll never hit with her again," he said, using slightly spicier language.

We worked on Andre's game. We pulled him up to the baseline, then inside the baseline, got him hitting everything on the rise. Others played behind the baseline, but Andre would come forward, challenge the ball, and hit the bloody hell out of it. When we worked on Andre's return of serve, we had the server stand a step or two inside the baseline to test and quicken Andre's reflexes. We marveled at his forehand and drilled and drilled him on his two-handed backhand.

When Andre turned sixteen in the spring of 1986, he was also ready to turn pro. I called a good friend of mine, Bill Shelton, who had worked on tennis camps with me, represented Prince in the early days of the oversized racquets, and then become a player agent for ProServ, the company, directed by Donald Dell, that was representing me. When Shelton left ProServ to join a splinter group, Advantage International, I stayed with ProServ, but Bill remained my friend.

RAISING ANDRE

"Bill," I said, "I've got somebody for you. I've got tennis's next superstar."

"Who's that?" he said.

"This kid," I said, "Andre Agassi. He's been at the academy for a few years, and now he's ready to play professionally. Get some contracts and get down here."

Bill Shelton quickly got together with Andre, and they hit it off right away. Bill became Andre's agent, Phillip was his brother and his road manager, I was the coach, Raul Ordonez the hitting partner, and Fritz Nau the ball feeder and bullshitter, the liaison between me and Andre. Team Agassi quickly took shape.

But Andre's professional career did not get off to an auspicious start. Late in July, he played in the Sovran Bank D.C. National Tennis Classic in Washington and he got beaten badly in the first round. He hit moon balls. He double-faulted. He missed easy shots. He looked like he was going to cry. He stormed out of the stadium and threw away his racquets and told his brother and Bill Shelton that he was never going to play tennis again. They found me, and I tracked down Andre and asked him, "What's the matter?"

"I can't make it," Andre said.

"Yes, you can," I said, "and you will. Do you see me wearing a watch?"

Andre looked at my wrist. "No," he said.

"You know why?" I said. "Because there's no time clock on you. I'm going to stay in your corner and we're going to battle and we're going to make it. You have everything you need to become a star."

Andre stared at me. "You really mean that, Nick?" he said.

"I mean it with all my heart and soul," I said.

"Jesus Christ," said Andre, "that's great!"

The next week, he went to Vermont for the Stratton Mountain Classic. Andre won his first three matches, and one of his victims was Tim Mayotte, a real gentleman who was then ranked among the top twenty players in the world. "If he continues to play the way he did today," Mayotte said after the match, "he'll be quite a player."

In the quarterfinals, Andre met John McEnroe, the No. 1 player in the world for much of the 1980s, the three-time Wimbledon and four-time U.S. Open champion. McEnroe was making a comeback at Stratton Mountain. He had taken a six-and-a-half-month vacation from tennis to revive his body and his mind, to rekindle his enthusiasm.

McEnroe knocked Agassi out of the tournament, 6–3, 6–3, but not before he saw one of Agassi's forehand returns-of-service go whizzing past him. "That's one of the hardest-hit balls I've ever seen," McEnroe said.

John McEnroe advanced to the semifinals at Stratton Mountain, where he, in turn, was beaten, by the reigning Wimbledon champion, a German teenager named Boris Becker.

WIMBLEDON: THE BREAK

At the end of the fifth game of the second set of the Wimbledon men's semifinal, NBC Sports, before going to a commercial, trained one of its cameras on the courtside box filled with friends and family of the players. The camera zoomed in on Brooke Shields and me. She was radiant, shaking hands with a friend. I was to her right, wearing a gray Adidas shirt and a wan smile.

When Agassi, leading, 4–l, served to start the sixth game, Becker hit a backhand return wide. Fifteen–love. The sixth straight point for Andre. "This is really a scary exhibition of tennis so far," John McEnroe told the NBC audience. "I mean, Agassi is jerking him around, and Becker must feel like a yo-yo."

Three years earlier, in the 1992 semifinal at Wimbledon, Andre had routed McEnroe, 6–4, 6–2, and 6–3. John had not forgotten. "I know how Becker feels right now," he said.

Then, suddenly, the big man came alive. Boris pounced on Andre's second serve and won the next point. Fifteen–all. Andre again missed his first serve, and Becker moved to the net aggressively and won the point. "A couple of loose points, rare loose points, for Andre," said McEnroe, who had counseled Andre on his game and who, I always felt, would've loved to have become Andre's coach.

The next point lasted twenty-five seconds and ended when Andre hit a shot long. Ahead, 15–40, double-break point, Boris set himself to receive the next serve. He wiped the sweat from his brow, blew on his fingertips.

Agassi saved the game with a beautiful backhand winner,

slicing the ball across the court. "That's impossible," said the announcer, Dick Enberg.

Andre served again. Becker hit a forehand return, Agassi a forehand, Becker a backhand, Agassi a backhand, Becker another backhand, Agassi a low crosscourt forehand, Becker a crosscourt forehand, Agassi a short forehand, Becker a rocket, a winner. Andre couldn't get to the ball. A service break.

Boris raised his arms triumphantly. Mocking himself, mocking his frustration, he smilingly acknowledged the crowd, then began to turn to the baseline with his arms still held high. Enberg suggested that this might be Boris's last chance to cheer.

As Boris turned, he caught a glimpse of Andre, spotted a smile on Andre's face, and interpreted the smile in his own way. He thought Andre was saying, "Slow down, man, You may have a game, but you don't have the match." He thought Andre was making fun of him. It was all right for Boris to make fun of himself. It was not all right for anyone else to make fun of him.

The smile vanished from Boris's face. In the next forty-six seconds, he held his serve at love.

Suddenly, Andre wasn't smiling either.

I couldn't see Andre's eyes, but I could read his body language. I could tell by the way he was staring across the net that doubt was starting to creep in. I could imagine a familiar blank look sweeping Andre's face, a look that used to haunt me but now gave me hope.

I knew then that Boris—that *we*—had a chance to win.

2

MY EARLY
YEARS

MY EARLY YEARS

When I was growing up in North Pelham, New York, I never imagined that someday I'd be sitting at courtside at Wimbledon. In fact, if anyone had suggested that I would make a living in sports, the last sport I would have thought of was tennis.

North Pelham wasn't a tennis town. Tennis was for the kids in the wealthier Westchester communities, the more affluent New York City suburbs, like Scarsdale or Pelham Manor. I grew up playing football, baseball, and basketball, games I've always loved.

Besides, who ever heard of an Italian-American tennis player?

We had produced great baseball players, like Joe DiMaggio, and great basketball players, like Hank Luisetti from Stanford, and great football players, like Angelo Bertelli from Notre Dame. But tennis? Not one.

My grandparents came over from Italy. One grandfather was a butcher, the other a farmer and winemaker. Several of my uncles were cops. My parents were born in the United States, and my father, who was a very handsome man, worked his way through Fordham University and became a pharmacist. He owned a drug store in North Pelham, which went out of business because he gave credit too freely to too many people. He was a good pharmacist, but he wasn't a very good businessman, which is one of many things I inherited from him. He also spoke softly, a trait I did not inherit.

My mother was a typical Italian mother; I think she wore the same dress for twenty years. She fed us and worried about us. I had an older sister, Rita, and a younger brother, Jimmy. He was the scholar in the family, quiet and sensitive, and one day, while my mother was doing the laundry, he slipped and got his neck twisted in the clothesline and accidentally choked to death. He was only fourteen years old. My son is named after him.

We lived in a mixed neighborhood, Italian and black and Irish, and we grew up playing ball together, all getting along. I was lucky; I never had any prejudices, never judged people by their race, religion, or nationality. We certainly weren't poor—I suppose we were middle class—but in my mind, I felt like a kid from the wrong side of the tracks. Yet I always had high expectations, wild dreams. I had no idea what I wanted to be, but I always knew I wanted to do something exciting, I wanted to take chances.

I wasn't much of a student in high school—I was much more into sports than into studies—but I was a hustler, a wheeler-dealer. I would steal lilacs from one of our neighbors' garden, then knock on her front door and sell her a bouquet. I would take candy from my father's drugstore and sell it to my buddies. I sold lemonade. I caddied at the golf club. I washed cars. I worked as a lifeguard. I liked being outdoors. I loved getting a tan.

Many years ago, when I read Nick saying in an interview that he was the gutsy kind of kid who would snitch flowers from your backyard and then sell them to you at your front door, I predicted that with that chutzpah, he had the potential to become the world's most notorious tennis coach and a living legend. And he did!
—Dennis Van der Meer
President, Van der Meer Tennis University

I played basketball and football in high school, and I was no threat to Luisetti or Bertelli, even though I got a couple of scholarship offers to play quarterback at small colleges. But my father wanted me to get a good Catholic education, and he pointed me toward Spring Hill College, a Jesuit school in Mobile, Alabama. One of his classmates from Fordham was on the Spring Hill faculty; I guess Dad thought Father Colkin would see to it that I studied.

I entered Spring Hill in September 1949, and I majored in Spanish and philosophy, social life and practical jokes. I studied my professors more than I studied my courses, their styles, their reactions, their likes and dislikes, just the way I later studied tennis players. I figured out how I could reach them, and I always seemed to get good grades. I dated the prettiest southern belles and occasionally took exams for my friends. I took educational trips to Florida and to New Orleans, and still had enough energy to play four years of intramural football, basketball, volleyball, and baseball. In my freshman year, I tried golf. I played one round. I played so badly I wrapped my new clubs around a tree, threw them away, and never played golf again at Spring Hill.

In my senior year, I had a light academic schedule, so I decided to go out for the tennis team. I'd played a little tennis the summer between high school and college—I had a rich uncle who belonged to the New Rochelle Yacht Club, and I hit a few balls with him—but I really didn't know what I was doing. I just hustled, chased everything, kept the ball in play, and prayed for my opponent to miss it. Somehow, I made the team. I played No. 6 singles and, before the season was over, worked my way up to No. 5. I may not have known much about the game, but I knew enough to realize I was not going to be the first great Italian-American tennis player.

In 1953, right after I graduated from Spring Hill, I went to New Orleans, took an exam for the Naval Air Corps—and flunked. I'd misread the directions. For more than forty years, one of my few regrets was that I never became a navy pilot. Every time I heard a plane fly over me, I looked up and dreamed I was in the cockpit. Finally, in the spring of 1996, I fulfilled my dream. I flew a navy fighter plane. It was one of the most thrilling, most rewarding days of my life. I flew with the Blue Angels.

I was invited to join the Blue Angels on April 9, 1996, at the Naval Air Station in Pensacola, Florida. Two of my children, my older daughters Danielle and Angel, accompanied me; so did my Leah and two of my pros. First, we watched the Blue Angels prepare for and perform a practice show, F-18 jets roaring in tight formation, executing precision maneuvers, spinning and soaring and turning and rolling, shooting straight up, flying upside down. I was dazzled by the skills of the pilots and by the efforts of the ground crew. Every man knew his job. Every movement was coordinated. I listened to the debriefing. I was impressed by the honesty of the pilots and by their physical condition. They all looked like athletes, athletes who had just been through a Super Bowl or a five-set final.

Their flight was so draining, so demanding physically and mentally, that only a couple of the pilots had the energy to attend a tennis clinic I gave. Most of my audience came from the Blue Angels' support team. The resident tennis pro, Mario Alvarez, clearly remembered Andre Agassi coming to Pensacola as a fifteen-year-old and winning his match in jeans, high tops, and heavy makeup.

I had lunch at McDonald's, then sat by myself at the edge of the water and thought about the adventure I was about to embark on. I psyched myself up. I went to the briefing room, and when a navy officer reviewed the emergency procedures—how to evacuate, how to use our life jackets—my daughter Danielle turned pale. I didn't feel exactly perfect myself. I put on my flight suit.

My pilot's name was Scott Beare. His nickname, of course, was Yogi. We climbed into an F-18 Hornet, a two-seater, and I was strapped in so tightly, strapped in eight different places, that I couldn't budge, not an inch. They didn't want to take any chances. They didn't want me to bounce around and hurt the plane.

The helmet went on, I pulled down the visor, and Yogi Beare said to me, "Nick, we're about ready." Then the canopy came down, covering my head, and I realized it was too

MY ACES, MY FAULTS

late, I was committed. It was like hooking up when you're a paratrooper and you're going to jump. There's no turning back. I was in my twenties when I was a paratrooper. I was sixty-four now. But Yogi said he could tell I was in great shape.

My people waved to me and I nodded back. "We would like clearance for a technical takeoff," Yogi told the tower. He was terrific. He talked me through everything. "Nick, this is your day," he said. "We're going to let you do whatever you want. You're going to fly the plane. We want you to have a fun time."

We were ready for takeoff.

"Are you ready, Nick?"

"I am ready, Yogi."

In one second, we were doing one hundred miles an hour, then one-fifty, then two hundred. We took off, leveled off, and as we sped over the end of the runway, Yogi said, "Nick, when I give you three-two-one, we're going up."

"Whatever you say, Yogi," I said.

"Three–two–one ..."

He jerked that stick back and pointed that plane straight up, and we went up to about eleven thousand feet in a little more than thirty seconds. "Holy shit, Yogi," I said. "Holy shit, holy shit."

We flew over the Gulf for more than forty-five minutes, and for a good part of that time, I was at the controls, piloting the plane. Once Yogi took over and turned us upside down and said, "Nick, do you see the water?" and I lied and said, "Yes, I do, Yogi," but I had my eyes clenched shut.

We went faster than sound; we went so slow we almost

stalled. We turned. We rolled. We fought the forces of gravity. I tried to throw up and I couldn't. I was drenched in sweat.

"We have about five minutes left, Nick," Yogi said. "Is there anything special you'd like to do?"

"I think we can land now, Yogi," I said.

When we landed, I was happy to be on the ground, but above all, I was proud, proud of the Blue Angels, proud of Yogi, and proud of myself. Sure, I was scared, I was nervous, but not to the point where I was sorry I went. It was an experience I will never forget. I've seen my students win Grand Slam tournaments; I've jumped out of airplanes; I've skied the Rockies and the Alps; I've parasailed. But nothing ever gave me a rush, a thrill, like flying with the Blue Angels.

But I don't think I'll do it again.

My daughter Danielle said she was worried about me after I landed. Even my tan had turned pale, and I was so subdued I hardly said a word for two or three hours. Danielle said she had never seen me like that.

Back to 1953. After I flunked the test for navy pilots, I went and finished my ROTC training at Fort Story, Virginia. While I was stationed at Fort Story, I met a young woman named Phyllis Anne Johnson, who was spending the summer at Virginia Beach. I remember we went dancing the night we met and surfing the next day. In the fall, I went into the army as a second lieutenant, and we saw each other only occasionally during the next year while she worked as a lab technician and I became a paratrooper.

MY ACES, MY FAULTS

Nick was famous in our house not because of being a great tennis coach, but because my dad's cousin Cubby was Nick's commanding officer in the army. Airborne Division! That's right. Would there be any other place for Nick other than diving out of airplanes? Cubby, a West Pointer, used to say Nick was the craziest paratrooper in his platoon. He was always jumping out of the plane first.

—Luke Jensen

In September 1954, just before I was sent overseas, I decided I was going to marry Phyllis. My college roommate, Jerry O'Leary, tried to talk me out of it—"She's a nice girl, Nick, but I don't think you're ready for marriage"—but I wouldn't listen to him. Of course I was ready for marriage. I was always ready for marriage. My argument was simple: "But, Jerry, she's such a great dancer."

Phyllis flew to Seattle, Washington, and we were married. Three months later, she joined me in Japan. I had a great time in Japan. The Korean War had ended, and we lived in a small village at the foot of Mount Fuji, had a maid who shined my jump boots and polished my brass and served high tea. I supplemented my lieutenant's wages by jumping out of airplanes, which brought me an extra $150 a month, and by playing poker and gin rummy and teaching tennis, which brought me more. I told people I knew a lot more about tennis than I really did. Phyllis and I frequented the jazz clubs in Tokyo, and she stocked up on silk dresses.

We returned from Japan in the summer of 1955, and in November, our son James was born. I fulfilled my army obligation in the summer of 1956 and was ready, at the age of twenty-five, to take my father's advice and attend law school.

I enrolled at the University of Miami, which offered a good law school and great sunshine. I had a wife and a young son, and even with financial help from the G.I. Bill, I knew I needed a job.

Fortunately, one of my uncles was the assistant water commissioner in North Miami Beach, and he helped me get a job as a tennis pro at a public park, Victory Park in North Miami Beach. There were a lot of good pros in the Miami area at the time, and as far as knowledge of the game was concerned, I was certainly the low man on the totem pole. For instance, when people asked me to show them an Eastern forehand, I wasn't quite sure what they meant. I faked it. I used to send Phyllis to watch the other pros in the area work. She would take notes and then tell me what they were teaching, and I would copy them. Slim Harbett, who taught at Henderson Park, was a valuable source of information. So was Fred Perry, who had won eight Grand Slam singles championships in the 1930s. He was at the Diplomat, a fancy resort with well-groomed clay courts.

At Victory Park, we had two broken-down courts with iron-mesh nets. My pro shop was an old Pepsi cooler jammed between two concrete walls and an umbrella. I got a salary of $100 a week plus $1.50 per half-hour lesson. I could earn as much as $12 to $15 each weekday from lessons plus $50 to $70 on Saturdays and Sundays. I was averaging close to $300 a week, which I thought was pretty good, especially since I was working outdoors. My father had given Phyllis and me a $17,000 house as a present, and I had bought a 1952 Plymouth, so I had everything I needed.

On weekdays, I got up at 6 A.M., left at 6:30 to drive to

law school in Coral Gables, about fifteen miles away, got to school by 7:30, stayed till 2:30, drove to Victory Park, worked from 3:30 to 8 or 8:30, went home, ate, studied, and went to bed at midnight. Sometimes, at night, I strung racquets. I just guessed at the tension. Fifty pounds, sixty pounds, I'd just try to come close. Phyllis would sit in one chair and hold the racquet, and I would sit and face her and do the stringing. I didn't complain about the schedule, but Phyllis did. She thought it would be nice if I at least spent some time with her and Jimmy Boy on Saturdays and Sundays. I preferred to go out with my buddies and drink and listen to jazz and party on the beach. Phyllis put up with me for an amazingly long time. Then one day I came home at 5 in the morning and found all my clothes, all my belongings, in the middle of the front yard with a note saying, "Nickie, I wish you well." I went and moved in with my buddies on the beach, eight of us sharing two bedrooms at the Sun City Hotel. We supported ourselves as lifeguards and bartenders.

Phyllis eventually became a model, got her college degree, and did a wonderful job of raising our son, Jimmy Boy. Now, more than thirty-five years after our divorce, we're still friendly. In fact, I'm friendly with most of my former wives.

I kept up my crazy schedule through one full year of law school, then decided that, as much as my father wanted me to be a lawyer, that's how much I wanted to be a tennis coach. I wanted to be Fred Perry, not Perry Mason. "Dad, I'm gonna become the number one tennis coach in the world,"

MY EARLY YEARS

I told my father, and he didn't argue with my decision. He just said, "If anyone can do it, son, you can."

I coached my first two aces at Victory Park, a girl named Sheryl Smith and a boy named Brian Gottfried. Sheryl started coming to the park in 1959 when she was eight years old. She lived only three blocks away, and she used to bring her Barbie dolls to tournaments. In 1961, she became my first national champion by winning the girls' eleven-and-under title.

I played college tennis and coached high school and college tennis, and I always loved to name drop when people asked me where I learned the game. I told them I learned from one of the best coaches in the world. Nick was always willing to give his time if you were willing to give yours.

—Sheryl Smith Craig

The same year, nine-year-old Brian Gottfried showed up at Victory Park. I didn't have the slightest clue that he was going to be my first pupil to be ranked among the top ten players in the world. Brian was all feet, but those feet never stopped moving. When he was twelve, we went to a junior tournament in St. Louis, and Brian defeated a local boy who was about half a year younger, a kid named Jimmy Connors. I made a remark afterward to Jimmy's mother, Gloria, that Jimmy would always have a hard time with Brian. I certainly had a keen eye. I think they played twenty more times in their careers, and Brian never won again. When Jimmy was the No. 1 player in the world, I apologized to him for that prediction.

MY ACES, MY FAULTS

Nick threw away my favorite tennis hat, which I had refused to wash. He tried to get me to eat tomatoes, which I still don't, and he made me spend long hours on the court. That was the part I did like.
—Brian Gottfried

Brian and Raul Ramirez of Mexico won three Grand Slam doubles championships, and in singles, Brian rose to third in the world during the 1977 season. I actually taught another player who ranked among the top ten for several years during the 1970s, but I'm too modest to take credit for his success. A man asked me to hit with him one day in Miami Beach, and while we were hitting, his seven-year-old son sat next to the court and watched us. "Has the kid started playing yet?" I asked the father.

Lenny Solomon said, "No," and I said, "There's no time like the present," and I gave Harold Solomon his first tennis lesson, the only lesson I ever gave Solly. Years later, I got handsomely paid for that lesson; Lenny Solomon donated a library to the NBTA.

From Victory Park in North Miami Beach, I moved down to the Sahara Hotel in Miami Beach. The courts were across Collins Avenue from the hotel—two Har-Tru courts with no Har-Tru left on them. There were also no nets and no net posts. After alimony and child support and Coppertone, I didn't have any money to buy equipment. But I did have my cousin Kenny, the son of the assistant water commissioner.

Kenny and I borrowed a pickup truck, and our first stop was the Hollywood Beach Hotel, a resort that was well equipped with Har-Tru. Somehow, several hundred-pound bags of Har-Tru found their way onto our pickup. It wasn't easy for them to find their way, because it was late at night and dark. Still, we managed to fill our truck twice. The next day, Kenny and I put the Har-Tru on the courts at the Sahara and watered and rolled them. That night, we went out to see if there was any place we could find two nets, two sets of posts, and two sets of lines. We got lucky again. We found just what we needed at the 125th Street Tennis Center. We loaded it all onto the truck very quietly, and within a few days, my tennis center was in operation. I was soon able to pay all my bills and support my ex-wife, my son, and my partying. My cousin Kenny went on to become vice mayor of North Miami Beach.

In the heat of summer, of course, no one played tennis in Miami, so, like the tourists and the waiters, I headed north, to be the resident pro at the municipal courts in Springfield, Ohio. I learned a lot in Springfield. I learned that a city recreation department needed a dedicated person behind it; Springfield was lucky to have Dr. Howard Dredge. I learned, too, about mass teaching, the system that later became one of my trademarks: Each Wednesday and Saturday, six hundred boys and girls came to our park by bus, and I taught them in groups of forty and fifty. I also learned you made more profit at the concession stand if you sold pop in cups filled with a lot of ice and just a little soda.

Springfield was considered a tennis hot spot, the site of the Western Juniors, a warm-up tournament before the nationals in Kalamazoo. I coordinated the tournament, which attracted all the best young players in the country. I first met Stan Smith there and Charlie Pasarell, Roscoe Tanner, and Arthur Ashe.

Arthur was a teenager when I met him, and our friendship lasted more than thirty years. I never met anyone so thoughtful, so decent. We shared many dreams; together, we founded the ABC program, Ashe–Bollettieri Cities.

> *ABC had its germination one day at Roland Garros Stadium in Paris in 1987, when Nick and I sat together watching one of his charges play a match at the French Open. Between points, we were talking about the deteriorating conditions in American cities, about violent crime and drug abuse and rampant juvenile delinquency, when Nick turned to me almost explosively.*
>
> *"Arthur," he blurted out, "we've got to help those kids! We've got to do something for those kids!"*
>
> *"What do you think we can do?" I asked.*
>
> *"Well, let's think about it. I know we can do something!"*
>
> *We thought about it over several weeks, and slowly came up with a plan. Our idea was to use tennis as a way to gain and hold the attention of young people in the inner cities and other poor environments so that we could then teach them about matters more important than tennis.*
>
> *In 1988, we launched the ABC program. Ironically, we launched it the same week that I discovered I had AIDS.*
>
> —Arthur Ashe, *Days of Grace*

The ABC program, under the direction of Bob Davis, Arthur's longtime friend, still flourishes in several cities. Bob runs the program from his office at the NBTA. We both miss Arthur. Tennis misses Arthur. He was so much bigger than the sport.

With his enormous talent on court and off, Arthur broke

down the racial barriers in tennis, so that today pros like
MaliVai Washington and Chanda Rubin are thought of primarily as players, not as black players. The country club
world within which tennis often operates may not be the
most integrated of worlds, but this doesn't have much impact
on the touring professionals. In some sports, like baseball and
football, black players have a tendency to hang out with black
players and white players with white players. But that's not
true in tennis. In tennis, the top players don't hang out with
anybody, black or white. It is the ultimate *individual* sport.

Besides meeting Arthur and so many great young tennis
players in Springfield, I also met a woman named Nancy
Nolan. She was a telephone operator in Springfield. She loved
to play tennis, and I loved to make long-distance calls. It was
a perfect match. Free tennis for her. Free phone calls for me.

Nancy became my second wife. She almost became my
third. It's a complicated story. You see, Nancy came to Florida and spent the winter with me. In the spring, she went
back to Springfield, and I was going to join her there. But
before I left Florida to go north, I happened to meet another
woman. Her name was Shirley, she was on vacation and she
was from Indianapolis. On my way to Springfield, I stopped
in Indianapolis to see Shirley. We got along so well I decided
I was going to marry her. But a snowstorm prevented us from
getting a marriage license, and I told Shirley that I had to
go to Springfield but that I would come back the following
weekend and marry her. I went to Springfield, saw Nancy,
and married her instead. I didn't dare go back to Indianapolis
for several years.

My big break, perhaps the break that shaped the rest of my life, came when a woman walked into my Springfield pro shop during the Western Juniors and asked if she could use some practice balls. I gave them to her, and when she brought them back, she asked me what the fee was. "No charge," I told her. I was just happy having all the big-name young players in my city.

She thanked me and asked me my name, and a few weeks later, this woman called me and asked me if I would be interested in being the pro at a famous resort in Puerto Rico called Dorado Beach. She lived in Puerto Rico, her name was Dora Pasarell, and her son Charles was one of the best young players in the world.

I told her I would love to be the pro at Dorado Beach, but I didn't think I had much of a chance of getting the job. I wasn't exactly a big name in tennis. I had never played at Wimbledon or Forest Hills. I was, in my own mind, still just a guinea kid from North Pelham.

I didn't know that Mrs. Pasarell was close to Lawrence Rockefeller and his wife and that Mr. Rockefeller and his family owned and operated the Dorado Beach Hotel.

Soon I got a phone call from Dorado Beach, telling me that I was one of three people being considered for the job. They asked me what I expected in housing, transportation, and salary, and I told them the truth: I didn't have the slightest idea; I'd be happy with whatever they felt was fair.

To my amazement, I got the job.

Nancy and I flew to San Juan and were met by a driver. In a little more than an hour, we arrived at Dorado Beach and were awed by its beauty. I was even more impressed when I met the manager and found out that I would be paid a salary of $3,500 for the five winter months, November through March, plus all of my lesson money (I had just raised my rates to $5 per half hour) plus I would own the pro shop and its considerable profits plus we had a beautifully furnished condo with maid service and all our meals free in the employees' dining room.

I was in paradise. I was in the big time.

WIMBLEDON: THE BOYS

They were close to Centre Court at Wimbledon, and yet they were a million miles away. They were on court 2, only a few hundred yards from where Andre Agassi was playing Boris Becker, but Gregg Hill and Tommy Haas, another American and another German, were playing a very different game for very different stakes. The two young men, prize students at the NBTA, were, at the age of seventeen, playing in the quarterfinals of the Wimbledon junior doubles championship.

If Andre, at the age of twenty-five, represented my past, and Boris, at twenty-seven, my present, then Gregg and Tommy represented my future.

Gregg was from North Carolina. He had come to me in 1988, when he was ten years old, with incredibly fast hands and a supportive family who had approached me at the U.S. Open that summer and had asked me if I would take a look at their son. During his first few years at the academy, Gregg had watched Andre Agassi, who was still a teenager, polish his skills; he had even, on one or two occasions, hit with Andre. Gregg had attended tournaments wearing blue badges that identified him as a guest of Andre Agassi.

Tommy was from Germany, and in 1989, when he was eleven years old, he and his sister Sabine, both junior champions in their own country, had visited the academy briefly. Tommy was invited to stay, but he was young and spoke no English, and he chose to go home. He wanted to become a great tennis player like his idol, Boris Becker.

Two years later, in 1991, Tommy decided to come and

live at the academy, and almost immediately, he and Gregg, my two best thirteen-year-old boys, my young aces, became friends and doubles partners. Gregg helped Tommy with his English. I brought both of them along slowly. I knew they were not going to turn pro at sixteen, as Agassi had. The game had changed too much for that. They were not physically mature. They were not mentally mature either.

In the spring of 1995, a couple of months before Wimbledon, I decided to take the boys to Europe to use them as sparring partners for Boris Becker. Tommy and Gregg were getting a little arrogant, a little too impressed with themselves. They needed to be cut down to size. Boris was just the man to do it.

One on one, of course, the boys couldn't stand up to his strength, to his experience. So, usually, they played two against one, which made Boris work for his points, helping his conditioning and his game. Still, he wore them down; when they were exhausted, he was still fresh. The experience of facing a player so powerful and talented as Boris clearly forced the youngsters to learn, to improve. Besides, Boris took the time to offer them advice and encouragement. He showed them by example how a professional acts on and off the court.

Tommy could remember that not even a couple of years earlier, at the end of 1993, when Boris tumbled out of the top ten in the world for the first time in almost a decade, when his skills seemed to be eroding, no one in Germany believed that he would ever regain his form, ever become a great player again. Then, at the beginning of 1994, I started coaching Boris Becker; by the end of the year, he had bounced back to No. 3 in the world,

Gregg and Tommy were both rooting for Boris to beat Agassi at Wimbledon, partly for his sake, partly for my sake, and mostly, I think, for the academy's sake. Boris represented the academy, and so did they.

Hill and Haas were seeded third in the junior doubles, and they were facing the best French team, Bachelot and Cadart. Ken Merritt, one of my top aides at the academy, my chef and housemate at Wimbledon, was at court 2, watching the boys, cheering them on. They had one eye on their opponents and one on the scoreboard.

Their match began just as the first set between Andre and Boris was coming to a one-sided close. Gregg and Tommy looked up and saw the result and both had the same thought, the same uneasy feeling that Andre was going to sweep Boris in straight sets.

Hill and Haas beat the French boys in their first set, and when they looked at the scoreboard once again, they saw that Boris had rallied from 1–4, from two service breaks down, and had taken the second set on Centre Court into a tie-breaker. Minutes before Gregg and Tommy won their second set and finished off the French team, Boris Becker crushed Andre in the tiebreaker, 7–1. The men's semifinal match was tied, one set apiece.

Ken Merritt relayed a report of the doubles victory to me as I sat at Centre Court, and I was delighted for both Boris and the boys.

3

CHI CHI AND LOMBARDI

CHI CHI AND LOMBARDI

W hen Nancy and I got to Puerto Rico, the first thing we realized was that Dorado Beach was primarily a golf resort, not a tennis resort. Chi Chi Rodriguez was the local golf prodigy, fresh out of the caddie ranks, just beginning to show his great talent. Chi Chi and I have been good friends over the years, and he must be a far better teacher than I, because I now play golf in the high seventies and low eighties if you play by my rules, and Chi Chi still can't hit a tennis ball worth a lick.

Dorado offered two championship golf courses, thirty-six magnificent holes, but only three tennis courts, which were bordered by the most beautiful shrubs, trees, and flowers. Nancy and I figured out quickly that guests at the hotel had to walk past the tennis courts to get to the golf courses, so whenever we saw a guest heading our way, we grabbed our racquets, ran onto a court, and started hitting balls back and forth. We wanted people to know that tennis was alive and well in Puerto Rico.

Slowly, our business began to build up, and soon our courts were filled most of the time. One day, a man called the pro shop and told Nancy he wanted a court at 9 the next morning. She said she had nothing open till 3 P.M. She told me about the call over dinner, and I asked what his name was, and she said, "Jay Rockefeller," and I just about choked on my rice and beans. I rushed to the phone and called Jay Rockefeller and told him that a court had opened up for him at 9 A.M. Jay, who later became the governor of West Virginia and then a senator, was the best tennis player of all the Rockefellers.

In the summers, the Rockefellers asked me to spend some time as their family pro at Pocantico Hills, their sprawling estate near Tarrytown, New York, not far from where I grew up. Pocantico Hills beat the hell out of North Pelham. The Rockefellers had their own security force and their own golf course, and, of course, each of the Rockefellers—Nelson, David, Lawrence, and the others—had his own mansion. There were a pair of immaculately groomed clay courts, with vines scaling the walls around them, and members of the Rockefeller family would call me and book court times and lessons.

My son Jimmy Boy often stayed with me at Pocantico Hills, and his favorite place was the Playhouse, a huge old Victorian building that accommodated two bowling lanes, an Egyptian tiled pool, and a gym equipped with rings, ropes, a horse, and a trampoline. There was also an ice cream parlor— imagine!—a family ice cream parlor. (I have one now in my condo in Bradenton.) Outside, above the clay courts, were a croquet field and a pair of swimming pools that were shaped like ships. I loved to play croquet and I loved the huge terrycloth towels the Rockefellers scattered at the pools. I took a few of those towels home with me every summer. I figured they wouldn't miss them.

Brian Gottfried accompanied me to Pocantico Hills. In fact, Brian accompanied me almost everywhere I went in the 1960s: to a variety of tennis clubs in the East and the Midwest, from the Woodmont Country Club in Rockville, Maryland, to the Bath & Town Club in Lake Bluff, Illinois; to the Nassau Country Club and the Port Washington Tennis Academy on Long Island.

I didn't stay anywhere too long, but I think they remember me at all the clubs. At Woodmont, I urged all the members to use the racquet, the line of clothing, and the tennis shoe I recommended; if they didn't, I booked them on the courts at the hottest hours. In Lake Bluff, I once asked the members to come off the courts so that they could be watered for afternoon play, and when the members were slow getting off, I turned on the sprinklers anyway. In Port Washington, I gave Hy Zausner the idea to build his tennis academy. A few years later, when Antonio Palafox was the resident pro, a kid named John McEnroe came out of there.

Nick's son, Jimmy Boy, spent the summers with us. Nick was crazy about Jimmy. He wanted him to be a tennis player, but Jimmy would hit the ball, drop the racquet, and run around the court as if it were a baseball field.

—Nancy Nolan Bollettieri Chaney

My second marriage ended fairly quickly. I can't remember exactly why Nancy and I broke up, which is probably why it broke up. By the fall of 1964, I was single, and Chi

MY ACES, MY FAULTS

Chi Rodriguez and I were in Des Moines, Iowa, giving golf and tennis clinics. We went to dinner at a restaurant across the street from the airport. I happened to notice that the woman who was the hostess at the restaurant was quite attractive, so, of course, I asked her to marry me. Not that night, but not that long afterward.

Her name was Jeri Sylvester, and she was a senior at Drake University. She was working at the restaurant and also at a local radio and TV station. I persuaded her to visit me in Puerto Rico during the winter, and once she got there, I wouldn't let her go home until she married me. We were married in a judge's office in Old San Juan, and our daughters, Danielle and Angel, were born in 1967 and 1969. Our marriage lasted twelve years, which was, and is, a record for me.

My tour in Puerto Rico lasted even longer, seventeen years, from 1959 into 1976, and it was at Dorado Beach that I first began to realize that I could be somebody, that if I put in enough effort—which, to me, always meant working longer and harder than anyone else—that if I surrounded myself with the right people, with loyal and committed assistants, with influential and supportive friends; that if I learned from my defeats and mistakes, and refused to accept being told that I couldn't do something, then I would make a great deal of money and, more important, I would make an impact. I really wanted to be the best, the most famous, the most important tennis coach in the world. I admit I also wanted to be rich.

My Dorado Beach pro shop, a handsome round glass building with a spacious deck, was a big moneymaker, and

I spread the money around. I tipped generously—waiters, housekeepers, everyone. They loved to see me coming. I tipped as well as most of the wealthier guests and better than some. My father always told me to go first class, and I always tried to. I loved feeling like a big shot.

At Dorado Beach, I got to know so many people who were instrumental in nurturing my career. Louis Marx Jr., for instance. I had met him on the tennis courts at the Rockefeller estate in Pocantico Hills—we played doubles, and I gave him a few tips on his game—but it was in Puerto Rico that I spent a great deal of time with him and his family. His father had founded the Marx toy company, and Mr. Marx had gone to Princeton. He had two daughters and two sons, all good tennis players, all students of mine. Mr. Marx, who is chairman of the company that distributes Swiss Army knives and watches in the United States, seemed to bail me out whenever I got in trouble financially or maritally. And his palatial suburban home provided a base for Andre Agassi during several U.S. Opens, a place to practice and relax in privacy.

I also got to know Dan Lufkin and his four children—he and Mr. Marx were good friends and business associates—and the Nelsons, Doc and Marilyn, who were from Minneapolis. Marilyn's family, the Carlsons, owned hotels, restaurants, and travel agencies around the world and, at one time, considered buying the Dorado. I had met Nate Landow, a real-estate developer, in Rockville, Maryland, and he and his family followed me to Dorado. Two of the three Landow children worked for me as counselors and camp directors. Monte and Susan Horowitz and their three children also vacationed in

Puerto Rico and became my students and my friends; he was in the construction business in New York. These people not only encouraged my dreams, but generously financed them, helped pay for the training of the Agassis, the Couriers, and the Seleses. I visited them, lived in their homes; they lived in mine. I treated their children as if they were my own, maybe even a little better.

You never knew who might show up at Dorado Beach. One day, when I was teaching tennis to a group of youngsters, a short, squat fireplug of a man stopped to watch my class on his way to the golf course. I didn't recognize him, probably didn't even take a good look at him. "Young man," he said to me, "you belong with children, teaching them." He was a teacher, too, he said, and a coach. His name was Vince Lombardi.

Lombardi was, of course, the coach of the Green Bay Packers, the team that won five National Football League championships in seven years in the 1960s, a record no team has ever matched. After the football season ended, usually in January for him, he took vacations in Puerto Rico. He stopped by the tennis courts almost every day, and we became friends. I used to send him bags of golf balls, and he offered me tickets to Packer games.

In 1967, Vince Lombardi and another Dorado Beach friend of mine, Art Nielsen Jr., from the television ratings family, recommended me for a job in Beaver Dam, Wisconsin. They told the headmaster of Wayland Academy, a private school in that small town, they thought I would be the right person to run a summer tennis camp on the school's campus. I had to give the school references. I gave them four: Vince

Lombardi, Nelson Rockefeller, David Rockefeller, and Maxwell Taylor. I had met General Taylor, the former chief of staff of the U.S. Army, when I was in the service. I wasn't certain he'd remember me, but I figured it wasn't a bad name to use.

The headmaster and president of Wayland Academy was a man named Ray Patterson, who had grown up in Beaver Dam, attended Wayland and the University of Wisconsin, played college and professional basketball, then returned to his hometown and his former school. Patterson presided over Wayland through most of the 1960s, then left in 1968 to become the president of a new National Basketball Association (NBA) team called the Milwaukee Bucks.

Patterson had the wisdom and good fortune to win the NBA draft lottery in 1969 and to select a tall young man from UCLA named Lew Alcindor, who soon changed his name, radically, to Kareem Abdul-Jabbar. The Bucks won the NBA championship the following season, the fastest any expansion team ever won a title in any major professional sport. Later, Patterson ran the Houston Rockets and, with the same blend of wisdom and luck, won the draft lottery again in 1984. This time he selected a tall young man from the University of Houston named Akeem Olajuwon, who also changed his name, barely, to Hakeem Olajuwon. In the 1990s, Olajuwon led the Rockets to back-to-back NBA championships. I couldn't help but learn from Ray Patterson and Vince Lombardi.

My first year in Beaver Dam I agreed to go up in April to coach the girls' tennis team at the school. I lived on the bottom floor of the girls' dormitory. We had four indoor courts then, and between April and June, we built eleven outdoor courts, finishing the last one at 3 P.M. on the Sunday the camp opened. It started to rain at 3:15, and it rained for a full week. I had to share the indoor courts with a brand-new basketball camp run by the coach at Marquette University, Al McGuire, who won the National Collegiate Athletic Association (NCAA) championship almost a decade later and then retired from coaching. Al was a lot like me. We both butchered the English language, but neither of us seemed to have any trouble communicating.

I operated the Nick Bollettieri Tennis Camp in Beaver Dam for twenty-five years. The camp opened in June and ran for eight weeks. Tennis in the sixties was still perceived as a sissy game. We made it a fierce sport, with strenuous workouts and strict discipline. The essence of our system was group lessons, teams of students and teams of coaches, although everyone at some time got individual attention, enough to assess his or her game. When our campers weren't actually hitting, they ran in place. They weren't allowed to twirl racquets or to chew gum. Any time I sensed that the students or the coaches weren't giving one hundred percent, I would stop the operation and make everyone, campers and staff, run laps on our quarter-mile track. The only time I would let up was when we got tornado warnings. Then I would make everybody drop everything and take cover. When I wasn't giving lessons or barking orders, I rushed around Beaver Dam in my sunglasses and my well-polished red Mercedes convertible. (The car was a gift from Nate Landow; seventeen years later, I gave it back to him as a fifty-fifth birthday present. It had only twenty-one thousand miles on it and was in super condition.) I loved every minute in Wisconsin. I even loved the campers' annual show; they mimicked my strutting, my screaming, and my suntanning.

Life was more of an adventure, full of excitement, when Nick was here. They were splendid summers we spent together. I will never forget them.
            —Gordon Kotinek
            Tennis coach Beaver Dam High School

In Beaver Dam and Puerto Rico, I was blessed with assistants and associates who shared my dreams and enthusiasm, who were willing to keep up with me and put up with me. They had to be coaches and baby-sitters, bus drivers and groundskeepers. Several of them remained with me for decades, humoring and protecting me.

I met Carolina Bolivar, for instance, in 1969, when she was twelve years old. Her father belonged to the golf club at Dorado Beach, and while he played golf, she hung out at my pro shop. I'd let her hit with the ballboys, and sometimes she'd watch one of my young daughters, Danielle or Angel. I also allowed Carolina to straighten out the hangers on the clothing racks in the pro shop. I told her I wanted two fingers between each hanger, all of the hangers straight, all facing the same direction. She aligned the hangers perfectly. I knew she had a bright future.

In the summer of 1972, when Carolina was fifteen, I invited her to Beaver Dam for three weeks. She attended the camp and still found time to help wash my cars, do my laundry, and take care of my children. After that, she came

MY ACES, MY FAULTS

back every summer. She taught tennis till she graduated from the College of New Rochelle with a degree in psychology and elementary education and dreams of becoming a schoolteacher with summers off. Instead, she came to work for me.

Carolina has been with me ever since, and she has occasionally had days off. Very occasionally. I did take her on the road with me one year. I took her to all the major tournaments so that she could be a nanny for Nicole, my fourth child. Now Carolina is the director of admissions for the academy. She interviews applicants, explains the program to them. She really believes in the program, and in me.

> *I've never worked for anyone but Nick in my life. He is a very, very generous man. He would give anyone the shirt off his back. As a matter of fact, he's always giving people the shirt off his back. Nick hates to wear a shirt. He's terrible with names. Sometimes he forgets my last name, my married name. I've been married for ten years now, and he still calls my husband Mike, and his name is Mark.*
>
> —Carolina Bolivar Murphy

Ted Meekma came to work for me when he was sixteen years old. He was from Beaver Dam, and in 1972, he started at the camp as a dishwasher. As he got older, he got more responsibility. It became his job to drive my red Mercedes into its very narrow garage. His mother was not delighted that he was working at our tennis camp. Ted's mom had heard all the Nick stories. I swore too much for her. I had too many wives for her. Ted came from a very proper background, and I think he told his mother he was going to change me. He's been with me now for almost a quarter of a century, and I haven't changed much. But Ted has. He's a lawyer and acts like one. He's an officer of the academy and of International Management Group, our parent company. He went to law school and coached tennis at the University of Arkansas and then came back to work with me, to help me through the latest mortgage or the latest marriage. He always wants me to have legal agreements, binding contracts. I've always preferred handshakes, conversations. I've always fought against prenuptial agreements and player–coach contracts. My theory is I've been screwed before, and if I want to get screwed again, I have a right to.

Greg Breunich joined me as a fifteen-year-old at Beaver Dam. His father and I had been high school football teammates in North Pelham; his father was a lineman, much bigger and better than I was. Greg was a student for two weeks in the summer of 1973, and the next summer he was a coach. He knew nothing about coaching, but like many of my instructors, he learned on the job and learned quickly. I had a core of teachers, experienced and expert, who know how to break in the novices. Except for a brief time at college, Greg's been with me since his teens. He's now the chief executive officer of the NBTA. He, like Ted, tries to keep me out of trouble, tries to get me to places on time.

I hired Julio Moros in 1973. He was a student at Pan-American College in Edinburgh, Texas, and I called his room at two o'clock one morning to offer his roommate, who had worked at Beaver Dam, a job at Dorado Beach. The roommate said he couldn't do it but recommended Julio. Julio worked two months for me without a day off before he asked me when and how much he was going to be paid. Julio stayed with me for fifteen years, then went off to launch his own tennis club.

Chip Brooks started with me in 1974, said he was from eastern Tennessee and wanted to see the world. He's still with me, directing the NBTA tennis program for adults.

In the early 1970s, as if the winters in Puerto Rico and the summers in Wisconsin weren't enough to keep me busy, I started a company called All-American Sports. For several years, we ran a series of tennis camps around the country, one of them in Amherst, Massachusetts.

Harry Hopman was the codirector of the Amherst camp. The former Australian Davis Cup captain, the man who led their great teams in the 1950s, lived in my apartment in Dorado Beach for several weeks before we opened the all-American camp; he was a great tennis strategist, a master motivator, but not a very good camp director. Hopman later wrote an article in which he said he hardly knew me. I still wonder why he said that.

I used to visit the Hopman/Bollettieri camp in Amherst a couple of times a summer. On my first visit each year, usually the second week of camp, I would take the entire staff, forty or fifty pros and office people, to dinner at a restaurant called the Steak Out. I would reserve the banquet room, and I would sit at the head of a long table—sort of like King Arthur and his round table—and I would order for everyone. I would say, "Waiter, everyone at the table will have a sizzler's steak—medium well—and everyone will have a Heineken." Once, when I finished ordering, one of the pros raised his hand and said, "Waiter, instead of a Heineken, I'd like a glass of red wine." And I said, "Waiter, that's fine, but the wine goes on his bill." From then on, everyone drank Heinekens.

In 1976, a *Sports Illustrated* management team convinced the Rockefellers that they could run Dorado Beach. They were going to put Butch Buchholz, who had been a well-known player, in charge of the tennis program—they said I could stay on under Butch—so I elected to leave. I didn't have a job, and between alimony and automobiles, I hadn't saved much money. I went to Miami to look around, and I heard from a friend named Al Lovetti that the Colony Beach and Tennis Resort on Longboat Key near Sarasota was looking for someone to run its tennis program. "Where the hell is Sarasota?" I said.

Mike DePalmer Sr., who lived close to Sarasota, which is right next to Bradenton, also heard about the opening at the Colony and thought of me. Mike, a former basketball coach, was then the tennis pro at the Bradenton Country Club. His daughter, Michelle, a nationally ranked junior player, had won a two-week scholarship to Beaver Dam a few years earlier, and she had enjoyed the program so much she had begun coming to Puerto Rico in the winters as well as Wisconsin in the summers.

Michelle's mother, Vicky, wasn't wild about her daughter chasing across the country and across the Caribbean for tennis lessons with a loud, excitable Italian. Vicky was a very devout woman, and she actually prayed every night that somehow God would bring me to Bradenton, would bring me to Michelle, instead of her coming to me. Her prayers were about to be answered.

With Mike DePalmer's help, I got an appointment to

meet with the owner of the Colony Beach Resort, Murf Klauber. The appointment was set for seven o'clock one morning. I partied in Miami till after 2 in the morning, borrowed a car from a friend and, with Julio Moros at my side, raced to Sarasota in not much more than three hours. I met Murf Klauber an hour later, and I could tell right away he was a wild man; he was as crazy as me. He gave me the job.

My days at the Colony were filled at first with lessons and clinics for guests of the hotel. When my pros weren't on the court, I had them picking up scraps of paper or pulling weeds, keeping the area free of debris. Mike DePalmer suggested that two or three nights a week I could put on clinics for adults at his place, the Bradenton Country Club. They proved popular, and so did the weekend clinics we started at the Colony for junior players. We ran them from 7 to 9 o'clock Friday nights, from 6:30 to 9 Saturday mornings, before the Colony guests came onto the courts, and then from noon to 1:30, the heat of the day, while the hotel guests ate lunch or went to the beach. We resumed at 7 at night till 9, then had another 6:30-to-9 session Sunday mornings and finished up from noon to 1:30. We charged only $35 for the weekend of tennis, and if the youngsters wanted to stay at the Colony, we got them a bargain rate. Sometimes six or eight juniors would share one room. Pretty soon, we had thirty or forty youngsters taking part in the program.

The first weekend set the tone for the program. Around 9 P.M., I went to Nick, who was running from court to court like a drill sergeant, shouting commands, and I said, "It's nine o'clock. Should we

CHI CHI AND LOMBARDI

quit?" He said, "Hell, no, we're just getting started. It might rain tomorrow. Let's do all we can tonight." His philosophy always was to give the customer more than he paid for. We charged $35 for the weekend, and Nick gave all the income to his pros, never kept a dime for himself.

—Mike DePalmer Sr.

During the summer of 1978, I told several of the families at Beaver Dam that I was opening a school in Sarasota, offering room and board and tennis. I lined up twenty children to start in September to live and train at my school. The only catch was that I had no boarding facilities. So half the kids lived in my house, and the others were scattered among the other pros.

We gave them breakfast each morning, sent them off to school, then, while they were gone, made sandwiches—peanut butter and jelly mostly—and lemonade, which we served them for lunch. After they ate in the parking lot at the Colony, they reported to the tennis courts. Ted Meekma gave lessons, then left the Colony early, went to my house, and prepared dinner for everyone. He had been promoted from dishwasher to cook. We rented two vans to shuttle the kids among their houses, school, and the tennis courts.

One of our earliest, and more prominent, live-in students was a lovely young woman from West Virginia, who several years later created a small crisis at Wimbledon. She shocked traditionalists by wearing a formfitting white bodysuit in her first-round match. Her name was Anne White—she was also a terrific basketball player—and she ranked among the top

twenty players in the world before her twentieth birthday.
Anne lived with the DePalmers.

*In the late 1970s, I was in a slump and I made arrangements
to go to Sarasota to play six hours a day at Nick's school and, with
some luck, get some pointers from him. At the time, I was certainly
not a star on the women's tour, but Nick found time to work with
me for an hour almost every day, usually at 7 A.M. As long as I
was eager and punctual, Nick was eager to help me.*

*Nick encouraged me to work harder than I had ever worked
before. He was full of positive remarks, and he suggested changes that
I felt capable of making. Often, well-meaning coaches can make a
player feel like there's nothing redeemable about his or her game, that
he or she needs a complete overhaul. Nick was the opposite. He made
me feel like I had a great game that could get even better with some
fine-tuning.*

*At the end of my stay, Nick would not charge me for his help.
I had to force him to take a token check.*

—Dr. Julie Anthony
Clinical psychologist

We watched our expenses pretty carefully in the early
days. Once, one of our girls, Susan Smith, a nationally ranked
junior, was playing in a tournament across the state, so I
went to see her in the finals. I drove my cherry-red 1972
Mercedes 450SL, and on the way back, I stopped for gas. It
was one of those self-serve gas pumps—they weren't so common then—and when I stopped the gas at $10, it may have
slipped over by a fraction of a cent. I sent one of my pros
in to pay for the gas with a $10 bill, and the guy who owned

the place said, "It's $10 and one cent." The pro came out to get another penny from me, and I exploded. I ran in and started shouting, "It's not a penny, it's not a penny, it's a half a penny, and you're either gonna put another half a penny's worth of gas in my car or you're gonna cut this penny in half." The guy got out a saw and cut the penny in half, and I took my half penny and got in my Mercedes and drove off.

We put our pennies and our half pennies into expansion. Mike and I bought a small club in West Bradenton that had seven courts. We named it the DePalmer Bollettieri Tennis Club, and Mike resigned from the Bradenton Country Club to run it. We still held our classes at the Colony, then ran our tournaments at the DePalmer Bollettieri Tennis Club.

The next thing we needed was our own housing facilities. One day Mike noticed a run-down motel on Manatee Avenue in Bradenton, stopped, and asked if it was for sale. He was told it might be.

Mr. Marx, who had followed me to Florida from Puerto Rico, was staying at the Colony Beach. I found him in the locker room, in the shower, and I said, "Mr. Marx, there's a little motel available where we could put our students. Could you help me?"

"How much do you need?" he shouted.

"I need fifty thousand," I said.

"You got it," he said, and we bought the motel.

The motel was in terrible condition. It was one of the grossest places I had ever seen. Mildew everywhere. We had to scrub the tubs

and the toilets, Ted and Greg and Julio and me. We scrubbed and scrubbed and scrubbed while Nick was on the court, giving lessons.
                                    —Carolina Bolivar Murphy

Carolina had to run the motel the first year. Then I brought in a retired army officer named Bill Baxter. Colonel Bill Baxter. He was in his fifties, a Special Forces veteran, a green beret who had fought in Korea and in Vietnam. He was straight out of *Apocalypse Now.* He called our students "messy-assed kids," and he told them that the greatest sound in the world was "hearing the bullets fly over your head, 'cause as long as you hear them, you know you're alive."

Colonel Bill was a fitness fanatic, a master of one-armed push-ups; he could even do more than I could. He wanted us to give up our buses and march the students from the motel to the tennis club and back again each day. He thought it would save gas and build character. He ran fifteen miles a day himself, and he told us he had celebrated his fiftieth birthday by running fifty miles. He made the kids sweep the driveway of the motel till there wasn't a grain of sand in sight—in a beach town! He made me look kind and gentle. He was particularly tough on one kid just because the kid came from Iran, and it was the time of the hostage crisis.

Once Colonel Bill brought his son Jay to the academy, and introduced him to Greg Breunich by saying, "Greg, I want you to meet my boy, Jay. Jay, at ease." When he left the academy, he went to Africa and trained mercenaries. When he found out that the men he was training were supposed to assassinate political figures, he quit. Colonel Bill came back to the States, and the last I heard, he was in Waco, Texas, selling used cars.

> *Colonel Bill once told me to scrub a peanut-butter-and-jelly stain off the floor in the dining hall. I told him it wasn't a peanut-butter-and-jelly stain; it was a shadow. He said it was peanut butter and jelly. I scrubbed and scrubbed and waxed and waxed, and of course, it didn't make any difference. The shadow didn't go away.*
>
> —Frank Falkenburg

Frank Falkenburg, who lived in the motel as a student, went on to become a champion, not at tennis, at Ultimate Frisbee, then a lawyer. Now he's back at the academy, as my personal manager.

Paul Annacone and Eric Korita also checked into our motel. Korita was one of the nicest kids in the world and one of the most talented. He had a huge serve, and on a good day, he could beat anybody. But he had no burning desire to excel, no killer instinct. He really didn't like tennis that much. Eric did like to eat. Actually, he inhaled, and the whole tablecloth came up. The beds in the motel weren't big enough for Eric. So he slept in a top bunk with his feet out the window.

Paul Annacone loved tennis, went on to the University of Tennessee, played for Mike DePalmer, made All-American, and spent a decade on the pro tour. He once ranked No. 12 in the world, and he won a Grand Slam doubles title. When Tim Gullikson, Pete Sampras's coach, got sick in 1994, Paul took Tim's place. Paul is proof that you can be calm and modest and be a good coach.

He still phones me regularly. He's not looking for advice, just saying hello, but we do talk about Pete. I'm a big Sampras fan. I've never coached him, but he has trained at the academy, has used our courts and our workout facilities, and whenever I see him, I tell him, "Pete, let your shoulders sag, and let your tongue wag. Don't ever change."

The most amazing thing to me is that people see Nick as this disciplinarian drill sergeant who has the kids hit balls until their arms fall off. I can't tell you how many times Nick would come running out to the courts of the Colony and call off practice because the surf was up. It was hysterical to see this little band of kids charging off the tennis court and down the beach, led by the biggest "kid," Nick. Clothes and racquets would be randomly discarded along the way so that no good waves would be missed.

—Paul Annacone

Not long after Carolina and the guys made the motel livable, a producer from ABC-TV's *20/20* program happened to be vacationing at the Colony Beach. His daughter played tennis. While I was working with the kids one day, yelling and screaming as usual, feeding them balls as fast as I could, the producer and his daughter passed the courts and caught my performance. Her father asked how much it would cost for her to participate in the program, and I said, "Nothing, get her out here," and after a while, the producer came over to me and said, "How would you like us to do a story about you and your program on national TV?" I said I thought I would like that very much.

CHI CHI AND LOMBARDI

NICK BOLLETTIERI: What'd I tell you about pulling down? What'd I tell you about putting your head down?

TOM JARRIEL: Would you pay $12,000 a year to have this man abuse your child? Almost one hundred people are, and four hundred more are on the waiting list to get their youngsters into the Nick Bollettieri Tennis Academy.

It's the capitalist version of the communist East European approach to athletic training. Take promising young players, lock them together, away from family and friends, to concentrate on one thing: producing champions. But here, individual families rather than the state pay the training bills. The students, age seven to seventeen, from ten countries, live four to a room in a converted motel. The rules are strictly enforced: No smoking. No drinking. No drugs. No car. No television or radio. Or even phone calls from home. Except on weekends.

The 20/20 segment was a huge boost for the program. The demand was suddenly so great we had to start working longer days. Instead of fifteen hours daily, we worked seventeen or eighteen. During the school year, we worked nine straight months. My pros got a day off only if there was a major emergency. Their loyalty, their belief in what we were doing, was incredible.

TOM JARRIEL: It is ... a blend of verbal abuse, sharp criticism, and then praise. But mainly, dawn-to-dusk discipline. It is a controversial program, admittedly for the rich, with long separations from family and a one-dimensional approach to life—revolving around a tennis ball.

Of course the *20/20* story wasn't one hundred percent positive. When they started talking about my temper and my ego, my mother began swearing at the television screen in Italian. "Mary," my father said to my mother, "the important thing is, they're talking about your son." He was right. How could I complain? They were talking about me and the academy and the kids. I wasn't going to waste my time and energy defending myself. Every knock was a boost.

Besides, I deserve criticism. Yes, some of my students missed out on their childhood. Yes, some burned out early. Yes, some were pushed harder than they should have been, sometimes by me, more often by their parents. Certainly, I contributed to the practice of fourteen- and fifteen-year-olds going off on the road to play professional tennis. I'll take the blame for that and the credit. Many of them have gone on to fine productive lives.

Kathleen Horvath, one of my earliest aces, won a fistful of junior championships, including the Orange Bowl, played and won her first U.S. Open match a few days after her fourteenth birthday, turned pro when she was fifteen, and scored perhaps her greatest victory when she was only seventeen, when she beat Martina Navratilova in the fourth round of the 1983 French Open, the only match Martina lost that entire year. In 1984, when she was eighteen, Kathleen became the first female student from the academy to be ranked among the world's top ten. But then Kathleen stalled, never quite rose so high again. In her twenties, Kathleen put tennis behind her, went to the University of Pennsylvania, graduated magna cum laude, got her MBA from the Wharton School, and now is married and works for Merrill Lynch in New York.

CHI CHI AND LOMBARDI

TOM JARRIEL: Nick Bollettieri's reputation these days is that of a self-made millionaire. His staff of eighteen tennis pros polish his three expensive cars. They have actually built much of his sprawling five-bedroom home. They clean his swimming pool and do whatever Nick says.

20/20, exaggerated a little.

If Kathleen Horvath was the best of the girls in the early years of the NBTA, Jimmy Arias was the best of the boys. He came to the Colony on a tennis vacation when he was twelve years old. At the time, he was the U.S. fourteen-and-under champion, but I didn't know who he was. I didn't pay any attention to him until he got on the court to hit with Mike DePalmer Jr. Mike was three years older than Jimmy, much taller and much broader.

I watched them for a few minutes, and I couldn't believe the forehands the little kid was hitting. I'd never seen a twelve-year-old hit a ball so hard. I chased young Mike off the court and told Jimmy I'd be happy to give him a few tips. "What should I tell him he's doing wrong?" I whispered to Steve Owens, one of my pros.

I offered Jimmy a scholarship on the spot, invited him to come to Florida to attend Bradenton Academy and train at the Colony. I told him I'd find him a place to live. Jimmy loved the idea. He went back home to Buffalo, which was freezing as usual, and told his father that he was either going to move to Florida or he was going to give up tennis. Jimmy felt he wasn't going to get much better unless he regularly faced tougher opposition than he could find in Buffalo.

> *Tennis players are prima donnas. If you're great as a kid, you get treated like you're some special guy. People do things for you all the time, and you don't ever pay for anything. You start to think that's the way of the world. When I was No. 5 in the world, I wasn't as well known as McEnroe or Connors, obviously, but I would go to restaurants sometimes and the owner would say, "Don't worry about it." I'd get so many things for free. I'd go to a doctor and he wouldn't charge me. You get a warped sense of the world.*
> —Jimmy Arias

Jimmy moved to Florida and, at first, lived at the DePalmers' home. He was a cocky kid, very sure of himself, but after a while, he felt uncomfortable at the DePalmers, probably because he had displaced Mike Jr. as my most promising pupil, my favorite. Jimmy moved in with me and, at one time, shared my house with eleven young girls and a freezer full of pizzas. I wasn't as concerned with nutrition then as I am now.

Jimmy's father had taught him his forehand, programmed him to use a full follow-through. Mr. Arias was an engineer, and even though his knowledge of tennis was limited, he did understand mechanics. He couldn't understand why so many players used an abbreviated follow-through. He had little Jimmy hitting with all his might, actually leaping off his feet as he hit, which got him started on his recovery.

Jimmy arrived armed with the forehand and with great quick feet. But I was concerned about the rest of his game.

CHI CHI AND LOMBARDI

I wanted to change his backhand to a two-handed backhand, which I thought would compensate for his small stature, but his father, who was not an easy man, vetoed the idea.

I did persuade Mr. Arias to allow me to make one major change in his son's game. When Jimmy came to Florida, he was used to playing at the baseline or just inside the baseline. I convinced Jimmy and his father that he should move back, play well behind the baseline, the way Björn Borg and so many other successful players were playing at the time, particularly some of the shorter ones, like Eddie Dibbs and Harold Solomon. Mr. Arias argued that if Jimmy played up, he would get better angles, he would put away more balls.

Maybe Mr. Arias was right. I wasn't an engineer, and I was still learning the intricacies of the game in the early days of the academy. In recent years, with Andre especially, I've urged my players to be more aggressive, to move inside the baseline, to play the ball on the rise. Of course, the equipment today is different; it's designed more for a power game. But perhaps Mr. Arias was ahead of his time.

I think he was wrong about the backhand. If Jimmy had mastered the two-handed backhand, I think he would have had an even better and longer career than he had, and he did for a while rank as high as fifth in the world. No one had faster feet than Jimmy, and no one had a bigger heart, and no one used the one big weapon he had, the forehand, any better than Jimmy Arias.

NICK BOLLETTIERI (on 20/20): *If we could eliminate the parents completely, our job and the results of the job would be three to five hundred percent ahead of what it is right now. It's alarming. The letters. Some parents telling their children, "Do more than what Nick gives you. Do one hundred more push-ups." The parents put so much pressure on their children in sports today. It is absolutely unbelievable.*

Jeri and I got divorced in 1977 after twelve years of marriage and two beautiful children, and for the next several years, against all odds, I remained a bachelor, living a bachelor's life in and around Sarasota. I hated to go out alone. I always tried to take some of my pros with me. They had a tough time keeping up with Nick.

Every night Nick would go to this place called Big Daddy's, on St. Armand's Circle. He loved to drink Crown Royal and ginger ale with a twist of lemon. He also loved to dance. These were the discotheque days, and Big Daddy's had mirrors everywhere, on the wall, behind the bar, on the ceiling, smoke floating up from the floor— a regular John Travolta atmosphere.

One night, at about 1 A.M., after a few too many drinks and dances, Nick vanished. We hunted and hunted and hunted and couldn't find him. We thought maybe he'd found a girl and gone on home. But his car was still outside. We decided to make one more search— we had to be out on the courts early in the morning—and this time we checked out the bathroom, and there was Nick. He was leaning up against the wall and talking to the mirror. He thought he was having a conversation with somebody. We just about died laughing. We finally convinced Nick he was talking to himself in the mirror, and we all went home and were back out on the courts in a few hours.

—Chip Brooks

CHI CHI AND LOMBARDI

I was tough on my pros in the Colony days. I worked from sunup to sundown seven days a week, and so did they. It's hard to believe, but few of them complained. They seemed to thrive on the schedule, to take pride in the pace, just as I did. But sometimes I may have gone too far.

On Christmas Eve, 1977, I walked into the pro shop at about nine o'clock, and a few of my pros were sitting, catching their breath after their last lessons. I noticed that some of the tennis shirts on the shelves were not folded properly. I turned to the pros and said, "I want you to take all the shirts off the shelves and refold them and dust the shelves before you go home." I expected Christmas Day to be a big day in the shop.

The guys looked at me like I was Scrooge. Before they could protest, I started screaming at them, telling them what it was like when I was in the army. I got a little carried away. I told them what it was like to be in a foxhole in Korea, eating mud and rice on Christmas Eve. It wasn't exactly the truth. I was in a foxhole a couple of times but never in Korea, only in Virginia, and it wasn't Christmas Eve, and there were no bullets flying. The Korean War ended before I got to Japan. Still, I told my pros how good they had it, how lucky they were to be at the Colony Beach in Sarasota, Florida, how much people were paying to get suntans just like the ones they were getting for free.

I kept talking about Korea, and Chip Brooks raised his hand and said, "Nick, who cares about Korea? This is Christmas Eve, 1977, and we want to go home. We've got to be back here at sunup tomorrow."

I yelled at them for five more minutes, just for practice, and then let them go home.

A few months later, a man showed up at the Colony with his young daughter and asked me to hit a few balls with her. "What do you think?" the father said after we'd hit.

"I think she has a lot of talent," I said.

The father nodded and walked away, leaving the young girl to hang around the courts. After a while, I said to her, "Where's your dad?"

"He's gone," she said. "He's leaving me with you."

She told me her name was Carling Bassett, and her father's name was John Bassett, and neither name meant anything to me. I had no idea that Carling's mother's family founded Carling Breweries in Canada or that her father, once a highly-ranked tennis player in Canada, had owned the Memphis Southmen of the World Football League, the team that lured Larry Csonka, Jim Kiick, and Paul Warfield away from the Miami Dolphins in the mid-1970s.

Carling moved into my home—she and Jimmy Arias and Kathleen Horvath were all there at the same time—and her father eventually did return to see her. John Bassett became one of the academy's great benefactors. He bought us a bus, and he built a clay court at my home, which was not far from the academy. Mr. Bassett was a generous man who died very young. His widow, Susan, later married Murf Klauber, the owner of the Colony Beach and Tennis Resort, the man who had brought me to Sarasota.

Carling turned pro at fifteen, reached the semifinals of the U.S. Open when she was sixteen, and was ranked eighth

CHI CHI AND LOMBARDI

in the world at seventeen. She was a great competitor, an incredibly tenacious player whose game lacked only the trademark Bollettieri forehand. The forehand was for me what the Green Bay sweep, with the pulling guards, was for Vince Lombardi. My bread and butter. I'll never understand how Carling could live in my house and not have the forehand.

A model and an actress, Carling was only one of several beautiful young women who brightened the academy. Another was Lisa Bonder, who was five feet ten inches and also worked as a model. She broke into the top ten in the world in 1984, when she was eighteen. Once, when Lisa was playing on court 2 at the French Open, she kept looking into the stands, waiting for me to flash signals to her, to tell her how to play the match. It was against the rules, of course, but I was supposed to touch my nose if I wanted her to do one thing, rub my ear if I wanted her to do something else. But I'd left the card on which I'd written the signals in my hotel room, and I had no idea what meant what. Every time Lisa looked at me, I just looked away. She won the match anyway.

In the late 1970s, when the oversized Prince racquet came on the scene, I was one of its advocates—up to a point. The head of Prince offered to give me $25,000 apiece if I would persuade Jimmy Arias and Kathleen Horvath to use the racquet. I told him I couldn't do that. In the first place, I didn't think it was right for me to tell them to switch racquets, and in the second, Jimmy's father would have killed me. (I think Kathleen later chose on her own to use the Prince.) I did, however, agree to use the racquet myself. I was a little reluctant at first—I felt like a sissy using the big green racquet—

but my embarrassment turned to enthusiasm when they offered me $3,000 to play with the Prince. I guess they figured I wasn't quite as valuable a role model as the youngsters.

I was soon part of a Prince team, including my friend Bill Shelton, that toured the country, introducing the racquet. While I was on tour, I saw a magnificent tennis center in California called Los Caballeros, which had dozens of courts and a dormitory and a dining room, and I told Larry Ware, a great teacher who was working with me, "This is what I want someday."

I was willing to try anything to raise money to make my dream come true. Once, when I heard that American Express was going to have a company meeting at the Colony, I borrowed a videotape camera, enlisted two of my pros as cameramen, Steve Owens and Chip Brooks, and had them shoot me on the court teaching Jimmy Arias and Carling Bassett. As we finished the lesson, Jimmy and Carling grabbed their gear and shouted, "C'mon, Nick, we're late. We have to go." And as we all ran off, I turned to the camera, held up my American Express card, and said, "Don't leave home without it." We delivered the commercial to American Express. We never heard from them.

During Thanksgiving, 1980, Mr. Marx was vacationing at the Colony, and I was telling him how the junior program was expanding, how well the youngsters like Jimmy and Carling and Kathleen were coming along. I told him we really needed a new facility for the kids, a bigger place, self-contained, with courts and dormitories and a kitchen and a dining hall, and Mr. Marx said, "Build it."

"With what?" I said. My savings were at their usual level.

"With money," Mr. Marx said.

"Where am I going to get it?" I said.

"I'll lend it to you."

A few weeks later, we heard about an old tomato farm for sale, dozens of acres on 34th Avenue and 55th Street in Bradenton. I went to Mr. Marx and told him about the property. He didn't hesitate. He wrote out a check for $1 million, and with a million more from the bank, we started building the NBTA early in 1981. We opened in November.

The construction took longer than my fourth marriage. My fourth wife's name was Diane Day; she was a hostess at the restaurant at the Colony. I think we got married after the groundbreaking and divorced before the opening. I wasn't single for long, however; I started dating Kellie Handler, who was working in my pro shop, and I asked her to spend the summer with me in Beaver Dam. She told me her grandmother said it wasn't right for her to go away with me if we weren't married. I certainly didn't want to offend her grandmother, so I married Kellie before we went to Wisconsin.

The new, expanded academy attracted kids of varying levels of ability. I told them over and over how proud I'd be if one or two of them made it to the professional level. I tried not to encourage unrealistic dreams. I told a reporter that if I ever got to coach another Brian Gottfried, it'd probably be pure luck.

Some of the kids came because they wanted to be good tennis players. Some came because they wanted to be great players. Some saw the caliber of the opposition at the academy and adjusted their games. Some adjusted their goals. Some came to live out the dreams of a tennis parent. Some came because their parents didn't want them around and had enough money to send them to us.

We dealt with all kinds of parents. The best would come to me and say, "Nick, you're the boss. Take your time. I'm not concerned with immediate results." The worst refused to be patient, couldn't comprehend that early success, success achieved too easily or achieved at great physical or mental expense, might mean later failure. And, of course, I would hear, or overhear, children saying, "My mother wants to know why I lost. She wants to know why she's paying all this money if I'm losing."

Nick always got criticized for not being able to teach serve and volley. He was supposed to be just a yeller, a screamer, a motivator, hit your groundies and that's it. But he helped lay the foundation of my game, which was totally serve and volley. Brian Gottfried, Eric Korita, Mike DePalmer Jr., Anne White—they were all serve and volleyers, too.

—Paul Annacone

In 1982, I stumbled into an international incident. Jerry Glauser, my friend and Mercedes dealer, and I flew from Sarasota to New York one day to meet with Steve Ross, the head of Warner Communications, to ask him to make a sizable contribution to provide scholarships to the academy. Mr. Marx had arranged the meeting.

While we were in Mr. Ross's office, my agent, Donald Dell, called from Washington and told me I had to go to

CHI CHI AND LOMBARDI

Los Angeles right away. A talented young tennis player from mainland China, Hu Na, had defected during the Federation Cup matches in Santa Clara and was hiding out in Los Angeles. I was to pick her up and take her to Florida. She was going to train at the academy, and Donald was going to be her agent.

Jerry and I had no luggage, no clothes. We'd been planning to fly right back to Sarasota. Instead, we caught a plane to Los Angeles and, not long before midnight, checked into the Beverly Wilshire Hotel. Jerry Solomon, an agent who worked closely with Dell and later married the skater Nancy Kerrigan, was waiting to welcome us to Los Angeles.

At 4:30 in the morning, the phone rang. The State Department was calling just to let me know that they knew why I was in California. I started to get very nervous. In the morning, a man named Frank Wu came to our hotel room. I knew Wu because he was in the tennis-racquet business; I had met him at a junior tournament in Taiwan. I found out that Wu had orchestrated Hu Na's defection. Wu went to a travel agency in the hotel lobby and bought an airline ticket for Hu Na under an assumed name. She and Jerry Glauser and I were going to fly all night on the red-eye from Los Angeles through Dallas to Sarasota.

At the airport that night, we spotted Frank Wu in a telephone booth, like Clark Kent, looking around to make certain he wasn't being tailed or observed. Then he came out and introduced us to Hu Na, who spoke no English.

No one was supposed to know we were traveling with Hu Na, but when we landed in Dallas, I couldn't help myself; I called a reporter at the Sarasota newspaper, told him Hu

Na was with us, and told him when we would be landing in Florida. He met us at the airport and interviewed me.

Then we took Hu Na to the academy. My daughter Danielle became her roommate. A few days later, somebody called from the State Department and said they had heard rumors that the Chinese were going to try to kidnap Hu Na, that they might assault the academy and kill anyone who got in their way. I was terrified. The next thing I knew, a federal SWAT team descended upon the academy with machine guns and mortar shells. They were going to protect us.

The rumors were false. No one attacked. Three weeks later, I was out on the tennis court, yelling at some students, when I got a phone call. I was told it was from the White House. The operator said President Reagan was calling. "Yes, Mr. President?" I said.

The president told me he had heard that I was a very good tennis coach, but he would appreciate it if, in the future, I would stay out of diplomatic affairs. "Yes, Mr. President," I said.

Hu Na trained at the academy, then played on the women's pro tour for several years. She never became a star.

But Steve Ross did contribute a quarter of a million dollars toward scholarships to the academy.

When Nick reads this, he will find out for the first time that it wasn't President Reagan who called him about Hu Na. It was the brother-in-law of one of our pros; he happened to be a comedian who was very good at impressions. We were going to tell Nick it was a hoax, but he got so excited about the president calling and he told so

CHI CHI AND LOMBARDI

many people we didn't have the heart to tell him the truth. Or the courage.

—Anonymous

In 1983, one of our scholarship students, Jimmy Arias, at the age of nineteen, won four pro tournaments, beat Yannick Noah to reach the semifinals of the U.S. Open (where he lost to Ivan Lendl), and rose to number six in the world, the highest ranking any product of the academy, male or female, had achieved. Jimmy was not only good, he was a crowd pleaser. He loved an audience. He was bright and articulate and had a great smile.

Jimmy's career peaked in his teens. Shoulder problems and a debilitating bout with mononucleosis affected his forehand. Still, he did stay on the tour for more than a decade, and he did earn close to $2 million in prize money and probably millions more from endorsements and exhibitions. Yet, despite all the years we worked together, I never shared in Jimmy's earnings, not one cent. Looking back, I suppose I really did deserve something.

I understand where Nick's coming from. I would feel slighted, too, if I were working with a kid from the time he was twelve years old and he made it to number five in the world, and I never got a dime. But how do you write up a contract with a twelve-year-old? You don't.

When I was growing up, when I was a kid at the academy, I never even thought of paying Nick. He was my coach for free, just as, before him, my father had been my coach for free. They coached me because they wanted to coach me. When I got to the semifinals of

the U.S. Open at nineteen, the idea of giving Nick a tip, a bonus—
which I would certainly do today—didn't even occur to me. I just
didn't know. I can understand how he feels.

—Jimmy Arias

Jimmy had an exceedingly rare gift: He was willing to play tennis with anyone, male or female, old or young, talented or terrible, and he would make it fun for them without hurting his own game. I don't think he ever turned me down when I asked him to hit with someone. I guess that wipes the slate clean, that and the lunch he bought the last time we played golf together. It was the first time *he* paid.

As Jimmy's career slowed down in 1984, another one of our young students began to blossom—Aaron Krickstein, a sixteen-year-old from Grosse Point, Michigan. Aaron was brought up in a loving Jewish family, and as an only son with three sisters, he was babied for sixteen years. His father, who was a physician, wanted me to toughen Aaron up. He wanted me to make him into an Italian.

Aaron fashioned a truly remarkable career. Despite stress fractures in both feet when he was still a teenager, despite a lingering injury that occurred when a New York taxi he was riding in was sideswiped, despite problems with his wrist and his knees, Aaron has played the tour for thirteen years, and in each of those thirteen years, he has ranked among the top one hundred players in the world. For ten of those years, he ranked among the top thirty-five. He rose as high as sixth in the world in 1990, before he turned twenty-three. He has won nine tournaments, and he has earned more than $3.5

CHI CHI AND LOMBARDI

million in prize money, and he is still not thirty years old. He is, in fact, only a few months older than Boris Becker.

Aaron never created the excitement that Jimmy Arias did before him or Andre Agassi did after him, but in the long run, Aaron may be the happiest of the three. I think he played up to his potential, married a lovely woman, developed interests beyond tennis. He drifted away from the academy a long time ago—he's had several coaches since he left me, including Brian Gottfried, who also coached Jimmy Arias for a while—but he's always come back, and we've always had a special feeling for each other. I'm particularly proud of the reputation that he's earned over the years: Don't get yourself into a fifth set with Aaron Krickstein. Going into 1996, Aaron had a career record of 28–8 in five-set matches; only Becker, among active players, had won so often under similar pressure, and Boris's five-set record was only 28–13. Aaron never quit.

Things were going so well at the academy by the mid-eighties that I decided to buy a yacht and learn to sail. I bought a thirty-two-foot Wellcraft and hired a pair of experienced sailors to teach me to pilot it. After a few weeks, I was handling it pretty well, so they decided it was time for me to try docking the boat. It was a tight little spot, a foot to spare on each side, and as I attempted to slip it in, I made a mistake. I put one engine in reverse, and one in forward, and the boat began to spin around. I took off half the dock with the bow of the boat. I realized I was never going to be a great sea captain. I sold the boat.

I almost sold the academy, too. A well-dressed man showed up in Bradenton one day and told me he represented an Arab sheik who was interested in purchasing the entire academy so that he and his friends would have a place to improve their game. He said the sheik was thinking about building a castle adjacent to the academy. Cost was no object. I said I would be glad to show the sheik the academy.

The sheik himself soon arrived. He and a sizable entourage landed in Sarasota in a pair of private 727 jets. He had a personal staff of twenty Filipinos. When the sheik stepped onto the tennis court, he was accompanied by a small army of ballboys and an umpire. Every time an opponent's shot landed anywhere close to a line—within a foot or two would do—the umpire would shout, "Out!" The sheik's shots, of course, were always in.

After two weeks at the academy, with tennis and clothing and racquets and rooms and meals, the sheik had run up a bill of more than $25,000. I was a little nervous, so I called Mr. Marx and told him the sheik's name. Mr. Marx had him checked out and said he was certainly legitimate: He was a billionaire or better.

Still, when his majesty's account approached $100,000 and we had not received a dime, I told Julio to present him with a bill. The sheik was shocked. He told Julio that I had invited him to the academy, that he had presumed he was my honored guest, and that he never dreamed I would insult him with a bill.

The sheik and his entourage promptly vanished without a trace. I never heard from him again. I guess I had hurt his feelings.

In 1985, we may have had our greatest collection of talent at the NBTA. Jimmy Arias, who turned twenty-one that year, his last year ranked among the top twenty, was still using the academy as his base, and so were Aaron Krickstein and Carling Bassett, both teenagers. Agassi and Courier were fifteen-year-olds, David Wheaton and Chris Garner were sixteen, Martin Blackman had great promise, and so did Murphy Jensen, the younger of the Jensen brothers. Mark Knowles, a Bahamian, was fourteen; I had seen him play at the Orange Bowl in 1980 when he was nine and had offered him a scholarship. He moved to Bradenton from the Bahamas when he was ten and stayed until he went to UCLA and became an all-American. He is now one of the best doubles players in the world.

I offered Courier a scholarship in the fall of 1984, when he was fourteen. Jim lived in Florida, just about a hundred miles north of Bradenton, and he said it took him only ten minutes to decide to come to the academy. He started in January 1985 and stayed for more than four years. He and Andre even roomed together for a short time. Jim was a competitor, a real athlete who probably could've played and excelled at any sport.

Jim had an odd variety of grips when he showed up, but they worked for him. His strengths were never technical. He didn't care whether he hit the shot just right or not. He just wanted to hit a winner. He had to be pushed to practice. He didn't like drills. He wanted to play matches.

David Wheaton was just the opposite. Wheaton could drill for hours at a time without ever complaining. He wanted each shot to be a classic stroke. But he had to be pushed in matches. He didn't have the same burning desire that Agassi and Courier had.

Jim won the sixteen-and-unders at the prestigious Orange

MY ACES, MY FAULTS

Bowl tournament when he was fifteen and the eighteen-and-
unders when he was sixteen, a remarkable back-to-back double
that no one had achieved since Björn Borg. Courier was a
very serious, very organized kid. He would check in for a
tournament and unpack every bag, put every shirt, every pair
of socks, neatly folded, into a precise pile. He was the opposite of Andre in many ways, which made them natural rivals
on the courts of the academy.

> *I'll always be grateful to Nick for allowing me to bring my
> drums to the academy. My parents were grateful, too, to get them out
> of the house. I set my drums up in a garage, right next to Jimmy
> Boy's darkroom. I used to torture the other kids with the noise at night.*
> —Jim Courier

David Wheaton came from a religious and close-knit family, which actually moved from Minneapolis to Florida while
David was at the academy. His mother was a major influence
on him and on other young people. It was the Wheatons
who encouraged Andre's interest in religion; for a couple of
years, in his late teens and early twenties, Andre spent a good
deal of time reading the Bible and discussing it with David
Wheaton and Michael Chang.

Wheaton's best year came in 1991, when he reached the
semifinals at Wimbledon and the fourth round of the U.S.
Open and earned a cool $2 million for winning the Grand
Slam Cup in Munich.

My three teenage aces, Agassi, Courier, and Wheaton—I
predicted that all three would be top ten players—came in
different temperaments and different sizes. Andre was five

feet eleven inches tall; Courier, two inches taller; and Wheaton, two inches taller than Courier. But I drilled all three of them the same way, inside the baseline, barking at them over and over, "Don't back up! Shorter backswing!" I'd yell at their instructors, too. "Make him play aggressive! If he backs up, he loses!" I told them backing up was not permissible; footwork was the key.

In the first decade of the NBTA, I had three tall and remarkably gifted young black players, three scholarship students, first Rodney Harmon, then Chip Hooper, then Martin Blackman, each with enormous potential. They all played professionally, they all played well, but I was disappointed that none of them became a champion. It would have meant so much to me and so much to the academy. I wanted them to be Arthur Ashe's heirs, and in some ways, I guess they are. Harmon attended Tennessee and Southern Methodist University and is now the tennis coach at the University of Miami; Blackman, who played on NCAA championship teams at Stanford, is back in college; and Hooper, who graduated from Arkansas, is a schoolteacher and coach in Kansas City.

I view my experience at the academy as being positive, though traumatic. At thirteen, training and living like a professional athlete/ student, surrounded by boys older and tougher, under physically and mentally demanding conditions, is not easy. But I learned discipline, mental and physical, and how to earn and keep the respect of my peers. I learned how to take care of myself. Nick was tough, but he walked the walk and led by example. I will always be grateful to him for his generosity and leadership.

—Martin Blackman

Often, probably too often, in concentrating on the world-class players, I slighted lesser players, the nonscholarship students at the academy. I didn't totally ignore them—I popped into their classes, dashed onto their courts, shouted, made my presence felt—but I didn't give them equal time.

In the mid-1980s, I did ignore the financial management of the academy. I turned it over to other people. I had someone in charge I thought I could trust, and I was wrong. I never looked at the books, paid no attention to the money coming in or the money going out. When I finally realized I was on the brink of bankruptcy, I was too embarrassed to go to my friends, to Mr. Marx and Mr. Horowitz and Mr. Landow and Dr. Nelson, and ask them to help me out.

I know they would have done it, but instead, I decided to sell the academy to IMG, International Management Group, Mark McCormack's giant company that runs tournaments, produces TV shows, represents athletes and entertainers, once even represented the pope. IMG paid me $7 million, most of which went to pay off the debts the NBTA had accumulated. But at least I was able to send a check to Mr. Marx for $2 million to repay him for his loans and for his kindnesses.

I was terrified I was going to have to take orders from IMG. Nick, do this! Nick, do that! What would I have done? How would I have reacted? It would have been interesting. But IMG understood me and kept me in charge of the academy. Mark McCormack and Bob Kain, his right-hand man, gave me total freedom—in every area except, naturally, financial responsibility. IMG was going to see that money was spent and earned wisely. I was going to see that the academy kept turning out the best tennis players in the world. IMG did with me what I did with my players: They didn't try to change me; they built on my style.

In 1989, for the first time, a pair of graduates of the academy, Agassi and Krickstein, both reached the semifinal round of the U.S. Open. I dreamed of Andre and Aaron meeting in the finals: my former pupil, Krickstein, against my current pupil, Agassi. I can't tell you how much that would have meant to me. I put the Grand Slams up on a pedestal. They are monuments. But both Andre and Aaron lost in the semis to the top two players in the world: Agassi to Lendl and Krickstein to Becker.

Two years later, I was named the U.S. Professional Tennis Association Pro of the Year. I dedicated the award to my father, who had passed away. He always believed I would become the best tennis pro in the world.

Nick sees things other people don't see. He hears things other people don't hear. He can make anyone a better tennis player immediately. He can make anyone listen to him. He fears no one and nothing, except small airplanes. He can tell if someone is tired. He can tell if someone is lying. He can tell if someone is not giving one hundred percent. He can make anyone give one hundred percent. He can listen, think, write, and talk at the same time. He can't remember anyone's name, but he can tell you what grip they use on their forehand.

—Ken Merritt

I think I was starting to mellow. I was yelling less and encouraging more. I was beginning to wonder if maybe children were coming to the academy too young, before they were ready to leave their homes and their childhoods. I worried about burnouts. I knew better than anyone that we couldn't make all our pupils top pros, no matter how good they were at thirteen or fourteen or fifteen. Their parents didn't always know that. I wanted our students to be aware of more than tennis.

If I've grown a little, the academy has grown a lot in its first fifteen years. Tuition now runs close to $30,000 for nine months, September through May, either for a student who in the mornings attends Bradenton Academy or Saint Stephen's or for a student who is out of school, who plays tennis all day. If the student wants special individual coaching, it may cost as much as another $10,000. We have close to two hundred tennis players, most of them boarding students, perhaps twenty percent of whom receive full or partial scholarship help. We have seventy-five courts, four of them within our indoor training center, which is hung with banners, dozens and dozens of them, each celebrating a championship won by one of our students.

The academy's official name now is the Bollettieri Tennis and Sports Academy, and we offer golf, soccer, and baseball programs, all of which are growing, especially the golf and soccer programs. We have a fitness center and a rehab center. IMG often brings in athletes to recuperate from injuries. Young football players come in after their college careers end to condition themselves for the National Football League (NFL) tryouts.

We have some three hundred tennis players a week in our summer program, perhaps a hundred during Christmas vacation, and another hundred during spring break. We also

CHI CHI AND LOMBARDI

provide year-round adult tennis programs and access to an on-site language school, teaching youngsters from all over the world to speak English.

Students come to the academy from dozens of different countries. Angela Maria Lopera, for instance, came from Colombia to spend her summers with us. In June 1995, when her father brought her to Bradenton, he left a letter with her that she carried everywhere:

My Dear and Beloved Angie:

As you read this letter, you are fulfilling your dream ... "Bollettieri" ... fighting to achieve a goal ... a goal that you have dreamed of. I feel very happy to know that you are fighting with all your heart and soul to earn the right of your dream to become a beautiful reality. Now as I think with happiness of all the love that I feel inside for you, I feel certain that my spirit remains besides you, at your bedside so that I can guard your sleep, and at the side of the court when you are playing so that I can help you with my spiritual strength to be as happy as you can be. If you win or lose at the end is no concern because the most important thing is that you are happy playing your tennis.

I want you to keep this letter all through the summer, this beautiful summer for you and all of us who love you and are close to your heart. Read these lines each time you wish to speak to us, because through this letter, we can talk each time you wish.

Your mother and I long for all your dreams to come true and that you have every opportunity to be happy. We wish that life will be very generous with you. Now that you are far from home, you know how to behave and take care of yourself. We are sure that the values we have instilled in you will help and defend you. You are now fourteen years old, and your mother and I see you as a beautiful ... young lady ...

Your mother and I are praying to God that you have a beautiful and unforgettable summer, but also asking God that the summer is soon over and that you return home because we are already missing you very much. May God repay you for all of the years of happiness that you have given us.

I love you with my entire life ...

Papa.

A few weeks later, on her way to a tournament, Angela was killed in an automobile accident. It was the first fatality in the history of the academy. Angela loved the academy; her father said she waited all year for the summer. I've found a special place on the grounds where I've built a garden that will flower year-round, so there will be flowers always in memory of Angela. And each year one little boy or girl will spend a summer at the academy on scholarship, representing Angela, so that her dream will always be fulfilled.

WIMBLEDON: THE SIGNAL

Suddenly, in the third set of the semifinal match, Andre Agassi's return of serve, perhaps his most potent weapon, lost its customary zip. Andre seemed to have slowed up a step, and twice, on second serves, Boris Becker aced him.

During a changeover, Andre glanced up at our box, looked to Brad Gilbert for guidance, for reassurance. I looked at Brad, too, and maybe it was only my imagination, but I would almost swear I saw Brad signal Andre to take his time, delay Boris, slow him down. Brad wanted Andre to put his towel on his head, cool himself off, change the pace.

Brad, you got that from me, I thought with some satisfaction. Three years earlier, when Agassi met Goran Ivanisevic for the Wimbledon championship, I had told Andre to slow down the hard-serving Croatian.

Now Andre looked at Gilbert and nodded. He had received the message.

Barbara Becker turned to me and stage-whispered, "He's giving signals! He's giving signals!" She was outraged; she hated for *other* coaches to give signals.

"Barbara, the signals aren't enough," I said. "You've got to perform. You've got to execute."

I could tell from the way Andre walked back on the court that he had begun to doubt himself.

Outside Centre Court, behind court 6, Ken Merritt and Tommy Haas and Gregg Hill sat on a wooden bench and studied a distant scoreboard and imagined the action. When Becker would win a point, Ken would improvise. "Well, Boris hit a perfect drop volley there." When Agassi would win,

Gregg Hill would announce, "A perfect passing shot from Andre."

Boris won the third set, 6–4. He was one set away from the seventh Wimbledon final of his career.

The hard seats of Centre Court no longer felt so hard to me.

4

GOOD-BYE, ANDRE

GOOD-BYE, ANDRE

Andre Agassi and I were so close in 1987 we once shared a hotel room. Neither of us could have suspected that six years later we would be so far apart that when I decided I could no longer be his coach, I notified him by mail.

In his first full year on the pro tour, in 1987, at the age of seventeen, Agassi played tennis with varying degrees of success on four continents. He reached the finals of tournaments in Korea and Brazil and won his first professional championship in his final event of the year in Itaparica, Brazil.

On his way to his first title, Andre defeated the man who was favored to win the tournament, his future coach, Brad Gilbert. The victory enabled my teenage pupil to finish the year ranked twenty-fifth in the world, far ahead of Jimmy Arias and Aaron Krickstein.

I didn't travel with Andre all the time in 1987, but I did join him in Europe in the spring, and in May, he and I and his brother, Phillip, took a single hotel room in Florence. We didn't have a lot of money. Andre had won a total of $25,000 his first year on the tour, and the NBTA was at the time, even though I didn't know it, sinking deep into the red.

The one room was not a good arrangement. Andre and Phillip liked to sleep ten or eleven hours a night with the curtains closed and the room pitch black. I preferred to sleep three or four hours a night with the curtains wide open. They won the argument, but I won the war. We went to bed with the curtains closed, but I woke up early anyway, and when I started doing my laundry, they woke up. That was the last time we shared a room.

For entertainment, we pitched coins on our tiled floor until our next-door neighbors, a couple of women, complained about the sound of the coins stiking the tile. Then we switched to backgammon until Andre beat me so badly one night that I threw the set out the door and onto the street.

The following month, Andre made his Wimbledon debut, and it was not an auspicious one. He lost in the first round in straight sets to Henri Leconte of France. He did not fall in love with the grass or the ambiance. "That's it for me," Andre said. "I don't have to play this kind of tournament. This is bullshit. This isn't tennis." He had just turned seventeen.

A few weeks later, back in the States, Andre played in Boston. Because he was still relatively unknown and the audience was small, I was able to get away with sending him signals. Despite my advice, Andre was losing. Finally, he turned to Phillip, Bill Shelton, and me and said, "F——it. I did what you told me to, and it didn't work. Pack the damned bags. We're going home." And he dumped the match.

Andre matured the following year, at least on the tennis court. As an eighteen-year-old, he won sixty-three matches and six tournaments, played three Davis Cup matches and won them all, reached the semifinals of the French Open and the U.S. Open, and lost to Mats Wilander, the No. 1 player in the world, in one, and to Ivan Lendl, the No. 2 player in the world, in the other. Andre ended the year right behind Wilander and Lendl, ranked No. 3 in the world. His official earnings soared to $822,000. With his flamboyant style, his technicolor clothes, his flowing hair, his instant appeal to the young, his rebellious image, he was the hottest thing to hit tennis since Boris Becker won Wimbledon at the age of seventeen. Corporations lusted after his endorsement; his rivals envied his quick success.

Several of Andre's victories that year were special. In May, he won the U.S. Clay Court Championship in Charleston, crushing Jimmy Arias in the final. A week later, he faced Slobodan Zivojinovic in the finals of the Tournament of Champions at Forest Hills, and he knew that we had to catch a plane that night to Italy. Early in the match, he turned toward me and shouted, "Hey, Nick, don't worry about it, buddy, we're going to be on that plane," and dispatched Bobo in straight sets.

In July, he took on Paul Annacone in the finals of Stratton Mountain, only a few weeks after Paul had reached the fourth round at Wimbledon. Paul thought it was fun—"one of Nick's original students playing one of his young students"—and Andre, who won, thought it was even more fun. The final came on July 31, my fifty-seventh birthday, and after the match, they brought out a cake, and Paul put his arm around me and said, "Well, at least we kept it in the family." Then Andre and Paul and everyone else sang "Happy

Birthday" to me. On national television, Andre said, "I'd like to dedicate this victory to my coach, my friend, Nick Bollettieri. He's done so many great things for me."

One of Andre's defeats in 1988 was noteworthy, too. At Indian Wells, California, he played Boris Becker for the first time, and Becker, who went on to win the tournament, beat him, 4–6, 6–3, 7–5.

Strangely, the two matches I remember best in 1989 were both defeats: one in the third round of the French Open, the other in a Davis Cup match against Germany. In the French Open, Andre met Jim Courier in the third round, and I made a devastating mistake. I should have sat in a neutral corner, should have encouraged both of my students, but instead, I sat with Phillip Agassi and Bill Shelton. Courier, who was still playing out of the academy, looked at me and knew that I was rooting for Andre. It showed in my face. "I realized that Nick didn't want me to win," Courier said later, "and it kind of hurt me."

Courier responded just the way I would've expected him to: by playing fierce tennis, by whipping Andre and me, 7–6, 4–6, 6–3, 6–2. Jim felt, justifiably, I suppose, that he had been betrayed. His days at the academy were about to end. I hated to see him go, but I really couldn't blame him. I had messed up.

The other memorable battle, the Davis Cup match, pitted Agassi against Becker. Andre won the first two sets, both on tiebreakers, a remarkable display of courage on Boris's turf, in Germany. In the third set, Agassi was up, 6–5, on the brink of victory, but Boris saved the match with a typical

GOOD-BYE, ANDRE

Becker effort, a lunging, diving get that I didn't think was possible. Boris won the last three sets, 7–6, 6–3, 6–4.

That was what Davis Cup tennis should be—great tennis—but rarely is. Once, in the days when so-called amateurs played, the Davis Cup was a huge event, a meaningful championship. But now it has lost so much of its luster, largely because of the time-consuming schedule. If an Agassi wants to represent the United States in all its Davis Cup matches, he has to give up seven or eight weeks a year, which means millions of dollars, which is why too often lesser players end up playing for the United States. I'd like to see the Davis Cup held, say, every two years, all the matches in a two-week period, with every tennis-playing country represented by its best. Then the Davis Cup would regain its significance, its glamour. Now it's just an excuse for a few tennis officials to enjoy an occasional vacation.

Andre passed the million-dollar mark in earnings in 1989 in only his forty-third tournament, faster than any player before him, and he did score a few memorable victories. He won only one title all year, in Orlando, beating Brad Gilbert in the final, but for the second year in a row, he reached the semifinals of the U.S. Open. In the quarterfinals, he came from being down, two sets to one, to defeat thirty-seven-year-old Jimmy Connors in five sets, the first five-set victory of his career.

In the season-ending Nabisco Masters, Becker and Agassi met for the third time, and for the third time, Boris prevailed, 6–l, 6–3. Boris would not beat Andre again for almost six years.

Sure, I don't agree with Andre's stance on Wimbledon or his pink shorts or his strange hair. He is not normal. But thank God for that. Thank God he is different. He's very good for tennis. He'd just be that much better if he came to Wimbledon.
—Boris Becker, 1990

In 1990, Andre beat Becker three times, at Indian Wells in straight sets, at the U.S. Open in four sets, and at the Association of Tennis Professionals (ATP) Tour World Championships in straight sets. Andre won the World Championships, lifting his earnings for the year to more than $1.7 million, for his career to more than $3 million.

But even though he won three tournaments and ended the year ranked fourth in the world, Andre was disappointed. He had reached the finals of two Grand Slam events, and both times he had lost to players he thought he should have beaten, a veteran and a kid, thirty-year-old Andres Gomez in the French Open and nineteen-year-old Pete Sampras in the U.S. Open.

Andre, by this time, was deep into Christianity, influenced and encouraged by David Wheaton and Michael Chang. When the three of them would get together to talk about the Bible, I would sometimes sit in on the discussions, listening to them trying to figure out the meanings of different passages. I found the talks interesting even though I was not so committed to religion as they were.

My wife Kellie, however, was a born-again Christian, which, for a while, created a bond between her and Andre. He grew close to my youngest children, too, Nicole and Alex. They loved to go out with Andre and his girlfriend of the moment. They especially liked Wendi Stewart. Wendi was from Las Vegas, and she and Andre had known each other since they were kids. She was a beautiful young woman who not only understood Andre, but was willing to stand up to him. Mike Agassi, Andre's father, did not care for Wendi; as a matter of fact, he didn't care for any woman Andre cared for. Mike feared that a woman, or a relationship with a woman, would destroy Andre's career.

Despite Mike's opposition, Wendi and Andre had, and still have, a wonderful friendship, which, for a while, became more than a friendship. I always thought Andre would end up marrying Wendi, but my judgment is probably not the most reliable in that area. I was startled when Andre and Brooke Shields announced they were going to be getting married.

Andre had surprisingly few relationships, considering the number of women who wanted to be with him. Wendi, a young woman named Amy from Tennessee, and an older woman named Barbra from Hollywood were the only three during his teens and early twenties. The relationship with Amy was not an easy one. I remember once we were in Memphis, and I saw Andre outside his hotel room, leaning on a railing, tears in his eyes after a disagreement with Amy.

I applauded Andre because he didn't go around flaunting his relationships or bragging about them, not to me anyway. I also applauded him for not taking advantage of the endless opportunities he was offered. Some nights, he chose to read the Bible. Many nights, he preferred to watch horror films.

Twice, in Andre's early years as a professional, he surprised me with generous gifts. Once, on a plane returning from a successful Davis Cup match in South America, Andre turned to me and took the check he had received for representing the United States and stuffed it in my pocket. "Buy yourself a Bronco," he said. The check was for $20,000. A year later, Andre bought his-and-his Corvettes, the ZR-1, the new racing car, and gave me the first one that was delivered, a black one, for Christmas.

> *Nick and Andre knew they could always count on me for a hit. Once they asked me to hit, and I was struggling so badly with my forehand I had to play my butt off just to give Andre a good workout. Nick, who coaches the forehand better than anyone on the planet, and Andre, who hits it better, began working on my forehand. I was given more information to compute than a shuttle mission to space. Andre would say one thing, and Nick would come over and whisper another thing in my ear. I was trying my best, but to be honest, I was just enjoying being the guy in the middle.*
>
> —Luke Jensen

In 1991, Andre turned twenty-one and moved into his own home in Las Vegas. I turned sixty and moved out of my own home in Bradenton.

In May, Team Agassi checked into the Georges V Hotel in Paris, Andre and Phillip, Fritz Nau and I, Bill Shelton and Gil Reyes, a terrific guy who had replaced Andre's original conditioning coach, Pat Etcheberry. We were staying at one of the fanciest hotels in Paris, close to some of the world's greatest restaurants, and we were eating our meals down the block at McDonald's. Double Big Macs, Big Macs, cheeseburgers, fries, apple pie, Coke—we devoured everything.

GOOD-BYE, ANDRE

When we tired of the cuisine at McDonald's, we ate tacos. We brought the food into the hotel, and we all gathered in Andre's room. They all wanted air-conditioning, which I hate, and they cooled the room down to about forty degrees, and I would bring blankets and wrap myself in the blankets, shivering, my eyes popping out while we watched Freddy and Jason and Chuckie.

We didn't go out, we didn't go to discos, we just hung out together, the six of us. We entertained ourselves. Between Andre and Gil, who was the former strength coach at the University of Nevada—Las Vegas, they knew the lyrics of just about every song ever written (Andre has a fantastic memory; he can remember almost every match he ever played, every critical point), and Bill Shelton, who has a wonderful voice, something like Nat "King" Cole's, would also sing to us. We didn't talk much tennis. I'd give Andre one or two little tips, and that would be it. He'd stay up till 2 or 3 in the morning with his horror films. Then he'd sleep till noon, get up, and go practice for ten or fifteen minutes and be ready to play. That was his idea of heavy training.

Andre breezed to the semifinals of the French Open in May 1991, then crushed Becker in four sets and moved into the final against our old friend, my former pupil, Jim Courier. This was Jim's first Grand Slam final, Andre's third, and Mike Agassi, Andre's father, came to Paris and turned it into a vendetta, a grudge match, revenge for the defeat in 1989.

Andre won the first set, Courier the second. Andre took the third easily, 6–2. He was only one set away from his first Grand Slam title. Then the match was interrupted by rain, and in the locker room, during the delay, José Higueras, who had become Courier's coach, suggested that Jim move back, play farther behind the baseline. Andre didn't adjust, didn't change his strategy—I should have anticipated the move—and Courier suddenly turned the match around. Jim took the last two sets, 6–1 and 6–4. Andre took the defeat hard. The critics were saying he couldn't win a Grand Slam, couldn't take the pressure, and even though he said he didn't pay any attention to the media, he half believed them. Andre himself wondered why he couldn't win the big one.

Andre returned to Wimbledon; he had skipped the Championships, as the British call them, for three years after his brief debut in 1987. We had bullshitted the media. We had said Andre wasn't ready for the grass courts, he wasn't strong enough, he wasn't mature enough. But the truth was that, after being eliminated in the first round in 1987, he simply decided he didn't like the surface or the atmosphere. I should have argued with him, emphasized the significance of Wimbledon, but instead, I just went along.

Now Andre was stronger and more mature—and, most important, confident enough to believe he could do well on any surface. He dressed in Wimbledon white, charmed the press by saying all the right things about the tradition and magnitude of the tournament, and as soon as he got out on the grass courts, he realized that the surface actually played to his strength, rewarded him for moving in and hitting the ball on the rise as it skidded off the grass. Andre played his way into the quarterfinals, where he lost to his friend David Wheaton after leading two sets to one.

Soon after Wimbledon, shortly before my birthday, I

GOOD-BYE, ANDRE

went home and Kellie confronted me. "How much more traveling are you going to be doing?" she asked.

"Quite a bit," I told her. "You know, our livelihood depends on this." Kellie walked out of the room, and I thought she was dropping the subject.

But less than an hour later, she gave me the ultimatum: "us or Andre." I chose Andre. I didn't even wait for my laundry to dry. I put my wet clothes in plastic bags, took off, and moved in temporarily with Fritz Nau and his wife.

I couldn't leave Andre. Not now. He had just won the Sovran Bank Classic in Washington, his second championship of the year, and I had an obligation to him, to push him, to drive him to the top level of the game. When he lost in the first round of the U.S. Open, which forced him to stop and think about his game and his goals, I began pointing for 1992.

In November 1991, Andre beat Becker for the fifth straight time, in the ATP Tour World Championships, then was eliminated by Courier in the semifinals. When Andre returned to the United States, I peppered him with notes and letters and suggestions. I gave him a five-point workout program. I told him (1) not to be competitive with his hitting partner; (2) work on increasing racquet speed, with racquets up in tension from sixty-two to seventy pounds; (3) develop muscle memory on the serve motion, with power not the objective; (4) work on depth and accuracy; and (5) enjoy the workout and don't try to reach the very high point of performance.

Andre spent a lot of time hitting with Luke Jensen and Raul Ordonez, a young Colombian who had come to the academy not knowing a word of English. A lot of time, that is, by Andre's unusual standards. Raul and I traveled to Vegas to work with him.

Andre's schedule was different from anyone else's I'd ever seen in my life. He used to wake up at 11 in the morning, have breakfast, and just relax for a while, play golf, go to the gym, lift some weights, and then run. At 9:30 at night, he'd have something to eat, maybe watch a movie, and then play tennis. It was the latest I'd ever played tennis in my life. We used to practice at 1 or 2 in the morning and go to bed at 4. It was crazy. That was Andre.

—Raul Ordonez

By the spring of 1992, Team Agassi was having problems, members of the team vying for Andre's attention and approval, sniping at each other, each trying to establish or inflate his own importance. Mr. Agassi was involved, too, urging Andre to concentrate on increasing the power of his serve; Mr. Agassi thought Andre had to have a serve as strong as Pete Sampras's. "No one questions how well your father knows your game," I wrote in one letter to Andre. "He gave you a great start. But now we all have to put aside our own needs and do what is best for you. It is time that all members of the team, past and present, accept the fact that we all added something to your development. No one should be talking or even thinking negative thoughts about others in order to make points with you."

In the same letter, I offered a series of suggestions: "You must work on your serve every day and develop the slice serve.... In practice, do not try to reach one hundred and ten percent or anywhere near one hundred percent.... You cannot get better without losing points in practice, without being passed.... You need quiet time as well as work time." I also asked Andre to let me know what he expected from me during each practice session: (1) sit on the side and watch; (2) get closer to observe strokes and serve; or (3) just feed balls.

In the French Open, Andre wiped out Pete Sampras in straight sets in the quarterfinal. That was the good news; the bad news was that in the semifinal he had to face Jim Courier, who had knocked him out of the same tournament in 1989 and 1991. Andre had eliminated Courier in 1990. This was the fourth year in a row my two students met in the French Open, but this time, for the first time, Courier was the No. 1 player in the world and the defending champion. Andre was never in the match. Jim beat him, 6–3, 6–2, 6–2. He stuck it to Andre again and to me and went on to win his second straight French title.

Andre flew back to the United States to take a break after Paris. A week later, in mid June, only a few days before the start of Wimbledon, my phone rang at two o'clock in the morning. I knew who it was before I picked it up. Only one person called me at that hour. "Nick, what the hell are you doing?" said Andre.

"I'm not doing anything," I said.

"Coach, do you think we should practice some before Wimbledon?"

"Yeah," I said. "I don't think it would be a bad idea."

I asked Andre where he wanted to practice, and he suggested a tennis club in Boca Raton, which was operated by

Carling Bassett and her husband, Robert Seguso. The fact that Andre's girlfriend, Wendi Stewart, was staying with Carling may have had something to do with his choice.

The next day, Fritz Nau, Raul Ordonez, and I threw our golf clubs in my Bronco and drove from Bradenton to Boca, a couple of hundred miles away. As soon as we arrived, Andre was ready to start hitting—a golf ball. We played eighteen holes, and at about four in the afternoon, Andre said he was ready to start hitting tennis balls. He hadn't hit a lick since the French Open.

We found two hard courts in a private condo development. They were painted green, so we pretended they were grass courts at Wimbledon. Andre got on the court and hit with Raul and Seguso for about forty-five minutes. One of the many amazing things about Andre was that he could go for weeks, or even longer, without hitting a ball, then pick up a racquet and start hitting just as well as if he had played the previous day.

Andre looked at me and said, "What do you think, Coach? Should we practice some more?"

"Shit," I said, "I think you're ready."

Andre agreed. "Shit, I'm ready," he said. "Let's go on over there."

We flew to England the next day, and the following day we put on a clinic for Donnay, the racquet Andre was using, at a London department store. After the clinic, Andre faced the media.

"Andre," a reporter asked, "are you excited about Wimbledon?"

"Yeah, I'm really looking forward to it," Andre said.

"How have you been preparing for it?"

"I've been in Boca Raton," Andre said, "playing on grass courts for the past ten days. You have to get used to grass."

"How do you like it?" someone asked.

"It's a great surface," Andre said and turned and winked at me. It was all I could do to keep a straight face.

When the press conference ended, Andre walked over to me and said, "Well, what did you think, Coach?"

"That was a hell of a conference," I said. "They believe you."

"You've got to make them believe you," he said.

I didn't believe we had the slightest chance at Wimbledon. After one day of practice! After all that bullshit about ten days on grass! Besides, Andre was seeded twelfth, and no twelfth seed had ever won the tournament.

Right in the first round, Andre faced Andrei Chesnokov, a Russian who had ranked among the top ten in the world the previous year. The match began late in the afternoon on a dreary day, and before play was interrupted by rain, Andre lost the first set and got a warning from the umpire for using the "F" word on the court. Andre was no longer studying the Bible with the same intensity.

The match was halted because of darkness, and Andre went back to the apartment he had rented not far from the courts, and I went back to my hotel room downtown. The next day, he finished off Chesnokov in four sets.

Still, the players standing between Andre and the Championship were formidable. Courier was seeded first. He came into Wimbledon ranked No. 1 in the world with a twenty-three-match winning streak. Becker was seeded second; he had reached the finals at Wimbledon six of the seven previous years. And John McEnroe, at the age of thirty-three, was a sentimental favorite, playing in his fourteenth and final Wimbledon.

Andre and McEnroe became friends in 1992. They were Davis Cup teammates—Andre won seven of seven singles matches as the United States beat Argentina, Czechoslovakia, Sweden, and Switzerland to win the cup—and as doubles partners in the French Open, they reached the quarterfinals. I watched them hit together almost every day during the first week of Wimbledon, saw them encouraging and advising each other. "Mac told me I didn't have to serve and volley to win with my game," Andre said. "He shortened my stroke, showed me how on the grass every point counts." During the second week, they hit together again. But this time, they tried to crush each other.

Both Andre and Mac were in Courier's half of the draw, and when Jim's winning streak abruptly came to an end in the third round, snapped after twenty-five victories by Andrei Olhovskiy, a Russian who hadn't won a match in five months, both men's chances dramatically improved. In the fourth round, Mac beat Olhovskiy, and Andre beat Christian Saceanu, both in straight sets.

In the quarterfinals, Andre met Boris on grass for the first time. Grass, of course, was Boris's surface of choice, but this was the second week of Wimbledon, and in the second week, the grass courts turn brown and dry and begin to play like clay courts or slow hard courts. And Boris knew Andre had beaten him the last five times they'd played. "When Andre sees my face," Boris said, "his game goes up twenty levels."

GOOD-BYE, ANDRE

"Look, Andre," I told Agassi before the match, "he's probably going to stay back. So we show him that kick serve, show him those heavy spins, and run him side to side—you know, Bradenton to Las Vegas—and eventually, he'll make the mistakes."

Which was exactly what happened. Andre dropped only one set to Becker in the quarterfinals, McEnroe none to Guy Forget, setting up Agassi, the twelfth seed, against McEnroe, unseeded, in the semifinals, Andre's first at Wimbledon, John's eighth. "I don't think there's anyone happier for John than me," Andre said.

"These young kids always say how honored they are to play me," McEnroe said, "when what they really want to do is kick my ass."

Andre kicked ass. He won, 6–4, 6–2, 6–3. "Andre's taken the return to another level," Mac said. "The ball came back so fast, it threw my system off. My system was going crazy."

Now, Andre was going into his fourth Grand Slam final, and for the fourth time, he was opposing a player who, like himself, had never won a Grand Slam. For the fourth time, in fact, his opponent had never before played in a Grand Slam final. He was going to face Goran Ivanisevic, the Croatian who was younger than Andre (twenty to twenty-two), taller than Andre (six-four to five-eleven), and seeded ahead of Andre (eighth to twelfth). In his semifinal, Ivanisevic had delivered thirty-six aces and overpowered Pete Sampras, 6–7, 7–6, 6–4, 6–2. Goran and Andre had played twice before, and Goran had won both times in straight sets.

"If I serve well," Ivanisevic said, "I am not afraid of anybody."

MY ACES, MY FAULTS

"If anybody can break Goran's serve," McEnroe said, "it's Andre."

Pete Sampras said the match was "between the best returner and the best server in the game."

I told people the match was "between Andre and Isavinivich." I never could get his name right.

John Newcombe was in the locker room before the championship match. So were Tony Roche and Fred Stolle, all former Wimbledon finalists. They were talking tennis history, remembering great matches they had played and witnessed, and Andre was talking about his new souped-up Suburban, with its 550 horsepower and its $40,000 stereo system.

Two minutes before he was to walk out to Centre Court, Andre turned to tennis. "What do you think, Coach?" he said.

"Andre," I said, "I'm going to tell you two things, buddy. First, this guy's going to serve a bunch of aces, and you've got to accept it. Second, Isavinivich likes to play fast. Jack Nicklaus always used to play golf slow, and it irritated the hell out of his opponents. I want you to do the same thing to Isavinivich. Slow his ass down. And if you do it at a crucial time, I think it'll pay off for you. Good luck to you, buddy, you can do it. It's all in your hands."

I made my way to join Phillip, Bill Shelton, Gil Reyes, and Wendi Stewart in our courtside box. I looked around, at the royal box, at all the people filling the stands. I saw the players come out and go to their battle stations, Andre in his proper Wimbledon white, and I pinched myself, because this was the moment of truth, this was the finals of Wimbledon, the biggest tournament in the world. I had looked forward to this moment for so many years, one of

GOOD-BYE, ANDRE

my students playing for the Championship. I pressed into my seat, the last seat next to the wall. My lucky seat. Nobody else could sit in that seat.

The match began, and Ivanisevic's serve, as expected, was awesome. In the first set alone, he served eleven aces. The set went to a tiebreaker, and Goran won it, 10–8. The final point was an ace—on a second serve. But Andre refused to be flustered, maintained his confidence and his concentration. I had never seen him so filled with fight. He won the second set, 6–4, and the third by the same score. Once again, as he had been in Paris the year before, Andre was a set from a Grand Slam championship, and once again his opponent battled back. Ivanisevic whipped through the fourth set in seventeen minutes, losing only ten points, only one game. I studied Andre, searched for that scared look on his face. I didn't see it. His head was up. He wasn't panicking. "It wasn't like I didn't expect aces and love games," Andre said afterward. "I enjoyed watching Goran's serves myself."

Through nine games in the fifth set, through ten more aces for Goran, lifting his total for the match to thirty-seven, for the tournament to an incredible two hundred and six, the two players stayed on serve. "I kept telling myself Goran was capable of giving me a couple of free points," Andre said afterward. "If I could get him down to one final game, I liked my chances."

With Andre leading, 5–4, Goran, down to one final game, served, and double-faulted, not once, but twice, only his sixth and seventh double faults of the match. A couple of free points, and the score was love–30. But, as Andre said later,

"After what I've been through, I didn't hear the fat lady humming."

Goran hit two service winners, tying the game at 30. Then he hit a weak volley, and Andre responded with a forehand pass down the line. Set point. Match point. Championship point. I was hyperventilating. No preparation. No expectations. And now one point away from the greatest title in tennis.

Ivanisevic quickly got ready to serve, hoping to pound the ball left-handed into a corner at one hundred and twenty miles an hour or more. And Andre, moving into position to receive, looked over at Goran and said gently, "Slow down a second."

Slow his ass down.

Andre had done it. He had remembered. Goran looked annoyed, hesitated, then swung into his first serve and drove the ball into the net. "Holy mackeral," I said. "We're on the second serve."

"My eyes lit up," Andre said, "and I was really aware of the fact that it could all be done with one backhand return."

Ivanisevic served and charged toward the net, Andre hit a backhand return right at him, and Goran's volley dove into the net. I leaped up. Andre fell down. He crouched on his knees on the hallowed but withered grass of Wimbledon, and he began to cry, looked up, and said, "I'm the Wimbledon winner." I was accused of signaling Andre to stay down, remain kneeling, the way Björn Borg used to. Not a bad idea. But the truth is, the thought of signaling Andre never occurred to me. Besides, I didn't have a signal for kneeling.

Goran embraced Andre, and the duke and duchess of

GOOD-BYE, ANDRE

Kent applauded him. Andre had earned almost half a million dollars for his Wimbledon fortnight. He clutched the championship trophy, lifted the bowl high, caressed it, and kissed it. "You know," he said, "I really have had a lot of chances to fulfill a lot of my dreams, and I haven't come through in the past. But to do it here is more than I could ever ask for."

The feeling was unbelievable. I didn't walk back to the locker room. I flew, my feet never touching the ground. Andre and I met by the water fountain, and he said, "Coach, if we do nothing else, we've done it all. Thank you."

It was the happiest day of my life.

"I never felt the tension," Andre told the press. "I felt the ability." He was asked about avoiding Wimbledon for three years, and he said, "I am really kind of sad because, you know, the sport has offered me so much, this tournament has offered me so much. It's a shame that I didn't respect it a little earlier."

The following night, Andre put on a tuxedo, I dressed less formally and we went to the Wimbledon Ball, honoring the champions, honoring Andre and Steffi Graf, who had defeated Monica Seles in straight one-sided sets for the women's title. I was delighted by Steffi's victory, not because she had once spent a few weeks at the academy, but because Monica, who had spent several years at the academy, whose family had enjoyed hundreds of thousands of dollars worth of room and board, training, and perks for free, had turned her back on me and the academy, had announced that I had never been her coach, that I had had nothing to do with her development, her success. I wasn't as glad to see her lose as I was to see Andre win. But it was close.

Andre spoke at the ball, and he said, "There's a man in this audience who helped make all of this possible, my coach and my friend, Nick Bollettieri." Then Andre thanked Steffi Graf, too, for beating Monica Seles.

I still get chills thinking about that night. There is nothing, absolutely nothing, like the feeling of being the coach of a Grand Slam champion.

When I got back to the academy, the banner was already up, the most prominent among all the banners hanging in the indoor tennis center, honoring all the championships won by my students: Andre Agassi, Wimbledon Champion, 1992.

A few weeks later, his friends in Las Vegas threw a surprise party to celebrate Andre's victory, and it was a hell of a party. They had a drinking contest that started with beer and went to Long Island iced teas and then tequila. I caught one of Andre's friends just before he fell into the swimming pool. I had the honor of giving the congratulatory speech. Late in the night, Andre said he was thinking of taking his ten-seat Jetstar, his latest toy, and flying to California just to pick up one of his favorite hamburgers at a famous place called Tommy's. He settled for sitting on his lawn, looking up at the sky, naked.

The following week, he lost in the first round in Washington—he tanked; he didn't even pretend that he was trying to win—and just when people were starting to say, "Same old Agassi, Wimbledon was a fluke," he went to Toronto and won the singles championship in the Canadian Open, beating Ivan Lendl for the first time, and was the runner-up in doubles, with McEnroe as his partner. In the U.S. Open, he got only as far as the quarterfinals, knocked out once again by Jim Courier, who was still the No. 1 player in the world at the end of the year.

For Christmas that year, I sent many of my friends a framed set of photographs, one showing Andre kneeling on the burnished Wimbledon grass, one showing him hoisting the trophy, and one showing the two of us at the Ball sharing the trophy. "Please share the biggest thrill of my life," I wrote on the gift.

At the start of 1993, Andre Agassi was twenty-two years old and had already earned more than $5 million in prize money and at least as much, probably more, in endorsements. The academy and I had spent at least a million dollars on his development, on coaches, rooms, board, travel, and hitting partners, and in return, we had received a considerable amount of publicity and less than $400,000, which included the Davis Cup check and the black Corvette. It struck me that I had been generous, even lavish, in my dealings with Andre, and I didn't feel he had quite reciprocated.

Andre, nursing a case of bronchitis, skipped the Australian Open and the tournaments that led up to it and began his 1993 season in earnest in February. He got off to a strong start, won two tournaments in four weeks, then cooled off. Tendinitis flared up in his right wrist, forcing him to pass up the French Open. He did attempt to defend his Wimbledon title, but even with Barbra Streisand cheering for him— she seemed like a nice lady, and she loved to yell, but she didn't know much about tennis—he got only as far as the quarterfinals. He put on a gutsy performance in the quarters, coming from two sets down to force Pete Sampras, the eventual champion, to five sets before succumbing.

At Wimbledon, Andre and I had a talk, and he told me that Perry Rogers, his childhood friend who had become his business manager, was going to start monitoring his spending, cutting back on expenses, perhaps dropping people from the team, even putting Andre himself on an allowance. I felt uneasy. I wondered if Andre might be hinting that he was going to drop me. Not that that would've saved him much money.

I wasn't terribly happy with the way our relationship was going. Andre didn't seem to know who he wanted to be his coach. He had consulted McEnroe, he had courted the veteran Pancho Segura, he had sought out Brian Teacher in San Diego for advice on his volley. I felt my authority was being undermined. I felt that Andre was listening to everyone except me. I also felt betrayed by Fritz Nau, whom I had hired, trained, and teamed up with Andre. Fritz was supposed to be working for the academy and for me, yet he kept preaching Segura's philosophy to Andre.

When I got back to the States, I went to North Carolina to stay with the Hills, the parents of my talented junior, Gregg Hill. While I visited the Hills, I thought about my decade with Andre, reflected upon our shifting relationship, his changing attitude toward tennis and toward me. I was afraid he had gotten too big, too big for me, too big for himself. He was immensely talented, but he was unwilling to train properly, to commit himself to the regimen that would make him a champion. He didn't want to hear criticism, and I didn't want to be a yes-man.

GOOD-BYE, ANDRE

I was frustrated, angry with Andre, angry with myself for not being more forceful with him, more demanding. I decided we needed a separation. I knew it would be very painful for both of us—he had been like a son to me—and I knew that it could be permanent. But I felt it had to be done for Andre's sake and for mine.

I sat down and wrote him a letter telling him that I was resigning as his coach. It wasn't easy. It was like saying good-bye to my children after a divorce. I told him he wasn't applying himself to becoming the best player in the world, he wasn't focusing in on being a champion. I told him that as much as I cherished our time on the road, and as much as our partnership meant to my career and the prominence and success of the NBTA, I now wanted to spend more time with my children and my Leah and my students at the academy. I wished him well and said good-bye.

I wanted to be sure that I was the one who said good-bye, not Andre.

I should have flown out to Las Vegas and told him in person. I shouldn't have told him in a letter even though I had sent him so many letters before. I certainly shouldn't have told a newspaperman about my decision even before Andre received the letter. But I've never been very good at keeping my feelings to myself. "I felt that the role I was playing was not productive," I said. "I just hope he concentrates on what made him reach this level, and that's his tennis." I asked the reporter not to print anything before the letter got to Andre, but he felt he couldn't wait. Andre's feelings were battered. So was his wrist. He played in the

U.S. Open, only his thirteenth tournament of the year, and was eliminated in the first round. He did not play again in 1993.

He underwent surgery to remove painful scar tissue from his wrist, and by the end of the year, aching and overweight, up from one hundred and fifty-five pounds to more than one hundred seventy, according to some reports, Andre Agassi had plummeted to No. 24 in the world.

"I honestly didn't think he would ever come all the way back," said his brother, Phillip.

FOREHAND

Grip

A semi-Western, which he adjusts to hit a little flatter or to gain heavy topspin.

Backswing

A rather high circular backswing.

Forward Swing

Unbelievable racquet acceleration—even when he cuts down backswing.

Options

He can hit any shot from any position on the court.

1. Consistent crosscourts, down the lines with spin, heavy rolling spin, or just flatten it out.
2. Against net rushers, he can drive you crazy and make you gun-shy in one second.

Why?

1. He comes forward and makes contact well inside the baseline, which forces the volleyer to make contact at a very low level and reduces the chances for an offensive volley.
2. If you do manage to get in a few extra steps and you feel you now have Andre, just try volleying balls with heavy spin that will drop suddenly, like a knuckleball in baseball.

Add to this three more of his options:

1. He will smack it right at you, forcing you to make a reflex volley.
2. He will hit a topspin lob.
3. He will pass you down the line or crosscourt.

Note: If you play Andre to either his forehand or his backhand side, do not think or even hope that under pressure, even on match point, he will just push the ball back and hope you miss it. He will do what his father taught him to do: **Hit it and then hit it harder.**

BACKHAND

Grip

The bottom hand is not quite an Eastern backhand; it is a little closer to a Continental grip, which he might adjust for a one-handed slice. The top hand is just about an Eastern forehand.

Swing
Andre's backswing and preparation is as good as it comes:

1. A quick shoulder and hip rotation.
2. Racquet backswing level is waist high and then adjusted on the forward part of the swing.
3. He can drive the ball, making contact at ball height, then extending the arms out to the target.
4. He can get under the ball, accelerate racquet speed, follow out to target, but then continue around his left shoulder on the follow-through.

Note: Be careful if you get into a crosscourt backhand rally with Andre. He will burn you by coming in and hitting a winner down the line over and over and over.

SERVE

Andre's serve is one of the most underrated in the game. A few years ago, just by accident, his brother, Phillip, and I realized that when serving to the ad court Andre should hit a heavy kicker out wide. This became his new weapon. The ball bounced out so wide and high the opponent just about had to go into the stands to return it. All Andre had to do was run around and hit a forehand to the open court. If you try to move in on him, he will hit the big ball for an ace.

VOLLEY

Because Andre hits the ball so early, two to four feet inside the baseline, it has become a natural response for him to move forward a few more steps, and once he's in that close, he doesn't have to do much more than block the ball for a winner.

OVERHEAD

This is one of his best shots.

MOVEMENT

He can move in any direction at any time and hit offensive returns rather than just getting the ball back in play.

MENTALITY

Andre certainly thinks better on the court than he used to, and I think the credit should go to Brad Gilbert and to maturity.

SUMMARY

His ability, his clothing, his hairstyles, his Brooke, his charisma—he is one in a million!

GOOD-BYE, ANDRE

HOW TO BEAT HIM

When Andre decides he wants to win *and* believes he will win, he is almost unbeatable. You must refuse to lose. You must keep your head up. You must bring doubt to Andre's mind. That is the only way to make him vulnerable.

WIMBLEDON: THE WINNER

When they walked to the net at Centre Court, when the match was over, I knew that Andre Agassi wanted to say something, that he was about to speak. But Boris Becker never gave him a chance. He just shook Andre's hand and turned away.

Boris never gave him a chance either in the tiebreaker that ended the fourth set, ended the match, and ended Andre's string of eight straight victories over Boris. Boris won the tiebreaker easily, 7–1, and with his four-set triumph, 2–6, 7–6, 6–4, 7–6, advanced to his seventh Wimbledon final in eleven years, a record unmatched by a male player in the twentieth century. When he won the final point, Boris thrust his fist in the air and turned for approval to the people in his box, to Barbara, Mike, Ulli, Val, and me.

As I hurried to the locker room, my mind raced back to 1992, back to the match between Andre and Goran Ivanisevic. I remembered the exhilarating feeling when Andre won the Championship. I also remembered the terrible feeling more than a year later when Andre turned on me. When Becker reached the locker room, I hugged him and said, "Thank you, Boris. Thank you from the bottom of my heart."

I think I wanted this victory more than any other victory in my life, perhaps even more than Andre's victory at Wimbledon. I wanted this victory to show Brad Gilbert that a coach doesn't have to have been a great player to be a successful coach. I wanted this victory to show Andre Agassi, whom I had nurtured like a son, that I was not insignificant. I wanted this victory to show Boris Becker that he had been wise to entrust me with rebuilding his career.

"Coach, I won this one for you," Boris said.

"Boris," I said, "you lifted yourself to a new level today." I wanted him to know how magnificently I thought he had played. "I never knew you could play that well," I said.

When Boris went off to his news conference, when Andre came into the locker room, I didn't want to approach him. But as he walked past me, I said, "Sorry, Andre." I didn't know what else to say. A little later, as he left the locker room, I said, "Andre, I wasn't rooting *against* you. I was rooting *for* Boris." I definitely had mixed feelings. "I've never wished you any evil," I said. "I never said anything negative about you. Never."

"I know that, Nick," Andre said.

I hoped that he did. I hoped that he knew how difficult it had been for me not to fight back when he had said I never did anything for him, when he had said that I was selfish, that I was motivated purely by money. I've done a lot of things wrong in my life, but I've never been selfish. I've never been a taker. I've always been a giver.

"Nobody should underestimate me," Boris told the press. "He made a major mistake at 4–1 when he didn't finish me off."

"When that lead slipped away," Andre said, "I think Boris started playing a bit more aggressively, and when he got back on serve, I never quite had the confidence again."

"Once Becker bowled him over with his determination in the second set," Robin Finn wrote in the *New York Times*, "Agassi never recovered. The court, like his baggy tennis whites, simply looked too big for him, and so did the man across the net, a man who just happens to be coached by Nick Bollettieri, Agassi's mentor-turned-nemesis after their acrimonious split in 1993."

Boris and I didn't get out of the locker room until after eight o'clock. As we were driving back to our rented homes, Boris put his hand on my knee and said, "Mr. B, remember when we got the shit kicked out of us at Lipton in '94?"

Of course I remembered. Not only did Andre batter Boris in their match at Key Biscayne, but that was the day Andre told the media that I was insignificant.

"I made up my mind that day," Boris said, "that someday we were going to get even. I've been telling you for the past eighteen months that there was a big match coming."

The victory over Andre was so big that that night, Boris invited Leah and me and Mike DePalmer and his wife Angelique to celebrate with him and Barbara over dinner at San Lorenzo, our favorite Italian restaurant. Normally, Boris celebrated only championships. This was the closest thing.

5

HELLO, BORIS

HELLO, BORIS

In the spring of 1993, when Andre Agassi skipped the French Open and Boris Becker was eliminated in the second round, I was home in Florida, watching the tournament on television. Cliff Drysdale and Fred Stolle, the announcers, were talking about Becker's decline, interviewing his former manager, Ion Tiriac, and some of his former coaches, a lengthy list that included Gunther Bosch, Bob Brett, Tomas Smid, and Gunther Bresnik.

What was wrong with Becker? Everyone offered a theory. He was unhappy with his personal life, he was too wealthy to be motivated, he was too fat and too lazy to put in the work that was needed to get back in physical and mental shape. Boris's career, they suggested, was going down the drain.

What would they do if they were coaching him? No one seemed to have a constructive answer.

I got up and sent off a fax to Paris, to my friend Mary Carillo, the broadcaster. If I were coaching Becker, I told Mary, I'd ask him one question: Hey, Boris, do you want to play tennis anymore? And if Boris said yes, I would ask him one more question: Why?

MY ACES, MY FAULTS

Of course, never in my wildest dreams did I imagine that I would someday be coaching Boris Becker.

I had watched Becker win Wimbledon when he was seventeen years old and unseeded and again when he was eighteen. I had seen him win both Wimbledon and the U.S. Open when he was twenty-one. I remembered when he won the Australian Open in 1991 and rose, at the age of twenty-three, to No. 1 in the world.

I loved the way he leaped and dove to pull off miraculous shots. I loved the way he pranced around the court, tall and proud, like a young colt.

When I was traveling with Andre Agassi, whenever I saw Boris, I always said hello. Boris thought I was trying to con him, trying to get him to relax his guard. But I was just paying my respects. I thought then that I would always be with Andre.

After I said good-bye to Andre in July 1993, I intended to lay low for a while, sit back and analyze my career, perhaps plan my future. I had a good crop of young players coming up at the academy—Tommy Haas, Gregg Hill, a twelve-year-old Russian girl named Anna Kournikova. They would be ready soon.

Of course, as the summer went on, as the U.S. Open approached and passed, I began to get itchy. I was coaching Mary Pierce, who reached the fourth round at Flushing Meadows, but I didn't have anyone in the men's draw. For thirteen straight years, I had coached Jimmy Arias in the Open or Aaron Krickstein or Andre Agassi, sometimes even two of them, but now I had nobody. I felt left out. I missed the action.

Then, late in November, I received a phone call from Dr. Axel Meyer-Wolden, who was one of the people behind the Compaq Grand Slam Cup, the unofficial tournament in Munich that offered a very real $2 million to the winner. Dr. Meyer-Wolden was a lawyer, Boris Becker's lawyer.

I had met Dr. Meyer-Wolden at the Compaq Cup the previous year and had invited him and his family to visit the academy. He and his wife, Antonella, and their children, Sandy and Agi, spent three or four weeks in Florida in the summer of 1993. He watched me coach; he checked out our facilities. He assessed us.

"Boris Becker is coming over to the States," Dr. Meyer-Wolden told me. "He wants to look at your academy. Please take good care of him."

Boris was nearing the end of a terrible year by his high standards, his least successful since he was seventeen years old. For the first time since 1985, he had dropped out of the top ten in the world, was not even No. 1 in Germany, and had failed to qualify for the ATP Tour World Championships. He had not won a tournament in ten months. Besides, he was about to get married, and his fiancée was seven months pregnant. No wonder he wanted to get away from Germany for a few days.

Boris arrived in Bradenton with his personal trainer, Carlo Thranhardt, a German who was, in the 1980s, one of the world's two or three best high jumpers. Boris studied every court, every corner of the academy. When he spotted the banners hanging above the indoor courts, dominated by the banner commemorating Andre's 1992 victory at Wimbledon, Boris turned to me and said, "You know my game pretty good, huh?"

"What do you mean?" I said.

Boris smiled. "Well, every time Agassi plays me, he beats my ass."

I was smiling, too. "Well, Boris, it wasn't very difficult to do. You tried to beat him from the baseline, and very few people can beat Andre from the baseline."

Boris hit a few tennis balls with one of my pros and a few golf balls with me. He was just happy to escape from the reporters and photographers who followed him and his fiancée everywhere they went in Germany. I thanked him for his visit and wished him luck.

A couple of weeks later, I went to Munich to host a series of clinics at the Compaq Cup, and one day Dr. Meyer-Wolden invited me to join him for dinner at the house Boris was living in while his own home was being renovated.

Barbara Feltus, who was about to become Boris's wife, joined us. She is a very attractive woman, the dark-skinned daughter of a German mother and an African-American father. While Axel, Boris, and I talked, Barbara kept rolling around the room on a beachball. Of course, with her baby due in four or five weeks, she looked a little like a beachball herself.

We sat at the dining room table, and Dr. Meyer-Wolden brought up the fact that Boris was trying to decide on a new coach. Axel, as always, dominated the conversation, but I was able to mention the fax I had sent to Mary Carillo during the French Open. Finally, Dr. Meyer-Wolden looked at me and said, "Nick, I want you to be Boris's coach."

Without a second's hesitation, I turned my eyes to Becker and said, "Boris, do you really want to play tennis anymore?"

"Yes," he said. "I want to play."

"Why?"

"I want to win again," Boris said. "I want to compete again. I want to get back on top."

"Boris," I said, "you've got yourself a coach."

Boris and Axel may have discussed the possibility before, but not with me. I had not seen or spoken to Boris in the five months between the time I left Andre and the time Boris came to Bradenton. No matter what some people thought and wrote, Boris was not waiting in the wings for me.

We ate a magnificent dinner. It was easy to see that Boris loved good food and good wine. It was also easy to see that he was overweight.

We shook hands, and I said, "I'll be back in January."

Dr. Meyer-Wolden and Ted Meekma worked out a contract between Boris and me. I was to receive a salary of $15,000 a month, $180,000 a year, plus ten percent of Boris's earnings, up to $1.25 million a year. Because Boris had earned more than $1.25 million a year in each of the previous six years, the odds were that I would earn more than $300,000 a year. In addition, Boris would pay all of my expenses, including hotels, meals, and airline tickets, plus the expenses for hitting partners and a traveling coach.

Who would be the traveling coach? I had to make the choice very carefully. I needed someone with whom I could communicate and with whom Boris could communicate. I went over all my pros, and I picked David "Red" Ayme. He was a redheaded Cajun from Reserve, Louisiana, a baseball and basketball player at Nicholls State, a college on the bayou, who walked on to the tennis team, earned a scholarship, and, for a while, coached Nicholls's women's team. Red came to the academy in 1987 just for the summer, but he was so loud, so good, and so hardworking, I told him I wouldn't let him go back to Louisiana. He worked two years for me without taking a day off. He worked Christmas Day for seven straight years.

Red Ayme celebrated New Year's Eve, 1993, by flying to Germany with one of my students who would be hitting with Boris, a young Romanian named Gabriel Trifu. The other designated hitter, Tommy Haas, who was home in Germany on vacation, would join them in Munich. "What's Boris like?" Red asked me before he left.

"Red, I don't know," I said. "Just get him hitting lots of balls, getting the feel of the racquet again."

Over the holidays, I told my great friend Nate Landow, "I think I'm going to be coaching Boris Becker."

Nate looked at me. He didn't mince any words. "Don't do it," he said. "You don't need him. He's finished. You want to go down the drain with him? You got good kids coming up. Why don't you just wait for them to develop?"

"It's a big honor for me," I said, "and a big challenge."

I had never taken on a player of Becker's magnitude. His star may not have been rising, but he was still a monument in Germany, a national hero on a par with, or above, Franz

HELLO, BORIS

Beckenbauer, the soccer player and coach, and Katarina Witt, the Olympic figure skating champion.

Boris didn't want me to come to Germany right away. He wanted to have ten days with Red, Tommy, and Gabriel to start to get himself in shape, his body and his mind. He didn't want me to see him at his worst.

I arrived in Munich January 10. Boris, naturally, was wondering what I was going to be like. *What's he going to do, give me an Agassi forehand? Teach me a two-handed backhand like Krickstein or Courier?* I had my own thoughts. *Be careful, Nick. Be careful. Don't say very much. Get him to hit lots of balls. Get his timing down. Don't talk negative. Give him confidence.*

What I'm best at is making my players feel good about themselves. I try to get to their minds. Then I try to get more out of them than they think they have to give.

I stayed in Munich for ten days, and Boris amazed me with his work ethic. He worked his ass off. Our days started at 9:30 in the morning and ended at 8:30 at night. We couldn't train in Munich. The media would have been all over us. We had to drive thirty or forty minutes out of town to a place where Boris could have some privacy.

He stretched, practiced, ate lunch, napped on the floor, stretched, worked out, practiced, practiced, practiced. He certainly knew how to cover the court; he didn't have the quick feet of an Agassi, but he got there. When his son, Noah, was born on January 18, when he had to elude half the paparazzi of Germany to get Barbara to the hospital, Boris took half a day off. "Hey, Nick," he said, "do I have to have a baby any time I want half a day off?"

I was supposed to fly home the next day, but Boris, after

an understandably indifferent workout, said, "Nick, would you mind staying one more day, so you can really see me hitting the ball?" That was typical Becker, wanting to end every workout or every ten days of workouts on a high note, preferably with a perfect shot.

I stayed, watched, and said very little, which was, of course, against my nature. *What do I do? How do I change the game of someone who's won Wimbledon three times?* But I was starting to understand Boris. I realized that I had to have a good reason before I offered any advice, any suggestions. I had to be prepared to back up anything I said. Boris did not make decisions lightly. He had to think about it, weigh it.

On the flight home, I thought about Boris. *Jesus Christ, this is different for me, a guy who's very methodical, a guy who's very neat, who takes practice seriously, who likes to think before he acts. A grown-up.*

Boris wanted me to be with him for his first tournament of 1994, and I was so eager to get going, I left the States at 4 P.M. Sunday, January 30, two hours before the kickoff of my favorite event, the Super Bowl. I gave away my tickets, and I had great seats. I was somewhere over the Atlantic when Dallas came from behind in the second half and beat Buffalo.

Boris did better than the Bills. He won a couple of matches in Marseilles, won the next week's tournament in Milan, then the following week, in the quarterfinals in Stuttgart, beat Michael Stich, the man who had replaced him as the No. 1 player in Germany. Boris lost in the semis in Stuttgart to Goran Ivanisevic. I could already see how much winning meant to Boris. I could also see how important ritual was to him, especially in the last minutes before a match; he

HELLO, BORIS

always did everything the same way, very precisely, very calmly, never rushing, barely conscious of the referee coming into the locker room and announcing, "Five minutes, Mr. Becker."

Boris always took the full five minutes and usually more. He stripped off his clothes slowly, arranged them neatly in a pile. Then he took his tennis outfit out of his big Lotto bag, one item at a time, and dressed with great care, putting his sneakers on last. He went to the men's room, and when he returned, he put several extra tennis shirts, smartly folded, into his bag, packed two bananas and one hard roll, then turned to Ulli, who handed him five racquets, each hand-strung to his requirements, four of them wrapped in plastic, one, the one he would start with, ready for action. Then he would pack the racquets, zip his bag, throw it across his shoulder, and go off to work.

During practice sessions, I slowly summoned the courage to offer suggestions but never to give orders or make demands. "Something's on my mind," I'd say, and then when he'd ask me what, I'd say, "You know, Boris, as you move to the backhand, you might turn those hips and shoulders a little quicker so that the racquet is right there by your left shoulder when you get to the ball. Then all you have to do is the forward part of the swing." Half an hour to an hour before matches, Boris would say to me, "Mr. B., what's the plan for today?" and I would try to give him one little tip, one bit of strategy to keep in mind.

Boris called me the Old Fox. He said I had young eyes, said I saw things no one else saw.

In March, we went to Florida for the Lipton Championships in Key Biscayne. For the first time since I had teamed up with Boris, he and Andre were entered in the same tournament, each with quite a bit to prove.

For five straight years, from 1988 through 1992, both had been ranked among the top ten players in the world, Becker rising to No. 1, Andre as high as No. 3. Now neither was in the top ten, and neither was a favorite to win the Lipton. Becker was seeded tenth in a field of more than one hundred, Agassi twenty-fourth.

On the Monday before the tournament began, as I entered my hotel room around eleven o'clock at night, the phone was ringing. I picked it up, and it was Andre. We hadn't spoken since July. "I'm angry," he said. "I'm angry that you left me, and I'm angry with how you did it. I'm angry that you wrote a letter. I'm angry that you told the press before you told me. Nick, I have all your letters to me, all the letters you wrote over the years, all those nice things you said, they're all in my closet."

Andre said I had told him that I was leaving him to spend more time with Leah and my family and my students and then I had teamed up with Boris. "You talked out of both sides of your mouth, Nick," he said. "How could you do that?"

I let him talk and talk and talk, and finally, I said, "Can I talk now?" He said I could, and I said, "You know, Andre, I'd like to go back to the time when you were just thirteen, going on fourteen. You came to me, had a lot of talent, you and your father were going to kill each other, your father was getting in fistfights at the matches, fighting with everybody, and he asked me to help him out with his son. And

HELLO, BORIS

I took you, Andre, and I helped you in every way possible. I gave you my life. You say I talk out of both sides of my mouth. What about when you went out to Brian Teacher in San Diego and took lessons on your volley or when McEnroe had a press conference with you and you said he was going to be your coach? It hurt the shit out of me to hear that secondhand, but I wrote to you and told you that if that was what you needed to become the very best, I'd support you, I'd be all for it. I always sent you letters because I knew that you would take the time to read the letters through and through. You said that I would always be part of everything you did and that you would always take care of me. And you say *I* double-talked *you*. Andre, that's bullshit. When I left you, I wasn't planning to go with anybody else. But then, five months later, an unbelievable opportunity came up, which I thought was good for my career and good for the academy, and I took it."

We talked for fifteen or twenty minutes, and we both aired our feelings, our pain, and our anger. There was no yelling, and I thought we had cleared the air.

The next day, I saw Perry Rogers, Andre's manager. "You know, Perry," I said, "Andre and his father always said that I would be a part of their success. I feel that I deserve to be compensated for all the time and effort and financial support I gave Andre over the years. You know how hard I worked. Don't you think I deserve to be paid for all that?"

Perry didn't argue. "You've got a good point," he said. "Send me an invoice." When I did, Andre rejected it. He said he owed me nothing; he said I had been amply compensated in gifts and in publicity for me and the academy.

When the tournament began, Andre and Boris each drew a bye in the first round and an opponent they could handle in the second. Agassi eliminated Mark Petchey in three sets; Becker also needed three to beat Nicklas Kulti. They advanced to the third round to face each other.

I felt strange sitting at courtside, representing Boris Becker who was playing Andre Agassi. Fritz Nau was on the other side; so was Brad Gilbert, coaching Andre for the first time.

Andre not only beat Boris, he humiliated him. He made him look like a novice. The scores were 6–2, 7–5, and the match was more one-sided than the scores. Boris tossed away his baseball cap. He pounded his racquet against the ground. "I hit serves of one hundred and fifteen miles an hour," Boris lamented, "and he hit them back like they were nothing." When he was down, 2–6 and 0–2, Boris handed his racquet to a ball girl and suggested that she return Andre's serve because he couldn't. Andre tapped a gentle serve to the ball girl, and she hit it back.

When the match mercifully ended, I didn't go to the news conference. I didn't want to hear what Andre had to say. But he was asked about my presence, and he said, "Nick is insignificant to be quite honest. I feel like his knowledge of the game is limited, but he probably convinced Boris that he was the reason I beat Boris. He can sell himself pretty well." When he was asked about our relationship, Andre said, "I look out for myself and he looks out for himself."

As I was leaving the grounds of the tournament, I was told by a reporter what Andre had said and was asked if I had any comment. At first, I said no, but then I turned around and said, "Geez, if I was insignificant, and he went from nowhere to No. 3 in the world to three Grand Slam finals, won Wimbledon, became a Davis Cup star, and made $30 or $40 or $50 million, I wonder what the hell would have happened if I were significant."

"Is that all you have to say, Nick?"

"No, that's not all," I said. "I'm gonna put the rest in my book." And that was the first time I thought of writing this book.

Boris wasn't happy with the way he had played in his seventh straight loss to Andre, but he tried to console me. "Our day will come," he promised.

Andre had a remarkable tournament at the Lipton. After beating Boris, he defeated Cedric Pioline in the round of sixteen, Stefan Edberg in the quarterfinals, and Patrick Rafter in the semis. Which meant he had defeated five players in a row from five different countries—a Brit, a German, a Frenchman, a Swede, and an Australian—and in the final, he was going to face an American, Pete Sampras, the No. 1 player in the world.

Sampras woke up the morning of the final with a miserable stomach virus. "I was feeling nauseated, heaving and gagging," he said. "I didn't think I'd be able to go out and play." Pete was so weakened he couldn't make the scheduled 1 P.M. starting time for the match. Andre graciously agreed to a one-hour delay, and by 2 P.M., Sampras was strong enough to walk on to the court, strong enough to make the first set close before losing, 5–7, and strong enough to win the next two sets, 6–3, 6–3, and the championship. Andre lost the match but won admiration for his sportsmanship.

MY ACES, MY FAULTS

"I'm going to take my career to a place it's never been," he promised.

Boris struggled for the next couple of months but not for any lack of effort. He had taken off weight. He was moving better. "I've been working my ass off," he said to me before the start of the Italian Open in May 1994. "When are we going to start seeing some results?"

"Well, Boris," I said, "God has a strange way of doing things."

The Italian Open was played on red clay, a favorite surface for most Europeans, including, at one time, Boris. As a teenager, he had spent a great deal of time competing and winning on red clay. But as a pro, Boris struggled on the softer surface. In fact, he had won thirty-nine tournaments at that point in his pro career, not one of them on clay.

I always looked forward to the Italian Open, which may be my favorite European tournament, not because of the surface, but because of the crowd, because of the Italians, my people. I loved their enthusiasm, their cheering, and their special way of doing things. I remember once John McEnroe was playing a night match in Rome against a South American, an Argentine. The Italians loved McEnroe, loved his hot temper, his almost operatic passions, and of course, they wanted to see him win. But Mac was having an off-night and fell behind, clearly struggling and out of sync. Guess what happened? The lights failed. The match had to be delayed for twenty minutes, enough time for McEnroe to settle down, regroup. The match resumed, and John was still in trouble. Can you believe it? The lights went out again. When the power came back, so did McEnroe. He won the match, and my Italians cheered lustily.

In Rome, without divine help, Boris eliminated Karel Novacek of Czechoslovakia, Javier Sanchez of Spain, Pioline of France, Stich of Germany, and Ivanisevic of Croatia, all ranked among the top fifty in the world and almost all more comfortable than Becker on clay and more accomplished. Like Andre at Lipton, Boris had defeated five straight rivals from five different countries, and now, in the finals, he, too, had to face Sampras.

Pete won the championship decisively, but Boris had no complaints with his runner-up finish. He told Red and me to go home for a few days at his expense. "Regenerate your batteries," he said. "I'll see you in Paris Thursday."

We left Rome Monday morning, arrived in Bradenton Monday night, left Bradenton Wednesday night, arrived in Paris Thursday morning. Red said it was the longest trip he ever took just to get his laundry done.

Like all the Grand Slam events, the French Open has its own character and characters. Historically, the residents of Paris, probably for genetic reasons, do not warm easily to foreigners, particularly American foreigners. But once the Parisians step inside the grounds at Roland Garros, the site of the French Open, they are transformed. They become almost as friendly as Italians and just as boisterous, especially if one of their countrymen or countrywomen is playing. I thoroughly enjoy the first Wednesday of competition, which is children's day, with thousands of youngsters filling the stands, and I also enjoy the frankfurters with honey mustard.

On the eve of the 1994 French Open, Boris announced

that he had a back injury and withdrew. The strange thing about Boris's injuries is that the signal that he's hurting seems to come from his brain cells, not his bones. It's not that his injuries aren't real; it's just that they're not always visible. Tennis players, like all athletes, suffer convenient injuries when, for one reason or another, they want to take a week off.

Our next stop was England, which Boris considers his home for one month to six weeks every year. He lost in the first round on grass at Queen's Club, a Wimbledon warm-up he had won three times, and then turned his attention to the main event. Wimbledon is to Boris partly what Everest is to a mountain climber, a monumental challenge, and partly what Lourdes is to a believer, a sacred shrine. "Nick," he said, "this is very important to me. I've spent a good deal of my life for ten years preparing for Wimbledon. I like to do it in certain ways. I like to have the atmosphere quiet."

He also likes to do Wimbledon in style. He rented a beautiful house for me only two seconds from the All England Club, only a few minutes from his own rented house. I had a tennis court and a barbecue area, and through the bedroom window, as the tournament progressed, I could see people queueing up outside the club, most with umbrellas, some with tents, all prepared to spend the night on the sidewalk, waiting for a chance to purchase tickets. We had a rented car to get wherever we wanted to go. I had everything I could've wanted except the Sports Channel on the telly. I really wanted to see the last few games of the NBA play-offs, Houston against the Knicks. "Get it," Boris said.

"But it'll cost $700 or $800," I said.

HELLO, BORIS

"Get it," said Boris, who already had the Sports Channel at his house. He had to be able to watch the NBA, too, and the soccer matches he loves.

Boris was the only player I'd ever heard of who had his own personal practice courts at Wimbledon, three grass courts at a nearby college, courts he rented every year, so that he could prepare himself quietly, privately. He didn't want any of his rivals to observe his practices, to study his methods.

Once the tournament began, the pain in Boris's back subsided. The early rounds at Wimbledon are the dangerous ones, when the grass is thick and slippery, and obscure challengers know they can build an instant reputation by knocking off a champion. But Boris had both a good draw and good fortune. He got past the "red-light" rounds, avoided an embarrassing upset, but two other championship contenders did not. Michael Stich, seeded second, lost in the first round, and Jim Courier, seeded fifth, lost in the second, both of them in Boris's half of the draw. Boris beat David Wheaton, Arne Thoms, Javier Frana, Andrei Medvedev, and Christian Bergstrom, five different nationalities once again—only Medvedev was seeded—before he faced Ivanisevic, who was seeded fourth, in the semifinals. Goran won in straight sets, but Boris was heartened by reaching the semifinals and thanked all the members of his team for their contributions.

He sat down privately with me, even asked Barbara to leave the room, and said that he felt everything was moving in the right direction, but he wanted to make one change in the team. He wanted to replace Red Ayme. Boris acknowledged that without Red's prodding in the beginning he would not have gotten so far so quickly, but now, he felt, he needed someone a little more quiet, more relaxed. So Red went back to the academy with a bonus from Boris, and I brought Mike DePalmer Jr. in as the new traveling coach/hitting partner.

Ulli Kuhnel and Val Kliesing were the veterans of the team, dating back practically to the start of Boris's career. I don't know whether Ulli was the best racquet stringer in the world, but Boris thought he was, which was all that mattered. And it was very rare when one of Boris's racquets broke. Ulli was basically lazy—his girlfriend sometimes did the string-ing—and boorish, but he was absolutely dedicated to Boris. So was Val, who handled the taping and the massaging, was on call twenty-four hours a day, and, in effect, kept the big engine running. He was also Boris's yes-man; Val knew better than any of us that Boris did not like to hear what Boris did not like to hear.

Barbara Becker led her own team, nannies and cooks to make her life and Boris's more comfortable. Boris was not easy to be with after a match, especially if he lost or if he felt he didn't play up to his standards. He didn't take defeat easily. Usually, he just wanted to be alone, to sit quietly and brood about the match. Barbara's reaction was to go shop-ping, have massages and facials, and have her hair done. She went shopping almost every day. Boris didn't care. He just wanted his wife and son with him on the road, and he knew they couldn't hang out at the site of the tournament, where they would be hounded constantly by the media.

I saw Andre at Wimbledon, a brief but emotional meet-ing, and wished him luck. He beat Aaron Krickstein to get to the round of sixteen, then lost to Todd Martin in five sets after dropping the first two. Not long after the tournament, I

wrote to Andre, reiterating my belief that I was owed something for the years I dedicated to him. Again, I documented
the amount of money I had spent on him and the amount I
had received. Andre's reply was sort of like his forehand,
powerful and piercing:

Nick—

It has never been my style to communicate my
thoughts or feelings by writing a letter. I have always
preferred to allow someone to see my eyes when I open
a piece of my heart to them. If I lie, in my eyes you
would know. If I speak truth and sincerity, in my eyes
you would be sure. But since you have [always] chosen
to communicate with me by letter ... and especially
after your last letter to me based on the few moments
we shared in London just recently ... maybe if I write
to you, you can read it over and over and ... understand and see clearly ... who I am and the standards
and values I refuse to compromise in my life.

For me to try and recap [our] ten-plus years together could never do them justice. The memories,
Nick, I ... never want to forget. When I think of all
those years, a smile moves across my face.... With each
passing day, those memories become more sacred....

The break-up was hard on both of us.... You felt
justified in how it was handled even though I felt lost
and let down. My reaction to it, while justified by me,
left you confused and disappointed, I'm sure. Neverthe-
less, when I saw you in London, my heart was crying
out to the only father I felt like I ever had and to the

second father I felt like I had lost. I said to you, "I miss you, I want you to come to Vegas and play golf, there's a lot you need to catch up on, you know?" You smiled and looked at me with tears, you put your hand on the back of my head and gave me a hug, like you had done so many times, just as if our hearts were the only thing that mattered. I had to wipe my eyes as you walked away.

Then I received your letter. Just like a father: With one small effort, you gave me so much to believe in, and with an even smaller effort, you tore it all away. Your letter told me that I could have a father/son relationship with you, I would just have to be willing to pay for it. So sad ... So devastating. You have taught me so much through the years, Nick, but never this much. I have just now learned how to really appreciate the little good that is still left in the world.

There really is something I feel like I need to express to you ... You have [always] said that you chose me over your own children. Nick, you chose me over your children, and you chose money over me. To say it in the third person, like you say so many things, Nick chose Nick over his children. Whether you continue to live in denial or not, I won't accept any responsibility for your relationship with your kids. Nick, remember I've seen you at the mall, with Nicole and Alex walking steps behind [you, and you're] on the cellular phone while someone you employ takes them around. It's only been a year since you went [two months] from Rome through London spending only two days at home. I do not judge you for this because I love you enough to want for your life what you want for yourself. But please have enough integrity as a man to look in the mirror and call it like it is.

I want to end this so bad by saying if you ever need anything, please call me, but all that goes through your mind when I say that is dollar signs. So let me say this, and I mean this with all my heart, I want your friendship, Nick. Call me or write me or spend time with me on that level only.

I love you,
Andre

Andre's letter was remarkable, both the gentle words and the harsh. He moved me with what he said about our relationship and stung me with what he said about my relationship with my children. He was right, of course, about the cellular phone; he was wrong, however, about my emphasis on money. He hurt me much more by saying that I was insignificant than he did by not paying me. My little Alex, who loved Andre, asked me why he said unkind things about me.

Boris knew that he would have to play well in the second half of the year to be one of the eight qualifiers for the ATP Tour Championships in Frankfurt in November. He made a strong move in August, winning events in Los Angeles and in New Haven, but then in the U.S. Open, seeded fourth, he was wiped out in a five-set match in the opening round. Boris fought back from two sets down to even the match

MY ACES, MY FAULTS

before Richey Reneberg beat him in a tiebreaker. (It was an open of upsets; none of the top four seeds reached even the quarterfinals, and the championship went to the sixteenth seed, my former protégé, Andre Agassi.)

The next big tournament was in Stockholm in October, and Boris's first opponent, naturally, was Reneberg. The first set went to a tiebreaker, and this time Boris won it, breezed through the next set and his next match, and advanced to the quarterfinals.

Then Boris pulled off a feat that may have been unprecedented in tennis history. On three consecutive days—Friday, Saturday, and Sunday—he defeated the three top-ranked players in the world: Stich, No. 3, in the quarterfinals; Sampras, No. 1, in the semifinals; and Ivanisevic, No. 2, in the finals. The opening set against Goran was the only set Boris lost all week.

Barbara Becker sat through many of Boris's matches with me, and I don't think I've ever seen anyone suffer so much at a tennis tournament. Most of the time, she had her head down, as if she couldn't bear to watch. She looked as if she was praying, but often, she was pleading with me. "Nick, you've got to help my husband," she'd say. "He relies on you. You've got to help him."

"But, Barbara," I'd say, "I'm not allowed to say anything to him during a match. He'll get fined if I help him."

"Don't worry," Barbara would say. "We'll pay the fine and give them a $500 tip. You've got to help him get through these matches."

(Personally, I can't understand the rule against coaching, especially now that almost all of the fifty or hundred best players in the world have individual coaches, who know them and know their games. Coaching is permitted in Davis Cup competition and in college play, and I think they ought to at least try it on an experimental basis on the ATP tour.)

Boris was doing fine on his own, accepting my occasional advice, exercising extraordinary self-discipline to overcome his love for food and wine and beer. For him to keep his body down around one hundred and eighty-five or ninety pounds, he had to work very hard, which he did.

With a respectable showing the week after Stockholm in the Paris Open—he reached the quarterfinals before losing two tiebreakers in a row to Marc Rosset—Boris qualified for the ATP Tour World Championship. It was certainly one of his major goals in our first year together—the previous year, he had failed to qualify, which meant he wasn't able to defend the championship he had won in 1992—and helped solidify our relationship.

I thought the relationship was terrific. Boris was unfailingly polite and appreciative, always said, "Thank you." He was a loyal friend. When Axel Meyer-Wolden came down with cancer, Boris was frequently at his bedside. He was proud and focused. He was the first player I'd coached since Brian Gottfried who had a child, and I think it made him more stable. Boris was both gracious and generous. When he gave me or Red or Mike a bonus, he did it quietly, simply saying, "You earned it." When we flew, we went first class or business class or in a private jet. I felt it was important that I be a coach first and a friend second, but I enjoyed the way he would say, "Come on, big brother, let's get the wife and go have some pasta." He used to kid me about my outfits, too; my favorite suit is a sweatsuit. "Now, Mr. B.," he would say, "when we go out at night, you have to be dressed up because you're one of the great coaches in the world and you have to go out there and look smart and tall." He arranged for me to go on special shopping expeditions to the Boss factory.

I think Boris was also pleased with our relationship. "I can't believe it," Barbara would say to me. "I can't believe it. He's so happy."

The ATP Tour World Championship in Frankfurt was magnificent. There were, as usual, only eight players, the eight highest-ranked players on the tour, divided into two groups. Each player was treated like a king, with his own locker room, his own shower, his own massage table. The food was fantastic—pasta, turkey, ham—all good and plentiful. And the prize money was impressive, even to the millionaire players.

Boris was in one group with Ivanisevic, Sampras, and Edberg; the other group included Agassi, Michael Chang, Sergi Bruguera, and Alberto Berasategui. Each group played a round-robin and then the top two finishers in each group advanced to the semifinals, the winner of the first group against the runner-up in the second group and vice versa.

Boris barely won his first match, beating Ivanisevic in a third-set tiebreaker, then took Sampras in straight sets in his second match. When he started his third match, against Edberg, he was almost certain of a place in the semifinals. He was 2–0 in matches, 4–1 in sets; Sampras was 2–1 in matches, 4–3 in sets; and Edberg was 1–1 in matches, 3–2 in sets.

Edberg won the first set, 7–6, Becker the second, 6–4. If

Edberg won the third set, then he and Becker would have identical records, 2–1 in matches and 5–3 in sets, and they would both advance to the semifinals, eliminating Sampras. If Boris won the third set, Sampras would be in, and Edberg would be out.

The German crowd was almost as ecstatic as Sampras when Boris pulled out the third set, 7–5.

Becker beat Bruguera and Sampras beat Agassi in the semifinals, and in the final, Boris took the first set, Pete the next three and the championship. Pete collected $1,225,000 for his week's work (Edberg, who came so close to the semis, had to settle for $165,000, more than $1 million less than Pete) and thanked Boris for beating Edberg and giving him the opportunity to reach the finals. On television, Pete said he was so grateful he would buy Boris a condo; Boris, in response, said his lawyer had already picked out the place. Becker earned $665,000 for finishing second.

Afterward, our team celebrated over dinner and backgammon, and Boris stood up and toasted the rest of us. "I want to thank all of my team that made it possible for me to get back to play for the world championship again," he said. "I sincerely feel within myself that we have another two or three or four years to go. I'm happy to be competitive again. I love playing, and thank you all for getting me where I am."

Boris and I had a chance to talk before I flew home, and he asked me what I was going to do over the next few years. "I'm going to be with you," I told him.

"Good, big brother," Boris said. "I want you to be my last coach."

On the plane, I thought, *God, you've been fantastic to me. You helped me bring back a guy who so many people doubted.*

At the end of the year, Boris was ranked No. 3 in the world, behind only Sampras and Agassi, his highest year-end ranking since he was twenty-four years old.

In 1995, I went to the Australian Open for the first time—January is normally my month for skiing and the Super Bowl—to coach Boris, who was upset by Patrick McEnroe in the first round, and Mary Pierce, whose experience in the tournament was much more pleasant. My Leah went with me, and when I was busy with practice or with matches, which was most of the time, Leah found things to keep herself occupied.

For one, she worked on her tennis game, hitting with Jessica Stich, the wife of Michael Stich, a workout that later prompted Barbara Becker to say, "I can't believe you're playing with the enemy." Barbara is a very outspoken woman, especially after a long day.

"I'll hit with anyone who'll hit with me," Leah said.

"I can't believe you're playing with the enemy," Boris also said.

Leah and I met in August 1992 at six o'clock in the morning in the Tampa airport. I was heading to the U.S. Open, and if I hadn't missed my flight out of Sarasota the day before, I wouldn't have been in Tampa at 6 in the morning, and if Leah hadn't just driven from New York to Tampa, helping her girlfriend, the model Kim Alexis, move, she wouldn't have been at the airport at 6 in the morning. I struck up a conversation, found out she was a flight attendant for American Airlines and a tennis fan, and offered to get her tickets to the open. All I asked for in return was her telephone number.

Usually, I lose phone numbers. I also forget names. This time, I got lucky and smart. I held onto Leah's number, got her the tennis tickets, called her, and took her to dinner. Then we went to hear some jazz and ended up talking in a diner till 4 in the morning. To save myself from embarrassment, just in case I forgot, I carried a card in my wallet with LEAH written on it. We've been together ever since— I threw away the card after the third or fourth date—and I can't believe how lucky I am that this lovely and loving and energetic and sensitive young woman would spend her time with a guy whose track record is as bad as mine and whose pace is so hectic. She is wonderful with my children, they all love her, and so do I. I've given Leah a ring, but I've promised her I won't marry her. Still, I can't imagine living without my Leah. I call her Boo.

> *Nick is a very intense person and can make people crazy with his drive and determination. But he knows when to have fun, and he does have fun at almost everything. He's the most generous person I've ever met, and he's very approachable (even though it sometimes may not appear that way on TV). Our relationship is the best thing going.*
> —Leah Rhodes

With Red Ayme rotating back on the team because Mike DePalmer had to undergo back surgery, Boris enjoyed a profitable winter. He won in Marseilles, was runner-up in

Milan, and reached the semifinals in Stuttgart before losing to Jessica Stich's husband. Then he came to the States, to Indian Wells, California, a tournament run, incidentally, by Charlie Pasarell, the man whose mother had helped me get my job in Puerto Rico more than a quarter of a century earlier. In the semifinals at Indian Wells, Boris once again faced Andre: Becker, No. 3 in the world, against Agassi, No. 2.

With the score 4–4 and 40–15 in the first set, Boris served, charged to the net, and chose to let Andre's passing shot go by. Boris thought the shot was going out. An official said it was in. Replays later showed clearly that the shot was out, that Boris was right. Irritated by the call, Boris lost his serve, lost the set, and lost the match, 6–4, 7–6. Boris was not unhappy with the way he'd played, only with the decision that cost him the first set.

Andre lost in the finals to Pete Sampras. Then, in the Lipton Championships, a tournament run by Butch Buchholz, the man who replaced me in Puerto Rico (the tennis world really is small), Andre beat Pete in the final and, a few days later, for the first time in his career, ascended to No. 1. Andre and Brad could not resist taking shots at me. "Nick felt that if you went out and played well, that would be enough," Gilbert announced. "I'm more of a strategist."

"Nick's a selfish person," Andre told a reporter. "He thought that I wasn't going to do well anymore. But he didn't have the guts to tell it like it was."

Boris and I went separate ways for a month after Indian Wells. I had a whole month in the States; he went back to Europe. When he left, he told me that before the year was over, he wanted me to prepare him to win a tournament on clay. We agreed that I would rejoin him at Monte Carlo on the red clay. Excerpts from my diary in Monte Carlo reflect, I think, what life is like for me on the tennis tour.

April 17, 1995

Midnight
As I unpacked, I thought about Leah and how she always unpacks for me, carefully putting all my clothes away. Before long, who calls? You guessed it! My Boo! She called to make sure I had arrived safely.

10:30 A.M.
Boris, his trainer Carlo, Mike DePalmer Jr., Tommy Haas, Gregg Hill, and I went to the gym for stretching and three-on-three basketball. Carlo, Mike, and I were beaten by the younger boys. After the game, they did all sorts of exercises. Carlo put them through their paces for forty-five minutes.

12:30 P.M.
We returned to the hotel. The boys had lunch, but Boris asked me to see his condo and, of course, to visit with Barbara and little Noah, who now was walking. It was delightful for me, but it made me miss Leah. We always have so much fun playing together with young children, and she especially loves playing with Noah. Boris, Barbara, and I ate lunch on their nineteenth-floor deck, overlooking the ocean. We brought each other up to date.

3:45 P.M.

On our way to practice, Boris said his brain cells were sending him a message to take a break. He and the boys had been working four to six hours a day on and off court. When Tommy and Gregg heard this, they celebrated—by taking a four-hour nap. While they slept, Mike, Carlo, Barbara, Boris, and I headed up to the golf course. Mike drove a Jeep, and Boris his silver 600SL Mercedes convertible. Boris led us up—2,800 feet. We could view beautiful Monte Carlo and the harbor below, and we realized that one driving mistake could send us to our doom.

7:45 P.M.

We were all dead tired coming to the seventeenth hole, and the weather was turning bitter cold. On seventeen, Boris and Mike both had double figures, but we all laughed and walked in with the darkness.

8:45 P.M.

We were all so tired that we ate and immediately retired.

April 18

2:30 A.M.

My Boo called me to say good night, making my day complete.

8 A.M.

We were all up very early. Carlo, Boris, and the boys ran several miles.

My mother and father thought they were raising a lawyer, but when I chose the courts over the courtroom, they were my number-one fans.

My ROTC uniform in college. It wasn't the last time I wore a tie, but it was close.

I spent seventeen years in the sun at Dorado Beach, and I've never lost the tan.

When I drove my red Mercedes convertible around Beaver Dam, I was the King.

This was a group of elite students at the NBTA. Can you spot Brad Gilbert? Jimmy Arias? Tim Mayotte? Eric Korita? Aaron Krickstein? Lisa Bonder? Raffaella Reggi?

How Carling Bassett (with my arm around her) could spend so much time at the academy, and live in my home, and still not develop a booming forehand I'll never know.

Brad Gilbert still likes to flex his muscles, but he wouldn't be caught dead wearing a Nick Bollettieri shirt.

Jimmy Arias combined great heart and a great forehand to reach No. 5 in the world.

Arthur Ashe was a champion in every sense of the word. Tennis misses him and so do I.

My son Jimmy (extreme right) helped coach our traveling team. Jim Courier (behind me) helped us win.

Andre and Monica both came out of the academy and soared to No. 1 in the world.

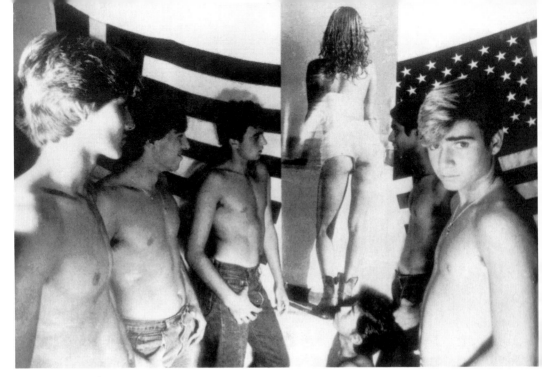

Andre and his roommates didn't think about tennis all the time.

Andre reminded me of myself in so many ways. Except, of course, in the way he played the game. My forehand wasn't quite that good.

Andre listened to me sometimes, even though I was "insignificant."

Andre dedicated his victory over Paul Annacone (left) to me on my fifty-seventh birthday.

Monica was the most dedicated player I ever worked with. She was just as dedicated as her family was demanding.

I put in hundreds of hours working with Monica, maybe thousands, but now she insists I never coached her.

With Boris, I always tried to stay in the background, to study him carefully before I made a suggestion.

I've always enjoyed listening to Bud Collins, and he says he's always enjoyed interviewing me. Neither of us is ever at a loss for words.

"Mary, dear..." When Mary Pierce heard those words, she knew I was starting another lecture.

I loved working with Mark Philippoussis. The only trouble was, I had to work with his dad, too.

Anna Kournikova came to the academy when she was nine years old. IMG had spotted her in the Kremlin Cup. They have eyes everywhere.

They may be my future—and the future of tennis: Anna Kournikova, Tommy Haas, and Gregg Hill.

I told Alex to keep her eye on the ball, not on the camera.

Leah Rhod‹

Leah Rhoc

Nicole is certainly better-looking, but I've got the better suntan.

My older daughters work with me now, Angel (on my right) at the Sports Grille and Danielle at the academy.

How can someone as beautiful and intelligent as Leah put up with me and my track record? I'm just lucky, I guess.

Danielle Bolletti

I dreamed of flying with the Blue Angels,
but I never dreamed the flight would leave me speechless—almost.

HELLO, BORIS

10 A.M.

We went to the gym, and everyone did some stretching followed by a three-on-three basketball game. Boris, Tommy, and Gregg won again. Afterward, Carlo put the three of them through rigorous exercises to develop spring in their legs.

1 P.M.

The sun broke through as we ate lunch beside the pool. I was so happy I put on my presun and soaked up the sunshine in a beach chair for two hours.

4 P.M.

We returned to the courts, and Mike put Boris and the boys through pure hell. Just when they thought they were finished, I had Boris do five two-minute drills. The boys admitted they could not keep up with Mr. B.

6 P.M.

We all went downstairs to the Monte Carlo gym where we worked out for another hour. Boris stayed on when the rest of us returned to the hotel, descending the hill on foot.

8:30 P.M.

Mike, Tommy, Gregg, and I ate at the hotel restaurant. The boys were ready to fall into their plates. They went directly to bed. Then my friend Gino came over and took us for a drive in his beautiful seventeen-year-old Rolls Royce. We stopped at an American sports bar to have one beer. Murphy Jensen was there. The smoke was so bad that we left.

April 19

8 A.M.
Boris, Carlo, and the boys ran several miles before we met for breakfast. Gregg and Tommy said very little. They were really hurting. Finally, I said my thighs were killing me. We could see the relief on their faces as they realized they were not the only ones suffering.

10:45 A.M.
Boris was away for the morning, so I put the boys through a workout for two hours and fifteen minutes. After lunch, the boys asked for a break.

4 P.M.
First we went to the tennis courts and practiced for an hour in a drizzle. When the rain got too hard, the boys wanted to go home, but Boris said, "Let's go to the gym and play a fifteen-point game." When we arrived, the gym was crowded with children, and we were told we couldn't play. My eyes lit up! Relief at last! But then—disaster! One of the staff recognized Boris and gave us a basketball court. Carlo, Mike, Barbara, and I played Boris, Gregg, and Tommy. They won, 15–13, and on the final point, Gregg bounced into a door and complained that his ribs were broken. I literally could not move and said, "Let's

all go home!" But Boris challenged Gregg to a one-on-one game. Gregg won, 5–4, ribs and all. I had to be helped off the floor, helped to the car. Billy-goat golf, workouts at the gym, basketball, and tennis did me in. I felt sixty-three years old.

7:30 P.M.

I needed a hot bath, and getting in and out was not easy.

8:30 P.M.

I couldn't move. The boys brought me a pizza. I will be all right by morning.

April 20

7:15 A.M.

I bounced out of bed bright and early, as always, much to my own surprise.

8:30 A.M.

We ate breakfast and went to the courts, but just as we arrived, it began raining. So we all went to the gym and worked out for about thirty minutes. Then Boris suggested that we all go to the big gym to play full-court basketball. Murphy Jensen and his coach joined us.

12:15 P.M.

I'm convinced that professional basketball players are the best-conditioned all-around athletes. Our game ended,

20–19, and at the end, I made two key baskets. I also tried to full-court press Boris. At least I slowed him down.

4 P.M.
We had to wait till the rain let up, but we were able to get in more than an hour on the courts.

9:30 P.M.
Mike and I had fresh bass for dinner; the boys tried steak tartar. I knew they wouldn't like it, and I was right. Gregg hid his under his lettuce, and Tommy piled french fries on top of his portion. Leah called after dinner and said she will be coming in tomorrow because she was able to exchange flights with someone. Then I watched the reports of the bombing in Oklahoma City on CNN. It is difficult for me to understand how anyone could do such a thing, especially to young children.

April 21

11 A.M.
We practiced for thirty minutes, and then it rained.

4 P.M.
Boris played a practice match for twenty minutes, and then it rained.

6 P.M.
Boris practiced with Pete Sampras for an hour.

HELLO, BORIS

7:45 P.M.
Leah arrived, and she and I ate dinner with Gregg and
Tommy. I had cold symptoms compounded by a fever.
Boris called during dinner to invite Leah and me over,
but as much as I wanted to go, I had to say no. Boris
knew how unusual it was for me to say I did not feel well.

9 P.M.
I took aspirin, and Leah kept putting cold towels on my
head. During the night, I felt my fever break.

April 22

8:30 A.M.
We all awoke to rain.

2 P.M.
It was still raining. Boris called and said take the afternoon off.

6 P.M.
It was still raining. Boris called and said he wanted to
play basketball in the big gym. I said fine even though
my cold had turned into the flu. I have been in Europe
for almost two weeks now [I was in Austria before Monte
Carlo], and there has been only one day of sun. This kills
me. In my entire life, I can't remember being sick more
than two or three times and then only with a cold and
only for a day or two. Without sunshine, this cold has

lasted seven days. If the sun doesn't come out soon, I'm leaving for the Sun Belt.

8:30 P.M.
The basketball game—Boris, Gregg, and Tommy against Carlo, Mike, and me again—almost ended in a fight. It was so bad Boris called afterward for exercise only.

9:30 P.M.
Leah and I ate alone—bad blood still flowed about the game. Then cold pills, aspirin, and bed.

April 23

8:30 A.M.
Dammit, rain again. My flu was no better without the sun. We planned to drive to a small Italian town that has a tennis center with an indoor red clay court where Boris can practice.

10:45 A.M.
Mike, Gregg, and Tommy drove to Italy in a Volvo wagon. Boris invited me to go with him in his silver 600SL.

12:15 P.M.
We all had cappuccino before going on to the court. Boris practiced against the boys for three hours with incredible intensity.

3:45 P.M.

Boris told the Volvo to go ahead. As soon as we sat down in the Mercedes, Boris told me to buckle up. I knew then that he was about to put this new car from his own dealership through its paces. When we passed the Volvo, our speed exceeded two hundred kilometers an hour, more than one hundred twenty miles. Suddenly, a BMW surged past us as if we were standing still. Boris kicked it into a lower gear, torquing up the four hundred horsepower engine. I felt my right foot braking reflexively, so much that my calf cramped. Boris just laughed. Fortunately for me, the BMW pulled off and Boris eased up. The Volvo took an hour and forty minutes to make the return trip. We made it in an hour.

6 P.M.

We went to the tennis center to see if we could practice outdoors, but the rain started again. Tommy and Gregg were delighted. Boris had already put them through hell. "Okay," Boris said, "let's go play basketball." When we got to the gym, we found it was closed on Sundays. Everyone except Boris rejoiced.

8 P.M.

Leah had been reading all day, so even though I was sick as a dog, I took her out, inviting Gregg and Tommy to join us for great pizza and Leah's favorite dessert, *tiramisu.*

11 P.M.

My nose was running and my eyes were watering, and I was so thankful to have my Leah taking care of me. Please, God, let the sun come out tomorrow.

April 24

Midnight

Before we went to sleep, Leah and I watched the memorial ceremony from Oklahoma City. It was so sad, and yet I felt so proud to be an American, to see our sense of unity in such a difficult time.

7:30 A.M.

More rain and more rain and more rain.

11 A.M.

We drove to Italy in the rain, and I put Boris and the two boys through two hours of constant, varying drills. I was very satisfied with their performances.

7 P.M.

For the first time, I had to tell Boris, "Count me out," when he said he wanted to play basketball. I showered and took Leah to dinner. The food was awful, and then we had to walk in the rain to catch a taxi—the end of another exciting day on the road.

April 25

7:30 A.M.
I was afraid to open my eyes this morning. I was afraid I'd see more rain. Finally, I looked. Rain. Not only was it raining, it was very windy and cold.

10:30 A.M.
The tournament started today. Leah and I went to the courts to see the Bjorkman–Roux match. Boris would play the winner tomorrow. The weather finally broke, enough for Bjorkman to win in straight sets.

6 P.M.
Leah and I went home and did some sit-ups, then took Gregg and Tommy out for a fantastic Italian dinner.

10 P.M.
I called Boris and told him he was the second match tomorrow and practice was at 10:30.

April 26

7 A.M.
With the shades up, as always, Leah and I were awakened by—the good old sun! I quickly shaved and sat on the balcony for an hour and a half of pure sun.

10:30 A.M.
The clouds and the cold weather were back, but Boris's practice with Tommy and Gregg was excellent.

1 P.M.
Stich, Medvedev, Edberg, and Larsson, all seeded, all lost the first match they played. Boris, however, was not ready to leave. He beat Bjorkman, 6–3, 6–1, and began preparing his brain cells for tomorrow.

3 P.M.
As we entered the locker room, Pete Sampras was leaving, on his way to play Paul Haarhuis. Pete won the first set, 6–4, and was moving along comfortably when a freak accident occurred. Pete tripped over his own foot. He had to be helped off the court. He defaulted and went to the hospital, all of us keeping our fingers crossed for him.

8:45 P.M.
Leah and I had a farewell dinner with Tommy and Gregg, who were off to Italy for their junior tour. Two weeks with Boris and being among the pros has done much to improve their behavior and has made them realize how much they must accomplish during the next few years if they ever wish to become pros.

Leah left the next day. Saying good-bye to her is always difficult. Not only is she my special lady, she is also my best friend. Once she was gone, the rest of the week was just tennis. But some of it was great tennis.

HELLO, BORIS

Boris's next match was against Alex Corretja, a clay-court specialist who was ranked in the top twenty-five in the world. Alex crushed Boris in Hamburg a year earlier. Before Boris went on court, he said to me, "Tell me, Mr. B.," and I told him he could control the game by constantly forcing the point, keeping Corretja off balance. I also told Boris to vary his serve and to come in behind it whenever he could.

Boris played one of the best clay-court matches of his career. He won, 6–2, 6–2, which put him in the quarterfinals against Richard Krajicek. My strategic tip was very simple. I told Boris to dominate the match, to be aggressive, to take it to Krajicek. Boris executed perfectly. His serve was fantastic, and his ground strokes were powerful. By the end of the match, there was no doubt in my mind: Boris was finally learning to play offensive tennis on clay. To my surprise, Krajicek, who was a veteran of the tour, was very upset after his loss. He sat in the locker room by himself for almost two hours, his eyes fixed on the floor. Now Boris advanced to the semis, ready to take on Goran Ivanisevic, only two victories away from that elusive first clay-court championship.

The next day, the sun was out, and after I played golf with Mike DePalmer Jr. in the morning, I went to watch the first semifinal, between Thomas Muster of Austria, the roadrunner, the king of the clay courts, and his practice partner, Andrea Gaudenzi of Italy, both of them coached by Ronnie Leitgeb, who obviously was in an awkward position. It was like Agassi against Courier when I was coaching both of them.

Muster won the first set handily, as expected, outlasting Gaudenzi in the long rallies. But in the second set, Gaudenzi began winning the long points, and they were long, incredibly long, and with the sun out, the temperature was rising. Muster began swaying on the court, exhausted, dried out, obviously ill. But there was no way he was going to leave the court except on a stretcher. The set went to a tiebreaker, and Gaudenzi took a 5–2 lead. Muster held onto the back fence, on the brink of collapse. Somehow, against all logic, against all physical evidence, Muster fought back and won the tiebreaker, and as he captured the decisive point, he fell to the ground. Medics and doctors rushed onto the court to help him.

Gaudenzi, stunned by the result, threw his racquet and spat toward the umpire, a gesture that would cost him a sizable fine. Then he walked over to Muster, who had stood up, shaking, and tapped him on the shoulder. The two walked off the court together, and as they entered the locker room, the players inside applauded Muster for his courage. Both he and Gaudenzi looked dazed, and their coach didn't seem certain which one to go to. Muster was taken off to the hospital, suffering from hypothermia and dehydration.

Boris and Ivanisevic had a tough act to follow. In the locker room, as usual, Boris said, "Tell me," and I moved close to him and said that he must not worry about Goran's big serve, that he must attack and, above all, must stay with him in the first set. Goran is a front-runner; if he gets ahead, he keeps rolling. I suggested that Boris keep coming in, even on his second serve.

The first set was unbelievable. Goran served for the set at 6–5, but Boris broke him with a jumping forehand volley. The tiebreaker was just as tense, but Becker won it, 9–7. In the second set, a dog began barking just as Boris was serving. The dog barked until it broke Boris's concentration. Then Goran broke Boris's serve and won the second set, 6–3. As the third set began, I sort of signaled Boris to become even more aggressive, to go for winners, and Boris responded perfectly. He seemed to turn on an afterburner and won the deciding set, 6–1.

Now, the final was cast: Boris, who had played forty-seven previous tournaments on clay without winning one, against Muster, who had won twenty-six championships on clay, more than any other active player. We knew that Muster would be out of the hospital, ready to play no matter how debilitated he felt.

We practiced in the morning. Boris hit with Guy Forget. Mike and I observed. At 2:15, fifteen minutes before the start of the championship match, which was to be the best three out of five sets, Boris and I met in the weight room. I told him to make the first set a long one, to drain Muster as much as possible. I reminded him that Muster would rather die than quit.

Becker won the first set, 6–4, and the second, 7–6. Two long, tight, demanding, exhausting sets. Boris was one set away from the first clay-court title of his career. I wanted it for him so much.

The third set was a quick one, and, remarkably, defying reason, it was all Muster. He suddenly sprang to life, began swinging as hard as he could and connecting, bewildering Boris. Barbara Becker was even more nervous, more hyper, than usual. She asked me how Muster could be almost dead one day and going into orbit the next. I told her he has the heart of a lion.

The fourth set was a long one, a tense one, everyone in the Monte Carlo stadium on edge, both players painted with sweat and red clay. I felt certain that Boris would win.

He went up a break. He was serving for the match. He got to match point, one successful swing away from the title. His first serve missed. Then he hit his second serve as hard as he had ever hit a first serve—and missed by inches. Deuce. Somehow, I sensed that the match was over.

Muster won the fourth set in a tiebreaker, and Barbara Becker got up and left. She couldn't bear the pain of seeing Boris come so close and lose. Boris changed into his seventh or eighth shirt of the day. Parachutists fluttered in the air above us. I found myself thinking that Muster, too, was flying. He won the fifth set in a breeze, 6–0.

I went into the locker room and sat down next to Boris. He was quiet. He had tears in his eyes. I mentioned the Oklahoma bombing, and I told him what President Clinton had said, that God has strange ways and that we must accept His decisions with faith.

I went to a telephone and called the academy and told them to order a banner for the indoor center, a banner celebrating Boris Becker's performance at Monte Carlo. To me, even if Boris was the runner-up, he was the winner.

"If I have to lose a match," he told me, "I want to lose it going for the big one."

Later, fatigued and frustrated, Boris complained to the media about Muster's stunning revival. "Yesterday he seemed to be dying," Boris said. "Now he's running faster in the fifth set than he was at the start of the match. Either he's a very good actor or something miraculous happened overnight. And I don't believe in miracles."

The ATP doesn't believe in one professional suggesting that another professional might be charging himself up by using illegal substances. Boris was fined $20,000 for his remarks about Muster, for "conduct detrimental to the integrity of the game."

Wimbledon was still seven weeks away, but it was already on Boris's mind and mine. I received a very flattering invitation to a pre-Wimbledon event:

INVITATION TO MR. NICK BOLLETTIERI
TO ADDRESS THE OXFORD UNION SOCIETY ON JUNE 13TH

Dear Mr. Bollettieri,

In its one hundred-and-seventy-year history, the Union Society has established itself as the foremost centre of political and cultural debate in the United Kingdom. Many British prime ministers and countless domestic and international statesmen have forged their political views in our Victorian Debating Chamber. Seven presidents of the Union have gone on to become prime minister of their country, ranging from William Gladstone and Edward Heath to Benazhir Bhutto.

Quite apart from the prestigious reputation the society has acquired due to the contribution of its past members to public life, the Union has built a name for itself as a forum of international importance. As the world's largest debating society with over 9,000 members, situated at the heart of the English-speaking world's oldest and most distinguished university, the Union has welcomed numerous guests of international stature, including Presidents Reagan, Nixon, and Carter, Prime Ministers Bhutto, Shamir, Fabius, and Hawke, as well as Her Majesty the Queen. In the last year alone, we have also welcomed no less than five winners of the Nobel Prize, including Mother Teresa of Calcutta and Archbishop Desmond Tutu. This term, we would be deeply honoured if you could address the society.

As a man who has coached a generation of champions and redefined the whole nature of the professional game of tennis, you have become nothing less than the guru of the modern game. You are a true innovator, never swerving from a challenge, a man who thrives on making incursions on convention. It would be greatly appreciated by the students if you could share both your unique pragmatic philosophy and your depth of experience with them.

Yours sincerely,

David Pinto-Duschinsky

President

It was probably the best write-up I had ever received. In fact, I was afraid it was too good. I called my lawyers, Ted Meekma and Frank Falkenburg, and my CEO, Greg Breunich. "Someone's playing a joke on me," I said. "Someone's pulling my leg."

Ted, Frank, and Greg were suspicious, too. They said they would make a few calls and check out the invitation. To their amazement and mine, it turned out to be legitimate.

HELLO, BORIS

I couldn't wait to go to Oxford. Boris, of course, was also invited to speak.

Our next stop was Munich, Boris's home, and he was anxious to show me his new flower garden. I had great Wiener schnitzel with Boris and Barbara and made the mistake of drinking two beers, one over my limit. I was up all night with an unbelievable headache.

The effect of the loss to Muster lingered. Boris lost in the first round in Munich, on clay, and in the first round in Hamburg, also on clay. He decided he needed a break; he needed to get away from tennis for a while. He told Mike and me that he would skip the Italian Open, that we could go home. He would meet us in ten days in Paris. As much as I like Rome and the Romans, I was delighted. I called my girls and Leah and I headed for home.

During the flight, questions kept popping into my head, thoughts about the demands of professional tennis, the toll the tournaments and the travel take on the minds and bodies of the players and their support teams. *How much longer can I continue packing and unpacking?* I thought of the thrill and satisfaction of being with Becker, of helping him renew his spirit and his confidence (not to mention his endorsement contracts). I thought of how our entire team always traveled comfortably, staying at the best hotels, eating the best meals, but this didn't make up for being away from my family, the academy, my friends, and, most certainly, my Leah.

Still, I know I'm not ready to give up the long days on the road, not completely, not yet. I have tournaments to win and champions to create. Besides, what would tennis be like without the crazy Italian in the coach's box with his Oakleys on, even if there is no sun?

Boris lost in the third round of the French Open and lost in the semifinals on the grass at Queen's Club, beaten by his friend Guy Forget. Boris strained a calf muscle losing to Forget on a cold, damp day and decided that he had to go back to Munich for treatment, that he had to cancel our appearance at the Oxford Union. The students were very disappointed, and so was I. I usually just wing it when I speak, just say whatever comes into my head, but I had been working on my Oxford speech for a few months.

"Distinguished guests, members of the Oxford Union Society, ladies and gentlemen," I was prepared to say, "how do I explain my presence here today? *I can't.* This is beyond any dream or any expectation I have ever had. I hope my message to you might give you insight regarding success and how *you* may achieve it."

I had been rehearsing for weeks.

(I was rescheduled for 1996; placed in the Oxford Union lineup just between Yasir Arafat and O.J. Simpson.)

Boris returned to England the Thursday before the start of Wimbledon. We scheduled our first practice for Friday morning, on the private courts that he had rented once again, three grass courts for three weeks, for approximately $8,000 to $10,000.

We arrived at the courts, and the familiar maintenance men were there, and the familiar wooden shack with the sign saying, BEND OR HIT YOUR HEAD. Boris stretched, then loosened up playing a little soccer. My eyes never left his legs. I saw absolutely no sign of injury. He practiced vigorously, then, after lunch, had another workout just as strenuous as the first. He looked to be in perfect condition. He said his doctor was fantastic.

Once again, we lived in luxury in the town of Wimbledon, four houses this time, one just to accommodate the security people the Beckers required. Ken Merritt, Mike DePalmer and his wife, Gregg Hill, and Tommy Haas shared my house. For the second year in a row, Ken was the head cook, serving, among other dishes, barbecued chicken breasts, corn on the cob, and Key lime pie with lemon sherbet. Mary Pierce and her traveling coach, Sven Groeneveld, came by for dinner; so did David Wheaton and his family. I delivered my Oxford speech for the Wheatons, then told them how easy I thought it would be for me to go to Hollywood and be another Al Pacino or Robert DeNiro. I sincerely believed this. I act every day of my life.

Boris must have spent at least $100,000 on the three weeks of Wimbledon. He said it was worth it to him to be comfortable, to be confident, to be in command.

At the club and in the locker room, on the tenth anniversary of his first Wimbledon triumph, Boris was, naturally, a great attraction. The locker room is ancient and so small that if you turn around too quickly, you will bump into someone, probably someone famous. Most of the lockers are along one wall of the room, with a few on the opposite side. Washbasins line the other two walls, with two simple rows of benches in the middle of the room. Two television monitors hang from the ceiling, updating the players on all the matches. I usually sat on the floor by Boris's two corner lockers, a tribute to his stature. The locker-room attendants sit in a tiny adjoining room and distribute the famous green Wimbledon towels. They probably start the tournament with five thousand, but by the end, there are few to be found. Agassi's championship Wimbledon towel hangs in the Bollettieri Sports Grille in Bradenton.

Uniformed security guards stand outside the locker room, permitting only players and VIPs with proper credentials to enter. John McEnroe often popped in, gathering information for his television commentaries; if a women's match came on the screen, John usually had a barbed comment. So did most of the other men; they are not big fans of women's tennis. When they weren't insulting the women, they were gossiping about each other. Rod Laver would come in and be treated like royalty. Ilie Nastase would come in and act like royalty. I had tried for years to resist the charms of Wimbledon, the strawberries and cream, the stodgy pomp and circumstance, but I was beginning to understand its allure.

This was the weirdest Wimbledon I had ever seen. An American player named Jeff Tarango charged an umpire with corruption, and after Tarango stormed off, his French wife stormed on and slapped the umpire. My friend Murphy Jensen got stuck in traffic and missed a mixed doubles match, which was so embarrassing Murph vanished for a few days, inspiring a flock of rumors. The Wimbledon officials introduced a new ball, supposedly less lively, to counter the increasing emphasis on power, and Goran Ivanisevic said, "I don't care if you put snow in the balls. I'll still get my twenty-five or thirty aces."

HELLO, BORIS

The drama built. Andre got more pressure from the media than from his early opponents. Reporters wanted to know about the do-rag that circled his skull and about his baggy and transparent shorts. "Are you aware that your shorts are see-through?" one journalist inquired. "Obviously, you are," said Andre.

He breezed through his first five matches with the loss of only one set, that one to David Wheaton in a match that could have been played ten years earlier on the back courts of the academy, the flamboyant Agassi against the straight-arrow Wheaton. This was no Bible class; this was a battle David could have won. He took the second set and was up a break in the third before Andre took control. In the quarter-finals, Agassi crushed Jacco Eltingh, setting up a semifinal match against the winner of Pioline vs. Becker.

Andre came into the locker room after his match as Boris and I were getting ready to go out. Andre walked over and handed me a roast beef sandwich. "I know you like this," he said and walked away, offering no further explanation. I was so hungry I wasn't going to turn it down. I had forgotten to carry any pocket money, and I was too embarrassed to borrow from anyone. I wolfed down the sandwich. As it turned out, I needed it.

Until he faced Pioline, Boris had lost only two sets in four one-sided matches, all of them against unseeded opponents. Pioline was also unseeded, and when Boris cruised through the first two sets, 6–3 and 6–1, playing as well as I had ever seen him play, the "dream" semifinal pairing seemed certain.

Then, abruptly, the match turned around. Boris's mind

started to wander, to drift toward the semifinals, and Pioline changed his tactics. He decided to stay back and, with nothing to lose, whack every forehand and backhand as hard as he could. Pioline won two straight spine-tingling tiebreakers, 8–6 and 12–10, and then, in the fifth set, went up a break, on the verge of knocking Boris out of Wimbledon, on the verge of erasing a Becker–Agassi semifinal. Barbara Becker was going nuts, hiding her head, twitching, groaning. She had to leave her seat for a while, anything to break the pattern.

Boris refused to quit, not in his tournament, not on his grass. *I am not going to lose this. You can't deny me my right to another semifinal, my right to play Andre Agassi. You can't take that away from me.* He battled back and won the decisive set, 9–7. It had been more than four hours since Andre gave me the roast beef sandwich.

We went straight to the first-aid room. Boris's toes were black and blue from digging into the ground, fighting for his life. In his news conference, of course, he gave no hint that he was hurting. Then Boris and I drove back to Boris's house in the big Mercedes, and Boris gave me a beer and said, "I thought I had that thing, but it almost drifted away."

On Thursday, the day after the quarters, the day before the semis, I saw Brad Gilbert being interviewed on television about the Becker match. Brad said that even though his man Agassi had beaten Becker eight straight times and even though Andre was the superior player, they were still taking the match very seriously. I looked up at Motormouth on the screen and said out loud, "You may have been with Andre the last year and a half, but, my boy, he spent half his life with me. And I think I learned a few things about Andre Agassi."

HELLO, BORIS

The same day, Boris and I sat down to discuss the Agassi match. This was a departure from our standard procedure. Usually, Boris waited until the final hour before he took the court to ask me for advice; usually, he wanted only a simple point or two that he could keep in mind during the match. But this was not the usual match.

"You've got to understand that it was quite easy for Andre to beat you," I said.

"What do you mean?" Boris said. His eyes opened wide.

My words were very similar to my words to Boris a year and a half earlier in Bradenton.

"You only had one plan," I continued, "one strategy to beat Andre. You thought you were just as good as him and you could stay back all the time and beat him. And then you also thought you could handle his heavy kick serve, which is far more difficult than most people think because it's tough to bring that serve down, and if you don't bring that serve down, little brother, if it falls short on Andre's side, he runs around the ball and hits the big forehand and you lose the point. You have to neutralize his ability to hit that big forehand."

For a change, Boris wanted me to talk more, to tell him more, but I pulled back, suggested it would be better to wait till the next day. I wanted Boris to think about what I'd said. I also wanted him to be eager to hear what I had to say next. The following morning, I got up early and, in the predawn darkness, wrote down a page of points to impress upon Boris. "Don't you dare put your head down if Andre beats the crap out of you in the beginning of the match. Don't you dare put your head down and let him think for one second that you've given up." I also told Boris that he shouldn't always stand in the same place to receive the serve, that he should move around, sometimes retreat well behind the base line, keep Andre guessing. And I told him he had to keep the ball deep, keep Andre at the baseline or, even better, three or four feet behind it, to remember that, unlike Pioline, Andre is at his strongest inside the baseline, where he can get the ball early, get it on the rise, use the opponent's power and catch him out of position.

In the locker room before the match, to my amazement, Andre again came up to me and again offered me a sandwich. *Jesus Christ, what the hell is this? Did he put something in the sandwich to make me sick?* I was only kidding. I thanked Andre and ate the sandwich. Forty-five minutes before the match was to begin, I handed Boris a folded piece of paper with a few final thoughts, reemphasizing my earlier suggestions. He read my note very carefully but did not say a word. Then he calmly went through his prematch ritual, and the two gifted players I knew so well marched out to Centre Court.

FOREHAND

Grip

An extreme Eastern forehand, close to a semi-Western.

Backswing

On the initial part of the swing, the left hand will sort of push the racquet head up and remains on the throat a little longer than most player's. His circular backswing will find the head of the racquet quite a bit above the right shoulder before starting its forward motion. Boris has both lower and upper body power, and this makes him very dangerous.

Forward Swing

Goes out to the target very well. He can hit his forehand with heavy spin or drive it for a winner. Note that Boris can hurt you with his forehand from any position on the court and then either sneak in or come to the net on your short returns.

Additional Comments

When Red Ayme and I first started with Boris, he was at a downpoint of his career and had let himself add weight to his already big frame. As he got into shape both mentally and physically, his movement and balance improved, which cut down on stroking errors. Balance and position are the most important factors that affect technique.

I soon noticed that Boris would hit more forehands when he had a choice, and his forehand was *big*.

BACKHAND

Grip

When I first started with Boris, his grip was an Eastern backhand. As we worked together, I suggested a little more turn to a semi-Western when more spin was necessary.

Backswing

Lendl, Edberg, Sampras, and Becker all have excellent backswing preparation: a quick hip and shoulder turn with the racquet immediately taking its full backswing. Because of this preparation, they only have to swing forward once they're in position.

Forward Swing

Even though Boris has the head of the racquet just about as high as on the forehand, he can adjust the racquet head to any height on the forward swing. The follow-through is long and classical, although it will be much shorter on difficult balls, including the return of serve and half volleys. He also pulls his shoulder away from the ball on contact. Very few players can do this and still make the ball go where they want it to go.

Backhand Underspin Slice

I've always urged my students not to use the slice as their fundamental backhand stroke. Becker is one of the few players who has the ability to hit over the ball, drive the ball, or slice the ball with offensive power. But when I first started with Boris, he was using the slice far too much, using it lazily. I counseled him to eliminate the slice until he got in perfect shape. As soon as he felt fit, he was able to use the slice aggressively.

VOLLEY

Boris Becker is and always will be one of the very best volleyers in the history of the game. His technique is almost flawless. Add to this the animal instinct he has to almost smell the direction of not only your first ball, but your second if you're lucky enough to have a second. And even though he has a six-foot-three frame, his legs are similar to Tomba's in skiing, which gives him that last split-second reaction, which at least once or twice in a match will produce that trademark dive for the ball, leaving you with that empty feeling, *I thought I had a winner.*

SERVE

He has that famous wind-up motion starting with his left foot almost on the line—with the umpire ready to yell out, "Foot fault"—but then as he starts his backswing, the foot pulls back several inches. Boris has all sorts of serves, including his big "Boom Boom Bomb," a kick serve and a slice serve.

And his second serve is not just a push hoping for an unforced error, but rather a potent weapon. He will go for the big one on the second serve over and over.

His grip is between a Continental and an Eastern forehand grip, quite different from the Eastern backhand used by so many players.

OVERHEAD

Don't try the lob. He goes up almost as high as his idol, Michael Jordan. Not only can he hit the overhead from almost anywhere, his completely extended arm and his racket extension make him look like Jordan going up for a dunk.

MOVEMENT AND BALANCE

This is where the Big Man fools you because of his big frame and lumbering movements. He was an excellent downhill skier, which requires powerful thighs, and Boris has them. Don't look for him getting to the ball too soon, but when it appears he will have no chance to make contact, he'll not only reach the ball, but will come up with a big one and be able to recover. Thanks to his stretching program, he is very, very flexible.

ATTITUDE AND MENTAL DISCIPLINE

This is the man you want next to you in a foxhole. He has come back time and time again when players felt they had him put away. Above all else, he believes in himself.

HOW TO BEAT HIM

You must get to his ego. You must make him want to show you that he can beat you at your own game. You must get him to play to your strengths instead of to your weakness. Think of two fighters, one a slugger, the other a boxer, power against finesse; the slugger's best chance is to get the boxer to slug it out with him. The difficulty is that Boris can both box and slug.

The miracle in the championship match was that Boris Becker won the first set from Pete Sampras. Boris won, 7–6, surviving in the tiebreaker, 7–5. Then Pete took over. The way he played reminded me of the way he beat the crap out of Andre in the U.S. Open in 1990. The scores then were 6–4, 6–3, 6–2. The scores now were 6–2, 6–4, and 6–2.

Pete hit sixty-eight winners and committed only seven unforced errors. His serve was clocked at one hundred twenty-nine miles an hour. Boris never once took Pete to a break point. "You just hope for rain," Boris said.

A victory would have lifted Boris to No. 2 in the world, ahead of Sampras, behind only Agassi. But the Big Engine was tired, drained physically and emotionally by his victories in the quarter- and semifinals. Still, I wouldn't have traded that engine for all the money in the world. I was so proud of him, so proud of the team, of Val, Ulli, Mike, Carlo, Red, and Barbara, of all of us who had contributed to Boris's success.

I was also proud of Pete. His victory, which he dedicated to his ailing coach, Tim Gullikson, gave him his third straight Wimbledon championship. He was only the third man and the first American to win three years in a row since World War I. The others were England's Fred Perry and Sweden's Björn Borg. It was probably just coincidence that both men were friends of mine, that I had stolen ideas from Fred when I was just starting out in Miami and that, more than thirty years later, I had offered ideas to Björn when he came to the academy to tune up for the ATP Senior Tour. It was probably just coincidence, too, that Pete had trained at the academy, and so had his traveling coach, Paul Annacone.

When Pete embraced the championship trophy, the crowd, which included Tom Cruise and Nicole Kidman, who were sitting a few rows in front of Ken Merritt and Gregg Hill, gave him a rousing ovation. But when Boris received the runner-up plate, the roar was even louder, a tribute to his history and to his courage. "Pete owns Centre Court now," Boris said, graciously. "I used to own it."

After the presentation, after we left the locker room, Boris and I drove to his house for a cold beer and a warm conversation. Then he told me to go home and shower and he would pick me up in a few minutes. When I got back to my house, the phone kept ringing, mostly friends calling to congratulate me for Boris's performances in the semis and the finals. One of the callers, however, was Michael Stich. The 1992 Wimbledon champion had lost in the opening round for the second straight year. He had not won a tournament in more than a year. He had been No. 2 in the world at the start of 1994, and now, a year and a half later, he had slipped to No. 9. Stich wanted to know if he could come to the academy to train. He said he knew he needed help with his game.

I was shocked. I didn't know how to react, how to answer. I told Stich to call me in Bradenton as soon as I got back to Florida, and he said he would.

Then Boris picked me up and took me to a news conference he had arranged, two or three dozen of the most important journalists in Germany. He introduced me to the group by saying, "This is the man who brought me back, the man who motivated me again, the man who made me want to play again."

I thanked Boris for his kind words and thanked him, too, as we Italians say, for "restoring the honor of my family." In the car, as he drove me back to my place, I told him about the phone call from Stich. "That's a compliment," Boris said. "Do it."

"No," I said, "I can't coach Stich. I'm your coach. But I might consider having him visit the academy."

Boris seemed comfortable with that idea, and we arranged to meet again at San Lorenzo for a farewell dinner. I never suspected that it really was going to be a farewell dinner. I mentioned the phone call from Stich during the meal.

"You mean that SOB had the nerve to call you?" Barbara Becker said. "He's the enemy."

My commitment is to Boris, I said.

6

TRAINING MARY

TRAINING MARY

Mary Pierce started playing tennis in 1985, the year that Boris Becker won his first Wimbledon championship. She was ten years old, the Montreal-born daughter of a French mother and an American father. Her father, Jim, quickly recognized her potential and became obsessed with molding her into a champion. He soon had her practicing eight hours a day, pounding ball after ball, developing a semi-Western forehand with dazzling power. Tennis was Mary's life, and Mary's tennis was her father's life.

When Mary was thirteen, in 1988, her father brought her to the academy. He remained her coach, but he felt the competition would be good for her. She lived in the dormitory for a couple of months and loved it. She said it was the first time she was ever really able to spend time with other girls her own age.

Monica Seles was training at the academy at the time. She was only thirteen months older than Mary, but the two never hit together. Monica never practiced with other girls her own age.

Jim Pierce, wary of anyone else's influence, soon took

Mary out of the academy. On the junior tennis circuit, she intimidated rivals with her forehand, and her father terrorized them. He openly cursed at her opponents, lashed out at their parents and their fans, physically attacked a few of them. "Kill the bitch, Mary," he commanded during a match between young teenagers.

Two months after her fourteenth birthday, Mary turned pro, the youngest ever at the time and went off to play the women's tour under her father's tutelage. Her game improved. His behavior did not. He turned his sharp tongue and his violent temper on Mary and her mother, Yannick. They fled from him, and he pursued and threatened them. He was officially banned from tournaments, his picture posted at the gate. Mary and her mother traveled with bodyguards.

When she was seventeen, estranged from her father and ranked among the top fifteen players in the world, I told Mary that if she ever needed a place to train, she was always welcome at the academy. A few days later, Mary called me. "Can we talk?" she said. She asked me if I would be her coach, if I would continue the work her father had begun. I said yes. One of the reasons I wanted to coach Mary, I'm sure, was that I hoped she might someday be good enough to beat Monica, who had turned her back on the academy and me. I've always believed in getting even.

Mary and I talked about her upbringing only once, during a four-hour drive from Miami to Bradenton. She told me in detail and in confidence what her life was like with her father, and I would never violate that confidence, never repeat the stories she told me.

Personally, I've always been able to speak to Mr. Pierce.

TRAINING MARY

I respect the work ethic he instilled in Mary, even if he did go overboard. I also respect the job he did in making Mary one of the biggest hitters in the history of women's tennis.

In 1994, our first full year together, Mary, a tall and lovely young woman, still only nineteen years old, climbed from No. 12 in the world to No. 5. In the spring, in Paris, fittingly, Mary, who is a French citizen, made a spectacular bid for a Grand Slam championship.

A couple of days before the French Open began, I offered her some undiplomatic advice. I thought she had been thinking too much on the court instead of trusting her instincts.

"Mary, dear," I said bluntly, "you aren't too bright on the tennis court. You might even be, well, *unintelligent*. So let's forget about the strategy and the finesse and do what you do best. Get up on that baseline and whack the crap out of every ball."

I gave Mary my best smile. "Don't think, dear," I said. "Just *hit!*"

During the next two weeks, Mary hit her way into the finals of the French Open without losing a single set. In fact, she lost only ten games in twelve sets in six rounds before the final. Her *average* score was 6–1! In the semifinals, she whipped the defending champion, the winner of four straight Grand Slam titles, Steffi Graf, 6–2, 6–2.

Pierce's performance, based so conspicuously on the power of sheer power . . . , confirmed Bollettieri's pre-eminence as a visionary of the contemporary game, despite the myopic complaints of a legion of detractors.

> —Peter Bodo
> *Tennis* magazine

I think that was a compliment.

In the finals, Mary's power failed her. Arantxa Sanchez Vicario outran and outlasted her, 6–4, 6–4. In a certain sense, the French Open was the story of Mary's year. She reached the finals of five tournaments and won none of them.

I advised her to play Wimbledon for the first time, but she chose not to after hearing rumors that her father planned to disguise himself to get into the tournament. In the U.S. Open, she reached the quarterfinals after a fourth-round victory over Iva Majoli, a sixteen-year-old Croatian girl who had been attending the NBTA since she was twelve. At the end of the year, Mary was ranked No. 5 in the world, but she knew she still had to elevate her game before she could compete with the top two women, Graf and Sanchez Vicario, on a regular basis.

I was determined to bring Mary up to the next level. On December 13, 1994, I sent her a letter:

Dear Mary:

After considerable thought and some conversations with Boris, I have come to the conclusion that 1995 is the first year in your career that a thoroughly thought-out plan is essential to your becoming one of the best women's players in the world.

TRAINING MARY

To accomplish this goal, the plan must be complete and well constructed, but most importantly, we must be fully committed to it and cannot alter our path once we have started down it. At the outset, you must answer the threshold question: Are you ready to be what you can be? To accept who you are—and not what you can be—is not and never will be my direction in life. In my discussion with Boris, we both questioned whether you fully understand what a top professional athlete is and has to do to reach the top and remain there. The simple answer is that you must be a professional both on and off the court 365 days a year.

What follows is an outline of a plan to which I feel very strongly that you must commit if you are to become a top professional athlete. Of course we can discuss these points and make minor changes. However, the bottom line is that if you accept the plan, I will help you, and if you do not, I will not help you. For me to be your coach only in part is not the way I can spend my limited time.

Mary, you will always be a very special young lady to me regardless of the choice you make. I truly hope that you are ready to accept your role in sports as well as life and that this letter will start you rolling in the direction of becoming the very best you can be.

Your friend and coach,

Love, Nick

I. *The Role and Responsibilities of Mary Pierce*
    You are the leader of a team that includes

your mother, brother, a manager, a full-time coach, and others who want to be around you. All of these people are a part of the plan. However, you and only you are the team leader. It is very important that you understand and accept this role because it means that you might very well have to say no to the ones you love and care about. You must always put your responsibility to yourself and your commitment first. You must require that those around you accept their responsibilities as members of *your* team. Ultimately, if they truly care about you and are committed to the goals you have set, they will accept their roles, and if not, you must be prepared for them to depart from your team.

II. *Behavior Both on and off the Court*

There is a distinct difference between the joy and excitement of a mature professional athlete and one who has not learned to accept and react to success. You must examine and adjust your reaction to success both on and off the court.

A. *On court.* You have a habit of looking to the box, raising your hands in disgust, or smiling, as well as a few other irritating habits. These must stop.

B. *Off court.* You must also behave like a professional off the court, for example, celebrating a victory during a tournament, such as having a party the night you beat Graf. What gives you the right to have a victory celebration when the tournament is not over? Aside from the lack of class this displays, your job is to win the tournament, not to beat any single player. This is the time to have a nice dinner with your team and enjoy the victory in a professional manner with the understanding that there is still more to be done.

In general, you are easily misled by the phonies who are attracted to you because of your success or who are not satisfied with their own life and want to be seen with you to satisfy their egos. These people do not care about you or your goals and will not be standing next to you when the chips are down. If you lead your team in a professional manner and learn to require those around you to live up to their responsibilities, you will be able to see these phonies for what they are.

III. *Your Personal Relationships*

The next two to four years offer you the very strong possibilities of

A. *Impacting the development of women's tennis, which has serious problems right now.* To be a truly great tennis player, you must care about your sport and its development. You have the potential to make a tremendous difference.

B. *Earning millions of dollars.* Your career is a business and you must treat it as such.

C. *Making a difference in the world.* Your status as a professional athlete affords you the opportunity to make a difference in any area you choose, underprivileged children or whatever.

In order to realize your potential, you must behave like a professional at all times. There have been and continue to be serious rumors about some of your evening activities. This is an extremely sensitive point, and I hesitate to bring it up. However, if our team is to function properly, we must discuss *all* issues that affect the team.

It appears that you are involved with someone from Paris. It is not for me to make any judgments about your relationships. However, as your coach, I feel that at this point this relationship and any others must be secondary to your career. If this person truly cares about you, he will understand and support your commitment to your career.

You must also take as a part of life that men have a tendency to boast and discuss with others relationships with the opposite sex. Remember, as your fame grows, so does the interest in your personal life.

IV. *Physical Fitness Program*

You must accept that your success depends on your strength and movement. It is essential that you spend time and effort and endure the pain of physical training. Even a small detour hurts you more than most people. You must commit to taking whatever steps are necessary to guarantee that no loss can be attributed to a lack of physical preparation. You must commit yourself financially to the selection of a trainer.

As a corollary, the proper selection of food, liquids, and supplements during tournaments and off-weeks must be made and *strictly adhered to.*

V. *Mental Outlook*

I am aware of some of your past and feel you must now open all the doors, no matter what you feel.

VI. *Mary Pierce's Present Game and Techniques*

A. The very second you step onto the tennis court, whether for practice or a tournament, all your thoughts and actions must be positive—no matter what happens, including the unexpected!

B. The French Open clearly demonstrated that your best position on the court is on or slightly behind the baseline.

C. From now on, in matches and in warm-ups, you will take option balls—and more—on the forehand side.

D. You will start coming to the net not only when they expect you to, but you will also sneak in when they don't expect it.

E. An offensive slice will become part of your game. If it is a one-handed slice, we will change your grip. If it is a two-handed slice, there will be no change.

Note: Please keep in mind that I will not

let you have an option of the slice because of *lazy feet!*

F. Your serve has improved, but still lacking are free points, whether coming from an ace, unforced error, or a short return that you attack. This cannot continue, especially against opponents who will attack.

G. Both rallying and playing sets, your practice partners must attack you, especially with slices and heavy spins. You have a tendency to wait for the ball and become very flustered.

VII. *Sven Groeneveld*

I would find it very difficult to find a coach more suitable to work with both you and me. Never, never lose sight of the fact that he is your coach first and a friend second. If this code is broken, everyone will suffer.

VIII. *Nick Bollettieri*

Both you and I know that we have a special feeling for each other, and hopefully, this will never change.

My 1994 schedule was not only a busy one, but kept me away from home, where I want to be more than ever before. I do not intend to take on more full-time students with regards to my personal supervision. I will take personal interest only in a select few, and you are among them.

Working with you and Boris Becker has been very fulfilling and was much needed due to the disappointment as a result of the end of the long relationship with Andre Agassi. I am now at a point in my life where I must focus on my personal financial security.

There are daily requests for me not only to take on new students, but to give clinics and motivational speeches. All of these offer substantial rewards. Accepting more of these opportunities would result in far less time for you and the few others of my select group. I suggest that you; your business manager, Gavin Forbes; and I sit down to discuss the terms of my time with you and come up with a financial plan, one that offers me a base and some incentives.

My report to you is only my side of the story, but you must be aware that, although I am open to adjustments, there are points in this letter that are a *must* for you to accept.

Two days later, Mary arrived at the academy in her light green Porsche convertible. I usually try to reserve the time around Christmas for my family, but I told Mary I would work with her every day until she departed on January 3 for an exhibition in Hong Kong on her way to the Australian Open. I also told her that Boris had asked me to go to Australia to be with him and that, of course, I would find time for her, too.

I decided that Mary was going to work her butt off, literally and figuratively, during the ten days before Christmas. She came to the academy between 9:15 and 9:30 each morning, stretched for half an hour, and took the court promptly at 10. For two hours or more, she practiced, usually one on two, and concentrated on her volley, shortening her stroke, and on her serve, lowering her toss. After lunch, she spent three to four hours each day in the gym, following a program designed by her new trainer, a member of the academy staff, José Rincon. I didn't have to set a curfew. She couldn't wait to get to bed each night.

After two days of strenuous work, Mary said very seriously that she wanted to discuss my letter. We went into my "office." My office, most of the time, is a picnic table on a wooden deck next to a flower garden brimming with roses of varying colors. I can tan and talk at the same time.

> *Man, I got that letter and I was like,* Jesus Christ! My God! I felt like, *That's me? You know? Things about my game and all that stuff is cool and I can deal with that, but then he started talking about other things, and I was like,* Whoa! That's not true! That's not me! I don't do that! *Those things hurt, and at first you're angry and you don't understand. But, then, it's so good for you.*
> —Mary Pierce

We went through my letter carefully, touching on every point and on a few raw nerves. I emphasized the importance of accepting a diet, eliminating the snacks and the junk food; I told Mary she had to get rid of the extra weight and body fat. I reminded her that, in 1994, at Amelia Island, her opponents tested her with thirteen drop shots, and she did not get to a single one. I told her she had to become "some kind of a physical animal" if she was going to be a champion. I warned her I was not going to give up my Christmas and take time away from Boris if she planned to just drift along and remain No. 5 to 10 in the computer rankings.

The way Mary looked at me I knew she was accepting the challenge. Still, a few days later, she got up the courage to ask me if she could have two and a half days off to spend Christmas in Paris. I just stared at her, and she went back to work. I could see her balance improving; she was moving better, covering more and more of the court.

Mary's traveling coach, Sven Groeneveld, took a few well-earned days off in mid-December, then joined us at the academy. Sven was an excellent coach, a Dutchman who had attended the University of Kansas and coached Sanchez Vicario and Kimiko Date. When he first teamed up with Mary, Sven himself was noticeably overweight at six feet three inches and a little over two hundred pounds. He quickly shed twenty-four pounds, an inspiration to Mary to curb her junk-food binges.

José Rincon told Sven and me that the exercise program he had devised for Mary would break her down in December, then build her up in January, and just as he had predicted, she complained about fatigue and her moods fluctuated. It's probably not politically correct for me to say this, but I've found that female tennis players are much more moody than males, with a few notable exceptions. Two of my favorite students, Raffaella Reggi and Carling Bassett, could fight off any mood, any distraction, and nothing fazed Monica, who simply created a world of her own. I suspect Monica could play through a tornado and then ask if it was windy.

When Mary, Sven, and José left for Hong Kong, Leah and I went to Aspen for a week of skiing. Mary beat Arantxa

Sanchez Vicario in an exhibition match, an important confidence booster, then arrived in Melbourne on January 11. Boris came in the same day, and I joined them on the twelfth.

I was disappointed when I saw Mary. She still wasn't as trim as I wanted her to be. I hate body fat. "Mary," I told her at practice, "with all the work you've been doing for the past month, you still haven't reached the level of movement and balance required to play and win long matches." She looked offended. Then I added, "You have to stop eating crap."

That night, I found out, Mary, with a little help from Sven and José, went to her apartment and threw away the junk food she had been hoarding in her refrigerator and hiding under her bed. She showed up at practice the next day with a whole new attitude. She even invited me to dinner that night and served a mixed salad with fantastic low-calorie dressing (the bottle with the label was right on the table), baked chicken, baked potato (dry), corn on the cob (no butter), and a fresh fruit salad. I took two pieces of chicken for myself, and I told Mary she could have one.

Boris lost in the first round—stubbornly, he thought he could beat Patrick McEnroe from behind the baseline, and he was wrong—but before he left Australia, he gave me orders to take Mary all the way to the championship. Mary won her first two matches easily.

The day before Mary's third-round match, I asked José Rincon to find out what court Mary's opponent was practicing on. She was a qualifier named Dally Randriantefy from Madagascar. I had never seen Randriantefy play, and I wasn't even sure where Madagascar was. José tracked her down, then led me to the court and pointed out the young woman. I studied her and reported to Mary that her next opponent "does not move too well and does not have much firepower."

The following day, when the two players walked on the court, I looked at Mary's opponent and did a double take. "Holy crap!" I told José. "We scouted the wrong girl!" The right girl had quick feet and smoked the ball. Mary looked up at me in the stands and rolled her eyes as if I were crazy. She started slowly but still beat Randriantefy decisively.

Mary had won her first three matches in six straight sets, giving up only ten games. It was Paris all over again. But in the round of sixteen, she would face Anke Huber, an improving young German player who had beaten Mary the last three times they'd played.

The night before the match, Mary, Sven, José, Leah, and I went to an Italian restaurant called Roberto's, and when we finished our healthy dinner, I turned to Mary and said, "Starting right now, everything you do, think, breathe, and dream will be pointed in one direction: *I will beat Huber. I will do whatever has to be done. I want to play her right now.*"

At practice the next morning, I told Mary, "Don't you put your head down, don't you blink an eye. Keep saying to yourself, *I want you! I want you now!*" I reminded her that Huber likes to go for a big first serve but usually does not come in behind it; if the game is close, she becomes tentative on her second serve; she loves to hit her backhand hard and down the line. She likes pace being hit to her on both sides but does not like high-bouncing balls.

Just before the match began, I turned to Mary and said, "How can you accept someone kicking your ass three times in a row?" Mary almost sprinted onto the court she was so pumped up. Early in the first set, Huber twice tried drop shots, and both times the new, slimmer, and swifter Mary got to the shots and put them away for winners. She whipped Huber, 6–2 and 6–4, and moved into the quarterfinals against the eighth seed, Natasha Zvereva of Belarus.

I was delighted for Mary, and I was worried. I was worried because if she beat Zvereva, I would have to miss her semifinal match. I wanted to stay in Australia, but I had committed myself to GTE to host a Super Bowl tennis tournament and clinic for the company's guests. I had to be in Florida the day of the semifinals.

We returned to Roberto's for dinner the night before the quarterfinals. Mary, Leah, and I had good high-carbohydrate, low-fat pasta. After the pasta, I ordered Leah's favorite dessert for her, *tiramisu,* and fresh fruit for Mary and me. When the desserts came, Leah offered Mary and me each a taste of her *tiramisu.* I said no, thank you, for both of us. Mary was not happy. She argued with me, said she'd burn off the calories, and besides, she said, she'd earned a taste. What Mary didn't understand was that once she started tasting, she didn't stop.

I won the argument, and Mary won her quarterfinal match. "Move her side to side and go after her weak serve," I counseled, and Mary played the first set to perfection, winning 6–1. But in the second set, Zvereva hit a few big shots and started jumping up and down theatrically, and the crowd got caught up in her enthusiasm, and before we knew it, Mary was reverting to her old ways, looking up at us in the stands for direction. She struggled but won the set, 6–4.

After the match, after being interviewed on ESPN by

Mary Carillo and Betsy Nagelsen, I walked down the corridor to meet Mary Pierce, to remind her that I was about to leave for the States. I knew it wasn't going to be easy for either of us. Mary ran up to me with a big smile, hugged me, and kissed me. She was so happy, so pleased with her performance and her prospects. "Let's go outside for a walk," I suggested.

She wanted to talk about self-confidence, about believing in herself, and I told her that once you conquer your fears and you realize you can do something, you can do it over and over and over. "Mary, you have very few, if any, technical faults," I said. "My only question about you is how you react when things aren't going your way. Can you handle adversity? Can you look to yourself—not look to the stands—and do it?"

Mary smiled, and I felt I had suddenly gotten through to her, and for a split second I thought, *The hell with GTE. I'll stay with Mary through the finals.* But I've always tried to honor my commitments. I told Mary I had to leave, I had to go home before the semis, and she said, "What can I do to keep you here?"

"Mary," I said, "you don't need me or anyone else to win this tournament. You have you. Accept the challenge for the first time in your life."

Mary had tears in her eyes. I had tears in mine.

We walked back to Sven and José and Leah, and Leah hugged Mary, and Mary thanked her for being her friend, for thinking of her as Mary, not as a tennis player. I hugged Mary again, and Leah and I rushed off. I didn't want to turn around and look at Mary, or I might have changed my mind. Of all the women I had coached, going back to Kathleen

Horvath and Carling Bassett, none had ever won a Grand Slam title, not when I was coaching them. I hated to miss Mary's bid.

Her opponent in the semifinals was Conchita Martinez, the No. 3 player in the world. I called Mary when our plane stopped in Hawaii and gave her the game plan:

1. Make her hit the ball on the run.
2. Move in when she hits a slice.
3. Because of your power, she will stay back, so use your angles, especially to her backhand side.
4. Get a big percentage of your first serves in, and get good depth on your second serves.
5. Power through her, and focus at all times, no matter what.

I got to Bradenton in time to watch the match. Mary dominated Conchita, 6–3, 6–1, running her streak to twelve straight sets without a defeat, without even a tiebreaker. Arantxa Sanchez Vicario won her semifinal, too, running her undefeated streak also to twelve sets. She beat one of my former students, Marianne Werdel Witmeyer, who had never before gotten past the third round of a Grand Slam tournament.

I drove from Bradenton to Boca Raton, which gave me plenty of time to think about Mary's match; participated in the GTE tennis activities; then called Mary to remind her that she had beaten Arantxa in Hong Kong and would beat her again if she remembered

1. Sanchez is very much like Michael Chang. She'll run your best shots down time after time, which can make

you impatient and make you try to hit even bigger shots, which causes unforced errors.

2. She will also start to break you down mentally because of all the work required to win a few points.
3. When she's running down your best shots, she has the ability to be quite offensive in a defensive way.
4. She thinks her backhand is her best shot and will come forward and be very aggressive with it. She will also follow it in with great confidence because of her high ranking and her experience in doubles.

Then I offered Mary a few suggestions:

1. When she runs your best shot down and comes back with a good offensive/defensive return, start the whole point over in your mind. Keep doing this until she starts giving ground, until she moves further back behind the baseline. When she backs up, she will make errors, especially with her forehand.
2. Even though you may be a little nervous in the first few games, try to maintain your high percentage of first serves.
3. Do not look to the coach's box for help. Look deep inside yourself. Even if I were there, there would be nothing I could do for you. It must come from you.

The day of the final, I played in a GTE golf tournament in Boca Raton, attended a GTE cocktail party, and then, when the start of the dinner was delayed, asked to be excused so that I could go back to my hotel room in West Palm

Beach and see the match. I made the drive in record speed and opened my door just as the first ball was being hit. For one set, I talked to the television screen as if Mary could hear me. Then I settled down and watched.

Mary did everything right. She beat the No. 2 player in the world, 6–3, 6–2, giving her fourteen straight sets on her way to the Australian Open championship. Her average score was better than 6–2, and not a single opponent won more than four games in a set. Best of all, Mary acted like a champion throughout the championship match. She kept her head high. She kept her poise. And she was only twenty years old. "Can Pierce become No. 1?" Sally Jenkins wrote in *Sports Illustrated.* "It appears so."

The whole Australian Open could hardly have gone better. Not only did two of my students get to the women's semifinals, Mary and Marianne Werdel, but three of the men's semifinalists trained at the academy—Sampras, Agassi, and Krickstein—and two of them were my former pupils. Plus Mark Knowles reached the semifinals of the men's doubles, and Jim Courier the quarterfinals of the singles. If only Boris had been the fourth men's semifinalist, instead of Chang, it would have all been perfect.

Not long after midnight, Mary called my hotel room. I was almost at a loss for words, which doesn't happen very often. I did manage to tell her how fortunate she was to have her support team with her, how much Sven and José had done for her. I also told her that I felt my departure had helped her, had forced her to stand up for herself. I suggested that she call her father, and I told her she had every right to go out and celebrate.

"Order the biggest *tiramisu*," I said, "and eat it all yourself. You've earned it."

U.S. OPEN: THE REMATCH

Andre Agassi was on one side of the net. Boris Becker was on the other. Becker used to be the No. 1 player in the world. Agassi was now the No. 1 player in the world. They were about to meet in the semifinals of the U.S. Open men's championship, the centerpiece of the final Grand Slam tournament of the year. The winner would play Pete Sampras for the title.

(Several hours earlier, Sampras had defeated Jim Courier in four sets in their semifinal match. I had coached three of the four semifinalists in the 1995 U.S. Open, and the fourth had trained at my academy.)

Only nine weeks earlier, Agassi and Becker had met in the semifinals at Wimbledon, and Becker had come from behind to win, one of the greatest moments of his career and of mine. Since then, however, Becker had slipped from a solid No. 3 in the world to No. 4, behind Thomas Muster, and Agassi had strengthened his grip on No. 1, ahead of Sampras. Andre had won five tournaments in a row since Wimbledon and twenty-five straight matches, the longest winning streak of his career.

Agassi and Becker had both reached the semifinals of the open without facing a player ranked among the top ten in the world. In his first four matches, Andre had lost only two sets, both to Alex Corretja. Plagued by sixty-seven unforced errors, back-to-back double-faults that ended the first set, and an obscene outburst that cost him a $2,000 fine, Andre had to overcome a two-sets-to-one deficit to beat Corretja. In the quarterfinals, he had defeated Petr Korda, a Czech who often trained at the academy. Boris had lost only one set in his first four matches, then, in the quarterfinals, had won a tense four-set four-hour match from the man who eliminated him in Australia, Patrick McEnroe.

At Flushing Meadows, unlike Wimbledon, the family and friends of the two semifinalists were sitting in separate court-side boxes. Brooke Shields, of course, was in Andre's box; so was his coach, Brad Gilbert. And Barbara Becker, of course, was in Boris's box; so was his coach, his new one, Mike DePalmer Jr.

Where was I? I was the ex-coach, the discarded coach. I was in Minnesota, not far from Minneapolis, on the shores of Lake Minnetonka, in the home of my friends, Glenn and Marilyn Nelson. I was watching the U.S. Open semifinal on television. At first, I didn't want to watch. *The hell with it*, I thought. *I don't care who wins.* But, somehow, I was drawn to the screen. Wendy Nelson, Glenn and Marilyn's daughter, my former student, said to me, "Nick, who do you want to win?"

"To be honest," I said, "I want Andre to win."

I wanted Andre to beat the shit out of Boris.

How could Boris have done this to me? I thought.

7

GOOD-BYE, BORIS

GOOD-BYE, BORIS

Boris Becker and I released a joint statement a few days before the start of the 1995 U.S. Open. "After a successful two-year relationship," the statement read, "Nick Bollettieri and Boris Becker have agreed that, beginning with the U.S. Open, Nick will no longer function as Boris Becker's day-to-day coach but will remain as Boris Becker's tennis advisor.

"The primary reason for the adjustment is that Nick cannot devote the time and travel that Boris Becker's schedule demands. Nick wishes to concentrate more time on the expansion at the academy.

"Mike DePalmer Jr., who has assisted Nick Bollettieri and worked with Boris Becker in the past year, will continue to travel and assist in the coaching of Mr. Becker."

The statement was pure bullshit from top to bottom. One, Boris and I never agreed on anything; he made a decision. Two, from that day on, Boris never sought my advice. Three, I was willing to devote as much time and travel to Boris as he needed.

The main purpose of the statement was to keep the media, especially the German media, from distracting Boris at Flushing Meadows, from asking him too many questions about our split. I went along with it partly because I respected Boris as a man and as a tennis player and partly because of my friendship with his advisor, Axel Meyer-Wolden.

It was Dr. Meyer-Wolden, in fact, who informed me of Boris's decision. He and his family were visiting the academy in August, and one morning he came up to me with tears in his eyes and, with no warning, said, "Boris doesn't want you to come to Flushing Meadows."

I was stunned. I was hurt. I was angry. And I was disappointed. I had put my faith and trust in Boris, and he had destroyed them. Suddenly, for the first time, I realized how Andre felt when he learned secondhand of my decision to end our father/son/coach/pupil relationship. I hurt him. It should not have been done through a letter. I should've gotten on a plane and flown out to Las Vegas and sat with him, eyeball to eyeball, and explained how I felt and listened to how he felt.

What went wrong with Boris and me? I had joined him when he was on the way down and I had brought his ass back. I had traveled with him, trained with him, planned with him, counseled him. I had sent my best pros to work with him. For twenty-one months, his needs, his desires, took precedence over the academy, over my children, and over Leah. Just what the hell did he want?

The problem, I eventually learned, went back to Wimbledon. First, Boris stewed about what I said to him right after he beat Andre: *I never knew you could play that well.* I meant it as a compliment. I meant that his blend of skill and courage that day was extraordinary. *I never knew you could play that well.*

He thought I meant that he had played above his ability, that I didn't think he was really that good. I meant I had rarely, if ever, seen anyone battle back so bravely from the brink of defeat.

Second, Boris, and Barbara, too, were irritated by my contact with Michael Stich. I hadn't searched out Stich. I hadn't solicited his interest. Even though Boris had at first indicated that I should be flattered by Michael's request, it had annoyed him. He and Stich might be countrymen, but they were also "enemies."

Right after Wimbledon, when I got back to Bradenton, I wrote a letter to Stich:

July 10, 1995

Dear Michael:

I have given considerable thought to what my obligations have been and always will be, and that is trying to help people reach their maximum potential not only in sports, but in life.

When I departed from Andre, there were thoughts in my mind for the very first time that I would give less time to the tournament circuit. Then, by chance, by accident, or by fate, Boris Becker and I joined together in a relationship that was questioned by many. Both of us had goals to achieve and nothing was going to prevent us from reaching those goals.

Today, we have achieved a great many things. However, we are not satisfied and will continue in striving for our goals together.

There is no doubt in my mind that you Michael

MY ACES, MY FAULTS

Stich have the qualities not to be just a great player, not to be in the top ten, but you have the qualities and talent to challenge for the very top. You must first accept this challenge from within yourself, and it must be a desire that burns within you to such a point that everything you do night and day is directed to your goal. This is easy to say, yet is difficult to achieve.

The next step is to surround yourself with people who believe in you and what you want to accomplish. They must also accept the challenge and know how to work with you to accomplish those goals. Not only must they be willing to work with you, but they (your team) must be willing to disagree with you in the interest of achieving this goal. Finding that combination is key to reaching your goals.

You and your team must then set to accomplishing your goals quietly, remaining focused and low key throughout. By remaining low key in your attitude and your activities both on and off court, you enable yourself to remain focused. I learned this tactic from my friend Boris Becker, who recently showed not only Andre Agassi, but the entire world that you will be a winner (even if you are getting beat in all ways) if you can hold your head high and keep your mind in focus.

You must do the same! This is a much more difficult task (if not impossible) if you have set yourself up in the spotlight. With the foregoing accomplished, I know you can challenge the top position in tennis.

For myself, I am honored that you have asked me to be a part of your career, and I hope you understand that I believe in you and your abilities as a person and an athlete. However, I cannot help you at this time. My energy, my commitment, and my bond belong to my friend and student, Boris Becker. Boris has provided me with the most satisfying and rewarding relationship of my entire thirty-eight-year tennis career, and I cannot let anything stand in the way of our quest to reach our goals together.

Thank you once again for the honor you do me by your request.

Warmest regards,
Nick Bollettieri

A few days later, I received a phone call from Stich. He understood that I could not coach him, but he wanted to know if he could use the facilities of the academy to train and practice. Axel Meyer-Wolden happened to call me the same day, and I told him about Stich's request. "Don't do it," he advised. "Don't have Stich come to the academy."

I said, "Axel, you don't understand my business. For thirty-eight years, this door has been open to everyone. When Jimmy Arias wanted to come back, when Aaron Krickstein wanted to come back, I welcomed them. If Andre asked to come back, or Monica, I would welcome them. This is what I've always done, and you want me to say to Michael, 'You can't come.' I'm sorry, I can't do that."

I told Stich that he would be welcome at the NBTA. He flew over within a few days and spent a little more than a week at the academy. Mary was taking time off, so Sven Groeneveld worked with Stich. I never spent any time on the court with Michael, but I did take him out to dinner and reiterated the advice I had offered in my letter. I don't know how much we helped him, but a week later, in Los Angeles, Stich won his first tournament in more than a year and moved up to No. 8 in the world. By the end of 1995, "the enemy" had hired a new coach: my friend Sven Groeneveld.

A month after our triumph at Wimbledon, Boris and I were together again in Cincinnati. He was seeded third, behind only Agassi and Sampras, but he lost his first match to Jan Siemerink. Stich, incidentally, beat Sampras in the quarterfinals, then lost to Chang in the semis. The following week, in New Haven, Stich went out early, and Boris lasted only to the quarterfinals.

I could sense in Cincinnati and in New Haven that Boris's attitude toward me was changing, that he was cooler toward me and less receptive to my suggestions. I thought it was probably just a letdown after the high of Wimbledon, but what I didn't know was that the team was turning against me, that Ulli and Val, in particular, whose livelihoods depended on their relationship with Boris, kept questioning my commitment, kept asking Boris whenever I went back to Florida or I worked with Mary, "Where's Nick? Why isn't Nick with us?" Then, when Ulli drank too much on the flight to New Haven and complained too rudely at the front desk of our motel, I turned on him and snapped, "You may represent Boris Becker that way, but you sure don't represent Nick Bollettieri that way." Ulli, I'm sure, resented my remark and voiced his resentment to Boris.

When Boris lost in New Haven, Mike DePalmer and I got a phone call from Val, telling us that Boris wouldn't be needing us for a while, that we could go home to Florida and he would call us when he wanted us to rejoin him.

The next word was from Dr. Meyer-Wolden, telling me I would not be needed at Flushing Meadows. Boris did, however, want young Mike DePalmer to work with him at the Open. He wanted Mike to continue to travel with him, to observe and coach him. If I had been Mike—remember, I had known him since he was about ten and I had matched him with Boris—I would've said no, I wouldn't have done it, but I could see Mike's viewpoint. He was divorced and recently remarried, paying alimony, and he was going to make at least $150,000 to $200,000 a year working with Boris. Where else could he make that kind of money? He asked me what he should do, and I said, "Go with Boris," and he did. I wouldn't have.

I went to the Open with Mary Pierce, who won her first two matches and then was eliminated at the end of the first week. I also started to work with a new pupil at the open, a teenage Australian with a powerful serve and a promising future. He, too, was eliminated in the third round.

The following week, at the Nelsons' invitation, I flew out to Minneapolis for a brief vacation. I was a thousand miles away from the stadium in Flushing Meadows, and yet I was hoping that Andre would beat Boris just as fervently as I'd hoped Boris would beat Andre at Wimbledon two months earlier.

How could I have switched sides so quickly?

Was I Jekyll and Hyde?

No. I was just human. I was hurt and instinctively striking back.

U.S. OPEN: THE WOMEN

Between the men's semifinals, between the Sampras-Courier and Agassi-Becker matches, I watched Steffi Graf play Monica Seles for the U.S. Open women's singles championship. When the two women took the court in Louis Armstrong Stadium in Flushing Meadows, New York, they had already won twenty-six Grand Slam events between them, seven Australian Opens, seven French Opens, six Wimbledons, and six U.S. Opens.

Graf owned most of the titles but only because Seles had given up tennis for twenty-eight months, had missed the last ten Grand Slam tournaments, recuperating, mentally and physically, from a madman's assault, a knife jabbed in her back at courtside.

The stabbing took place in Hamburg in April 1993, and when Monica screamed, women's tennis winced. The sport, too, was wounded. At the time, the best of the younger players, seventeen-year-old Jennifer Capriati, was on the brink of burnout, and the best of the older players, thirty-six-year-old Martina Navratilova, was on the brink of retirement. With Monica, Martina, and Jennifer all out of action, women's tennis by the spring of 1995 was deep in trouble.

Then Monica announced that her wounds, mental and physical, had healed, that she was coming back. She won an emotional exhibition match against Martina, five straight matches to capture the Canadian Open, then six straight matches to reach the final of the U.S. Open, to go up against Graf. In her first eleven official matches since she was attacked, Monica had not lost a single set.

U.S. OPEN: THE WOMEN

Graf and Seles once lived in the same room, although not at the same time. It was room A-203 at the NBTA. Graf came for a few weeks in the early eighties when she was thirteen years old, and I wouldn't even know she'd been there if her roommate hadn't been my daughter Danielle. Dani remembered Steffi; I didn't. Dani said she had a great appetite.

Seles came to the academy in 1986, when she was twelve, and she and her brother inherited Dani's (and Steffi's) old room, A-203. Monica made an unforgettable impression. She was the best player her age I'd ever seen—I told people she was "from another planet"—and for more than three years I provided her and her family with the finest facilities the NBTA had to offer, with a home and a car, with meals, equipment, and expertise. I spent hundreds of hours at secluded courts, usually guarded by screens or curtains, working with Monica and her brother, Zoltan, and her father, Karolj. I charged them nothing.

In the 1989 media guide for the Women's International Tennis Association, the year Monica turned pro, the year she won her first professional championship, her bio stated, "Coached by Nick Bollettieri." Within a year, she and her father were saying, "Nick who?" They insisted I had never coached her; they said I may have picked up balls for her. Karolj, a cartoonist by trade, said he had always been her coach; they had just used my facilities.

Yet I wanted Graf to beat Seles in the final of the U.S. Open, not because the Seles family had forgotten my coaching, but for the sake of women's tennis. If Seles won, if she dominated Graf, if she immediately reestablished herself as the No. 1 woman in the world, then critics would argue that women's tennis was a wasteland so short of talented players that Seles, even after a long layoff, even after gaining weight and losing a step, still was better than anyone else. I didn't want to see women's tennis tarnished. I had trained too many wonderful female players, had seen them work too hard to get to the top.

Still, I was delighted to see Monica reach the finals. My daughter Nicole and I had run into her during the first week at Flushing Meadows, and she had given Nicole a big hug and a kiss, and that meant so much to me. One of the reasons I have trouble being angry with Monica and Andre is that whatever disagreements I've had with them, they've always been kind to my children, and my children love them. Another reason is that they have both been good for tennis.

When Monica was hesitating about returning to competitive tennis, when her scars were still raw, I wrote her a letter:

Dear Monica:

It has been a good deal of time since we have spoken. I have missed this. In watching you last night on television, so many memories came back to me of the early days at the academy. You were so young and frail. Last night, I saw that, too.

Despite some differences and misunderstandings that have occurred between us, for me—and I hope you also—that is in the past. This letter is meant to be from Nick to Monica and comes from the heart.

I am very concerned for you. You have been so good and such a champion. You have been the wonder of women's tennis and have done so much to make it exciting and bring it back for the fan from the Chris and Martina days.

As someone who was instrumental in helping you in the early years, I want to write you now and tell you how important it is that you come back and play— both for yourself and for the game.

For you, Monica, I feel that playing again is critical. You have such a talent and so much time to prove to the world that you can achieve the titles and ranking that are rightfully yours. You are so young and have so much more time. Nothing is lost. This is something that you must do for yourself. You said that you are a fighter and not a quitter. You must come back and show yourself and the tennis world that you can do it again. The fans, the young players, your family, your sponsors—they all want to see you back on top.

Although your situation is devastating, it is not de-bilitating. So many athletes become injured or suffer losses from which there is no return. Certainly, it will not be easy, but you do have the opportunity, and that is proof that God wants you to play.

I would be very much interested if you would consider coming back to the NBTA to begin again. You are welcome to do this in any way that you wish—with or without my involvement but with the full support of the NBTA and our staff. Monica, if I can help, I certainly want to. You have always been very special to me.

Life goes on. I know that God has placed you on earth for a purpose, and although He has challenged you greatly this time, He still has left you with the opportunity to once again prove to the world who you are and what you do better than anyone else.

My prayers and encouragement are yours now.
Nick

Dear Nick:

Thank you very much for your letter and all of your well wishes. I am feeling stronger every day, and I would like to thank you for your encouragement to continue playing.

A month or so ago, I saw Danielle at the Opus store in the Gulf Gate Mall. It was wonderful seeing her. Please say hello to her from me. Please also say hi to Nicole and Alexandra. I'm sure I would not even recognize them now. I'm sure Nicole has grown into a beautiful young lady and that Alexandra is right behind her! Again, thank you very much for your letter, and I do hope to see you soon.

Monica

When Monica began preparing for the U.S. Open, guess who she used as her hitting partner? Jimmy Arias. In fact, when she arrived at Flushing Meadows, Jimmy was with her.

U.S. OPEN: THE WOMEN

The *New York Times* ran a photograph showing Monica and her father and Jimmy on the practice court. The caption said, "Monica Seles turns to Jimmy Arias for advice while her father shags balls." Of course, Karolj Seles promptly dismissed Jimmy.

I didn't watch all of the women's final on television, but what I saw of it, when I wasn't looking at the view of Lake Minnetonka, was magnificent. Monica had set point and was serving in the first set tiebreaker, but her bid for an ace landed wide by inches, and Steffi fought back and won the set, 7–6. Monica swiftly evened the match, winning the second set, 6–0, thoroughly dominating Steffi. But just when it seemed Graf's chances were fading, she charged back and won the third set and the title, 6–4. "The biggest win I have ever achieved," Graf said.

Three other women who have made their homes at the academy did not fare so well as Seles and Graf at the Open. Iva Majoli went out in the first round, and Mary Pierce in the third, and Anna Kournikova lost in the second round of the juniors.

Majoli had just turned eighteen, and Kournikova was only fourteen. They will have more chances in the future, and I suspect, so will I. During the Open, while I was walking around the grounds at Flushing Meadows, someone tapped me on the shoulder, and I turned and faced a woman I had never seen before. She was standing with a man and a very young girl.

"Mr. Bollettieri," she said, "my husband and I came all the way from Moscow just to see you. We would like you to meet your next champion." She pointed at the little girl. "She is eight years old," the mother said. "We would like to leave her with you."

I thanked her and explained that eight years old was a little too young.

A few weeks later, the little girl moved into the academy.

8

GROOMING MONICA

GROOMING MONICA

The first time I heard of Monica Seles, she was eleven years old and she was going to Disney World. Not to see Mickey. To play tennis. In a tournament named after Goofy.

At the time, we had a twelve-year-old at the academy named Kim Kessaris, who was, we felt, the best player her age in the United States. She played Monica in Goofy's tournament, and when my pros told me that Kim had lost, 6–1, 6–0, to an eleven-year-old from Yugoslavia, I said, "I've got to see that girl."

A couple of months later, in December 1985, I went to the Orange Bowl tournament in Miami with a man named Tony Cacic, a former soccer player from Zagreb in Yugoslavia, who had just moved to Bradenton so that his twelve-year-old daughter, Sandra, could attend the academy.

Cacic had heard of Monica Seles from friends back home, and when he saw her play, he turned to me and said, "I will buy plane tickets for her. You give her room and board." I told Tony that sounded good to me.

Cacic introduced himself to the Seles family and offered to pay for Monica to fly to the States. He explained that

Nick Bollettieri, the owner of the NBTA, would provide Monica with room and board and training facilities. The Seles family accepted. Tony bought two tickets, one for Monica and one for her teenage brother, Zoltan. The parents would come over later.

The youngsters moved into the dormitory at the academy, and Monica enrolled in Bradenton Academy. After several months, Monica's parents were ready to join them. Tony Cacic said he would pay for their tickets. By then, I knew how talented Monica was. I paid for the parents' tickets and gave Tony back the money he had spent on the children's tickets.

Incidentally, Tony's wife, Anna, came to work for me at the academy. She still works in the snack bar. Their daughter Sandra won the first tournament on the women's tour in 1996, a tuneup for the Australian Open, and moved into the top hundred in the world.

Early in her stay at the academy, Monica practiced out in the open on our showpiece front court, and she hit against Rafaella Reggi, Carling Bassett, and Lisa Bonder, young women six to eight years older than she, veterans of the professional tour. Monica wore them all out. She was the toughest twelve-year-old I'd ever seen. She had only one thing on her mind, and that was to be No. 1.

From the beginning, Monica did not believe in keeping the ball in play. She did not believe in rallying. She believed in hitting winners. She tried to put every shot away. This helped her become a great tennis player and a terrible hitting partner.

Soon, Monica stopped hitting against girls. She hit against

Agassi and Blackman, and wore them out, too. She beat up everybody. Even my pros hid when they knew I was looking for someone to hit with Monica. José Lambert, Raul Ordonez, and René Gomez, three of my elite pros, all served time as Monica's hitting partners. She aimed at the corners and ran them ragged. She not only wore them out, she wore out their shoes. A pair of tennis shoes didn't last a week against Monica. Yet Karolj Seles, Monica's father, was always scornful of the efforts of the pros.

Poppa Seles was not a tolerant man. He was tough on all my pros. I once saw José Lambert crying like a baby; he said he had never been treated like such shit. Poppa Seles was extremely paranoid about Monica's training. Once, he demanded that I fire René Gomez because he said Gomez was stealing Monica's drills, using the same drills with his own students. The truth is, he was. We had been using the same drills for years with all of our students. I didn't fire René.

What made Monica so special was not the drills, it was the effort she put into them. She was tireless, persistent, dogged. She worked hard from the moment she stepped on the court. From the first ball till the last, she was always focused. She would hit the same shot over and over and over till she had it down. Not for an hour. Not for a day. For weeks. She would hit nothing but two-handed backhands for two or three weeks, then nothing but two-handed forehands for two or three weeks, followed by nothing but overheads for two or three weeks. She practiced for three or four hours at a stretch. She wouldn't leave the court until she had hit the perfect shot. She once went more than a year without playing a single match. Monica spoke almost as rarely, but she listened. To her father and to me. And she hit. And hit. And hit. I couldn't have asked for a more dedicated student.

Once, when Monica was practicing on the front court, not yet into her teens, my friend Jerry Glauser, the Mercedes dealer, watched her and offered to put up $500,000 for an interest in her career. Another time, my friend Dick Vitale, the basketball announcer, watched me coaching Monica hour after hour and screamed at me, "When are you going to spend some time with my daughters?" Dick tends to scream when he says, "Hello."

Poppa Seles insisted that we move to a back court so that people would not steal his secrets and Monica's. He insisted that we put a fence and a canvas curtain around the court. A thick canvas curtain that no one could see through. We left openings in the corners of the canvas for the wind to blow through. Poppa Seles insisted that we close the openings to protect his privacy, and after we did, a howling wind blew the canvas and the fence down three different times. On windy and rainy days, we moved to the indoor center, and Poppa Seles demanded we put a curtain around the indoor court, too. He also wanted the music turned off at the nearby fitness center, and he told us to bar students from walking past Monica, detour them around her court; he would tolerate no distractions.

Poppa Seles insisted that we buy a thirty-five-foot-long rope and hang it from the ceiling of the indoor center. He wanted Monica to exercise on the rope. He explained she could develop upper-body strength holding herself out parallel to the ground, like an aerialist in the circus. The special sturdy rope cost more than $2,000, and when Greg Breunich couldn't get it installed quickly enough, Poppa Seles wanted me to fire Greg. Monica never used the rope. Nor did anyone else. It still hangs from the ceiling of the indoor center.

Often Monica hit with her brother, Zoltan, who was a good tennis player, willing to work endless hours without complaint. When Zoltan couldn't catch up to her shots, Poppa Seles was as tough on him as he was on my pros. Zoltan grew confused and depressed. His moods and personality fluctuated wildly. So did his appearance. One day, he had a goatee; the next, he shaved his head. One Christmas Day, he was so angry to find the pro shop closed when he wanted to pick up some restrung racquets he kicked the door down. "Each day you are an entirely different person," I told Zoltan, "and yet no matter who you are, everyone else is always wrong."

The Seleses were, by far, the most demanding family I ever worked with. Whatever we gave them—food, shelter, equipment, transportation, thousands of dollars worth of orthodontia for Monica, an operation for her mother—they wanted more. What they didn't eat in our dining room, they would throw into a big bag and take back to their condo, which we had already stocked with food. They were always demanding new tennis balls, and we hardly ever got used balls back. I still can't figure out where all the balls went.

One early letter from the Seleses said that they would stay and train at the academy *if* we provided an apartment, meals, schooling for Monica, preferably from 10 A.M. to 1 P.M. each day, medical care, jobs for her father and brother as coaches and trainers at the academy, working only mornings because in "afternoon, Karolj and Zoltan want to work, together with you, with Monica on a tennis court." They also wanted a job for Poppa as a cartoonist and training for Momma to work on computers plus a fistful of round-trip airline tickets between Yugoslavia and the States, and all of the aforementioned had to be guaranteed in writing. "Mr. Bollettieri," the letter stated, "we want from you to answer our every request, and if you have some better solutions, please contact with us. Please, Mr. Bollettieri, all these our requests you don't understand as our blackmailing, because these requests are the minimal conditions for a life and working in the U.S."

Over the years, their demands intensified and multiplied, and in 1988, when Monica was fourteen, I wrote to the Seleses:

I have done and am prepared to continue to do more for Monica Seles than I have ever done for any student I have ever coached, including Andre Agassi. But I *cannot* place one student in a position above that of the NBTA itself. This would be unfair to our parent company, to my staff, and, even more important, to my family and to myself.

I have already told you that Andre and Monica will always be my top priority, but I cannot refuse to supervise the training of anyone else. What about my traveling team students, Jim Courier, David Wheaton, and the countless other kids whose parents pay the tuition bills that ultimately allow me to feed, clothe, and house my family?

I will devote to you as much time as I possibly can. But ... I cannot guarantee that all your practices can be completely closed to the public. There will be times when we are so busy that this will be impossible!

I cannot kick everyone out of everywhere you are practicing, and it is not right of you calling them names. They are people and must be treated as people.

I put in hundreds of hours working with Monica, maybe thousands, as much work as I've ever put into a student. (Carling Bassett used to say, "Nick, you've given more time to Monica than you gave to me and Kathleen Horvath and Jimmy Arias put together.") I changed her backswing; she was using too much wrist, risking tendinitis. I changed her serve—the motion and the toss. I urged her to use a punch volley. I marveled at the two-handed forehand and backhand Poppa Seles had drilled into her. I encouraged her, applauded her, praised her. Once, while I was on the court with Monica, I was called to the telephone. Someone representing Jennifer Capriati was calling, asking me if I would be interested in working with Jennifer. I thanked him for the compliment, but I told him I had committed myself to Monica Seles and that I could truly focus on only one young woman at a time. I was as loyal as I could be to Monica, hardly suspecting that she and her family would abandon me as soon as they started making money on the pro tour, that they would state publicly that I had had nothing to do with shaping her talents or launching her career.

Monica's career skyrocketed. In 1988, after she turned fifteen, in only her second tournament as a professional, Monica beat Chris Evert in the final at Houston and won her first pro title. By the end of the year, she ranked sixth in the world. I kept offering her advice. Here is part of a letter I wrote to Zoltan early in 1989:

Backhand

The slice must become a weapon, not just getting the ball back.

Serve

The basic construction of her serve is letter-perfect. Ordinary development of the body will make it better, *but*
  A. We must now work on the kicker.
  B. She is now adjusting her grip just a little to hit the flat serve.
  C. She must develop the breaking slice as well as the jammer to the body.

Overhead

Must practice every day. Tends to get into position too quickly and then has difficulty when she has to make a last-second adjustment.

Angles

Letter-perfect.

Monica's Greatest Strengths

A. Return of serve!!!
B. Always forcing the opponent and moving forward.
C. Variety of strokes.
D. Serve technique.
E. Anticipation and movement.
F. Serve technique.

Comment

We all must never let her change the return of serve, which is the very best in women's tennis today.

When Monica was seventeen, she was No. 1 and already owned four Grand Slam titles. She won seven of the eight Grand Slam tournaments she entered before the stabbing in Hamburg, losing only at Wimbledon in the final. Before she turned twenty, she had already earned $7 million in prize money and millions more in endorsements. She could have given the academy a small token gift. Or at least said thank you. "It was a marriage of convenience," Karolj Seles told *Tennis* magazine when he was asked about his years at the academy. "We benefited from the facilities, and he benefited from the publicity." Chris Evert said on NBC television that she thought the Seleses were not giving Nick Bollettieri enough credit.

In 1989 and 1990, I don't know how many letters I wrote to the Seleses, offering to coach, to counsel, to be a friend and a second parent to Monica. I was willing to commit myself to her; all I wanted was a small sign of commitment from her family. I never got it.

Early in 1990, soon after she turned sixteen, Monica and her father and brother decided she would play tournaments in Chicago and Washington before she competed in the Lipton Championships. Monica did not play particularly well in those two events, and her family was dispirited.

I suggested that we cheer up, take a low-key approach to Lipton, remember that Monica was only sixteen. For the week before Lipton, I had Raul Ordonez working with her and with Andre Agassi, trying to get them both sharp.

A few days before we left for Key Biscayne, Poppa Seles and Zoltan came into my office and said they wanted to have lunch with me. They said they had very important matters to discuss. We went to Steak & Shake, and as we were eating, Mr. Seles took out a yellow pad that had several pages of notes written in both black and red ink. He said he had a few questions for me, seventeen or eighteen of them, as I recall, including:

How much time will you give to Monica?
Will you take any other students besides Monica and Andre?
Would you take care of Monica if anything happened to Poppa?
How would you market Monica?

Mr. Seles also talked about how I would be compensated for the years Monica had spent at the academy, for my work and my staff's. He said he would like me to reply immediately because he wanted to finalize an agreement before the start of the Lipton.

I paid for the lunch. Zoltan had forgotten to bring money.

That night, I sat down and answered all the questions in detail, reaffirmed that I would coach only Monica and Andre, that I would divide my time and my efforts between them. I delivered my reply to the Seles family the next day and waited to hear from them. Not a word.

We all went off to Key Biscayne, and when I saw the draw and saw the way they were playing, I had a suspicion that both Andre and Monica would win. I was right. Andre beat Stefan Edberg in the men's final, and Monica beat Judith Wiesner in the women's.

Two champions! I couldn't have been happier. I raced back to Bradenton, and the next day Poppa Seles came into my office and told me to get Raul ready to go to the next tournament. I asked Mr. Seles if he had read my answers to his questions. He said we would talk about it some other time. I pointed out that he was the one who had demanded my answers immediately, who had wanted to formalize our relationship so that there would be no misunderstanding. Mr. Seles said nothing.

"Until you tell me where I stand," I said, "I'm not going to be helping Monica anymore. Nor is the academy."

The Seleses moved out the next day.

Monica said she wanted someplace quieter to practice. She said it was a great move for her career, for her game, for her health, and for herself. Funny, but I didn't notice that her career, her game, her health, or herself had suffered during her four years at the academy.

SCOUTING REPORT: MONICA SELES

Born: December 2, 1973
Height: 5 feet, 10 ½ inches
Weight: 145 pounds

FOREHAND AND BACKHAND

She is a two-handed player who hits her forehand and her backhand with her hands in exactly the same position. Her swing is very compact, a smooth, circular motion, and she can adjust it to any shot coming at her, no matter the speed, no matter the degree of difficulty, in a fraction of a second.

She prepares early and, on contact, transfers her weight perfectly. Her follow-through is long and aggressive, helping her not only hit harder, but recover quickly.

She almost always makes contact inside the baseline and uses the opponent's power to magnify her own power.

Even though her ground strokes are hit with topspin, she still hits through the ball instead of excessively brushing up the ball. Her spin gives her control, but at the same time her ball is almost flat and runs away from her opponent.

No other player, male or female, has so many formidable weapons at his or her command.

SERVE

Her serve has improved greatly. She is no Brenda Schultz, with a big booming serve, but she gets excellent depth, and as a lefty, which is an advantage in tennis, she has learned to deliver a low breaking slice which is very difficult to attack.

RETURN OF SERVE

No matter how hard a serve is hit to her, no matter where it is hit, no matter how it kicks, it will come back. Her return makes you think that you need lessons on your serve.

VOLLEY

Monica can be quite effective with a full-stroke volley similar to Agassis. But often, because of her devastating ground strokes, which force a weak return, and because she takes the ball early, moving forward, it is easy for her to take another couple of steps to the net and win the point with a simple block volley or, at times, a swinging volley.

MOVEMENT

No matter what her foot speed may be, she anticipates the return and gets a very quick jump on the ball. Most often, she is coming forward, hitting the ball on the rise and catching her opponent out of position.

MENTALITY

Her will to win is unmatched. No one is more determined than Monica. No one is more difficult to distract.

HOW TO BEAT HER

There is only one way to beat Monica:

Our Father, Who art in heaven ... (use a variety of serves and come to the net on a few of them) ... hallowed be Thy name ... (try every shot you can think of, including at least a few drop shots) ... Thy kingdom come ... (be aggressive, gamble, go for the low-percentage shot because she's going to beat you a high percentage of the time) ... Thy will be done .... (If this doesn't work, try Hebrew, Islamic, and Buddhist prayers.)

U.S. OPEN: THE WINNER

For the second time in ten weeks, Andre Agassi and Boris Becker battled through four sets in the semifinals of a Grand Slam championship, and for the second time in ten weeks, the player I was rooting for won. This time, in the U.S. Open, the winner was Andre Agassi.

Strangely, I thought Andre was more impressive at Wimbledon. He never dominated Boris in New York the way he did for the first set and a half in London. As a matter of fact, Andre did not break Boris's service once in the first three sets in the open. Yet Andre won the first two of those sets, both in tiebreakers. When Boris took the third set, 6–4, I studied Andre on the television screen, looking for any sign of uncertainty. I saw none. Andre finally broke serve in the fourth set, won it, 6–4, and advanced to the finals against Pete Sampras.

Only in tennis could the two top players in the world, No. 1 Agassi and No. 2 Sampras, both still in their early twenties, have been playing against each other for more than a decade. As amateurs, they had probably both been outshone by Michael Chang; as professionals, they had met sixteen times, and each had won eight. In 1995, they had already faced each other four times, always in the final round, and Sampras had always won the first set, but Andre had won three of the matches. They had created a sensational rivalry that was helping to revitalize tennis.

I didn't watch much of the U.S. Open championship match. I really didn't care who won, or who lost. I had nothing but good thoughts about Pete, and I was grateful to Andre for beating Boris, for getting even for me.

Sampras won the first set and the match convincingly, 6–4, 6–3, 4–6, 7–5. Sampras hit twenty-four aces, and several other serves that Agassi couldn't return. Andre's winning streak came to an end after twenty-six matches.

For the third year in a row, Pete had won two Grand Slam titles. For the third year in a row, he was going to wind up No. 1 in the world. In his seven matches in the U.S. Open, Pete had never gone more than four sets, and he had lost the opening set only once.

The only time Pete Sampras trailed by a set in a match in the 1995 U.S. Open was in his third-round match against a six-foot-four, two-hundred-pound teenager, an eighteen-year-old Australian named Mark Philippoussis, who just happened to be my latest pupil.

9

HELLO, MARK

HELLO, MARK

Nick Philippoussis was just what I needed. Another tennis father. After Mr. Arias, Mr. Agassi, Mr. Seles, and Mr. Pierce. Strong-willed men, all of them. Demanding and possessive. I was warned that Nick Philippoussis made those four fathers look like pussycats. I was told that he dominated his son, distrusted outsiders, hated the media, and insisted that everything be done his way. *Watch out for his crazy dad.*

But then I met Nick Philippoussis. We got along just fine, for a little while. He was blunt, impatient, and opinionated. Great. So was I. Nick Philippoussis was also excitable. How excitable? So excitable that Mark said that I, of all people, was a calming influence on him. So excitable that before every match Mark played, Nick took a pill to get himself to relax.

But just like Jimmy's father and Andre's, Monica's and Mary's, Mark's father was totally dedicated to the success of his child and had spent endless hours grooming his child for that success. Jimmy came to me with his forehand, Andre with his hand-eye coordination, Monica with her work ethic and Mary with her power, all of them instilled by their fathers. Mark came to me with a sturdy arsenal of strokes, built around an awesome serve and a thunderous forehand, thanks, once again, to his father. I agreed with Nick that the serve was incredible; he had more faith in the forehand than I did.

I first met Mark Philippoussis when he was thirteen years old, when he came to the academy from his home in Melbourne, Australia, on a two-week scholarship. I followed his progress as a junior—he rose to No. 3 junior in the world—only from afar and through a friend, Marty Mulligan, an Australian, once a finalist at Wimbledon, who worked for Fila in the United States.

When I went to the Australian Open for the first time in 1995, Mulligan arranged for the Philippoussis family to talk to me. I met Mr. Philippoussis, a former soccer goalie who owns a Greek restaurant in Melbourne, and my first reaction was, He's different. In some ways, he reminded me of me. The old me. He never stopped talking, never let anyone else get a word in. He was wired. He made the Energizer bunny look like a loafer. And he believed that his son was special.

I saw Mark and Nick again in March, in Indian Wells, California, a week after Mark played a tournament in Scottsdale, Arizona. He was a qualifier in Scottsdale, an eighteen-year-old playing in only his fifth professional event (two of them had been Australian Opens, in which he lost in the first round), and yet he defeated two of the world's top thirty players in the quarter- and semifinals, then pressed Jim Courier in the final before losing, 7–6, 6–4, a performance that put him on the cover of *Tennis Week*.

HELLO, MARK

Mark and Nick were heading next to Florida for the Lipton tournament. I told them they were welcome to spend the week before Lipton using all the facilities of the academy. I had Tommy Haas practice with Mark, and Tommy managed to win a set from him. "I didn't have my son come here to practice with juniors," Nick Philippoussis snapped. I sent Bobby Bank, one of my elite coaches, to work with the Philippoussises at the tournament. I couldn't work with Mark myself; I was committed to Mary and Boris.

Mark beat Paul Haarhuis of the Netherlands in the second round of the Lipton, then lost in the third to Wayne Ferreira of South Africa. Our paths didn't really cross again until I arrived at the U.S. Open a few days before the first match, ready to coach Mary Pierce but without a player in the men's championships. Mr. Philippoussis invited me to spend time with him and his son during the Open to observe his game and assess his progress, perhaps even offer some advice. It was sort of a trial, to see how they liked me, and how I liked them.

I was impressed. Mark won his first two matches without losing a set, then moved into Louis Armstrong Stadium to face Pete Sampras, a duel between two young men whose fathers were born in Greece. Mark won the first set in a tiebreaker. He was able to keep the second set even through ten games. He was able to keep the match even through ten games of the third set. Mark ended up losing the match, 6–7, 7–5, 7–5, 6–3, but he won Pete's respect and he won thousands of new fans. Including me. I agreed to join the Philippoussis team. To be *part* of the team. Not to direct the team.

MY ACES, MY FAULTS

The next month, I went to Tokyo to be with Mark and Nick during the Seiko Open. Mark was coming off a terrific performance in Kuala Lumpur, Malaysia. In his second-round match against Byron Black of Zimbabwe, he set an ATP tour record with forty-four aces in three sets. He then beat two of the world's top thirty players, Haarhuis and Patrick McEnroe, before losing in the final to a fellow teenager, nineteen-year-old Marcelo Rios, a cocky and flamboyant Chilean who reminded me of Agassi at the same age. Of course, Rios liked to polish his game at the academy. Mark was the runner-up in singles and the champion in doubles, teamed with Patrick McEnroe.

In Tokyo, Philippoussis won his first match easily, then had to face Stefan Edberg, seeded fifth, once the No. 1 player in the world. Mark, Nick, and I ate breakfast together and shared a cab to the arena in time to stretch, warm up, and then practice with Paul Kilderry, an Australian who had once attended the academy. Nick and I had Mark work on his lob; we told him that Stefan would be coming in. We had Paul stand inside the baseline and serve a great many heavy kicks, then come in after them. We told Mark to charge the ball and hit over it before it reached maximum height. We also had him run around the backhand and hit his huge forehand for winners. Finally, we had him work on his serve for ten minutes, following it to the net to work on his volley. Afterward, Mark stretched, showered, and, at noon, ate some simple pasta with tomato sauce.

We watched my young friend Marcelo Rios play and lose. Then Mark lay down for thirty minutes, got up, had coffee and a few cookies, and was ready for his late-afternoon match. Nick and I offered him a few final reminders: (1) Reach all the way up with that big frame and hit big serves; (2) go for big returns; (3) watch Edberg's kick serve, go forward, and bring it down.

Edberg won the toss, served, and charged. Mark hit a thunderous crosscourt forehand winner. Edberg served again and charged again, and this time Mark's backhand return dipped down so quickly Stefan's volley sailed out-of-bounds. Mark quickly broke serve and began pounding his own serves in at more than one hundred and twenty miles an hour. He also outvolleyed Edberg, who was one of the best volleyers in the history of the game. Mark won point after point. Edberg changed racquets several times, tested the strings, shook his head. Nothing helped. I overheard players and coaches in the stands saying, "This can't continue." But it did. In the first set, Edberg won only seven points, not a single game.

Edberg did win two games in the second set. Nothing more. I was afraid to move, superstitiously afraid to alter anything, to break the spell. I wanted to move—the hated air-conditioning was aimed right at me—but I couldn't, not even if I came down with pneumonia. "I told you he would be a champion someday," Nick Philippoussis said to me.

The final score was 6–0, 6–2. It was a dream match, as close to perfection as I had ever seen, and incredibly, it was over in forty-three minutes. I walked over to Edberg, a man I have always admired and respected, probably more than any other recent champion, and I said, "I'm sorry," and Stefan said, "Hey, the kid played as well as you can ever play."

As I walked away, I thought, *If Mark reaches the top someday, I hope he can be the kind of champion Stefan Edberg has always been.*

Philippoussis won the next day and moved into the quarterfinals against another of the top fifteen players in the world, Richard Krajicek, at six-feet-five inches, one of the few players taller than Mark. It was power tennis at its most powerful. There were only two baseline rallies in the whole match, and Mark won both of them. There was only one service break, and it, too, went to Mark. He won, 6–7, 7–6, 6–3.

Mark won his semifinal match against a twenty-year-old German, then challenged Michael Chang for the championship, which was worth $153,000. Chang not only hit Mark's first three serves back; he whipped them past Mark. But Philippoussis battled back from love-40 and won the game. "I pretty much got a wake-up call after Mark's first forehand," Michael said. "I knew if I didn't start moving my feet, it could be over quickly."

It was over fairly quickly. Chang won, 6–3, 6–4. As runner-up, Mark earned $83,000 and moved up to No. 32 in the world, which is precisely where he finished the year. At the start of 1995, he had been No. 307. He had climbed two hundred and seventy-five places in twelve months. Coincidentally, Mark was also ranked No. 32 in doubles. He was the ATP's rookie of the year, the first rookie to finish among the top fifty in both singles and doubles in six years. He was the youngest player in the top fifty, the only teenager. (Rios turned twenty just before the end of 1995.)

I was delighted with Mark's success, his dramatic improvement, and I was pleased with how smoothly he, his father, and I were working together. Marty Mulligan said I brought peace to the team.

Nick Philippoussis was at war with the Australian tennis authorities. He was furious when the year-end rankings came out. Even though Mark was the top Australian in the world rankings—at No. 32, he was two places in front of Todd Woodbridge—he was ranked No. 2, behind Woodbridge, in the Australian rankings.

Mr. Philippoussis was also unhappy with the Australian Davis Cup coaches, with Tony Roche and John Newcombe. He felt they did not think highly enough of Mark, and he feared they would try to alter his game.

"I know my son's game better than anybody," Nick told me, "and I don't want them to take it over. However, with you, I feel I can turn over my son and step back for the first time."

I was flattered; I was excited. So many people had warned me that Nick Philippoussis would never step back. But he did, briefly. He actually skipped a few practice sessions. He actually let me me offer advice to Mark without interrupting me.

Nick had hired a trainer to work with Mark, an Australian rules football player named Todd Viney, who turned out to be a terrific guy, capable of hitting with Mark, and even coaching him, as well as conditioning him. I thought it was very important that Mark, because he was still learning to live with his size, have a fulltime trainer.

I felt we had a good team taking shape. Over the holidays, I faxed off to Australia one of the letters I traditionally send to my most gifted players:

I. *Establish Goals for 1996*
   A. To be the best you can be, but at the same time realize and accept the fact that it takes both ups and downs to reach another level and then challenge for the next.
   B. Continue to develop your techniques and accept the fact that strength and flexibility are part of technique.
   C. Eat a well-balanced diet that includes supplements, especially during long periods of tournaments and hard practice.
   D. Know who will direct your physical fitness, flexibility, and stretching on the road.
II. *Utilization of Your Weapons*
   In life as well as sports, you must try to do what you do best as often as possible.

Power First Steps

Because of your giant weapons, you will receive all sorts of defensive returns. It is imperative that you not only reach the ball, but have excellent balance when you do in order to put the ball away.

Volley

Never wait for the volley. Always challenge it. Move forward no matter what. This means you must be low and able to adjust in any direction without losing a split second.

Mental Attitude

You are no longer Mark the Rookie. You now must perform all of the time. You must do everything on and off the court like a champion. The other players must feel that you know how good you are—and you're going to kick them right in the ass!

Serve

Each day, you must capitalize on your reach and be able to put that serve where you want it. In order to gain respect for your second service, you must go for it and serve a few double faults.

Final Comment

There is no doubt in my mind or in your dad's that you will be a champion.

As the top-ranked Australian in the world, Mark Philippoussis was the heir apparent to a magnificent tennis tradition, to Hoad and Rosewall and Laver and Newcombe. He was ranked ahead of the Woodys, Todd Woodbridge and Mark Woodforde, who were the best doubles team in the world, and ahead of Patrick Rafter, who had been the great young hope.

In 1994, at the age of twenty-one, Rafter had ascended to No. 20 in the world, No. 1 in Australia. But in 1995, he didn't win a singles title, didn't even get to a final, and slipped to No. 68 in the world. "The pressure got to me," Rafter admitted.

It was my job and Nick Philippoussis's to see to it that the pressure didn't get to Mark in 1996, that he continued to grow, that he lived up to his billing. It was my belief that, with rare exceptions, like a five-foot-nine Chang or a five-foot-eight Rios, the big man, the power player, would dominate tennis in the future, and it was my hope that the big man among the big men, as we moved toward the twenty-first century, would be Mark Philippoussis.

FOREHAND

Grip

Contrary to the big, big forehands of today, almost all of which utilize grips ranging from an extreme Eastern to a semi-Western, Mark uses a Continental grip. Which demonstrates there will always be exceptions to the rule, even at the highest levels. Coaches must accept this—unless there is a very clear indication a change must be made in order to reach a higher level.

Backswing

Not only does he have a Continental grip but his backswing is all wrong—theoretically. He brings his elbow back first, he closes the face of the racquet, and he straightens his entire arm out, locking the elbow. His backswing starts very low, then ends up high, the racquet above his shoulders. At times, this unorthodox style works extremely well. But I can't help feeling that his forehand would be more consistent if he used a more compact circular motion.

MY ACES, MY FAULTS

Forward Swing

He will hit from a completely open stance (he does have hip and shoulder rotation), a partly open stance, or a closed stance. But whatever his ready position may be, his racquet speed will be so great that even a speed gun cannot measure it.

Note: Sometimes his stance is just too wide open and he stands too straight up. Mark needs to not only get under the ball for spin, but also to make contact with the ball at a greater height in order to drive the flat ball.

Special note: You will just about always see Mark hitting the hell out of the ball, and right during contact, he will start the recovery to a position far over to the backhand side in order to hit more and more forehands.

BACKHAND (One-handed)

Grip

Semi-Western and at times close to a Western. He will change this grip to an Eastern backhand for the slice and the chip and charge, which he often does.

Backswing

He has been working on a very quick hip-and-shoulder rotation, and this enables him to hit huge backhands in all directions, which includes very sharp, low crosscourt angles plus unbelievable topspin lobs from both the backhand and the forehand.

Note: We have been working on an aggressive follow-through plus excessive wrist acceleration on contact.

VOLLEY

Mark is a very fine doubles player who loves to come up and volley. But in singles, when he has to cover the entire court, his efficiency at the net suffers. He has to work on his movement and balance, and he has to learn to put a little more underspin on his forehand volley. On the backhand volley, he leads so much with his elbow that his wrist sometimes collapses, causing a very loose volley. He does have exceptionally quick hands for reaction volleys. Because his serve is so big and his ground strokes are so powerful, and because he clearly enjoys coming to the net, it is essential that he put in a lot of work on the volley.

OVERHEAD

Forget it. He is like a seven-foot-five center.

SERVE

His grip is very close to a Continental. His ready position and total delivery is quite classical, but because of his reach plus racquet acceleration, he has the ability to just beat you up in so many ways with this lethal weapon. Because of his height, he can slice the ball to the outside or jam you with the serve. He is like Sampras and Becker: Do not look for a push second serve.

Note: He will serve and volley, forcing you to go for a big return or you have no chance.

Special Note: Because his father talks to him constantly about his serve, even coughing during a match to signal Mark to increase his racquet speed, Mark sometimes gets confused, and when he is nervous or starting to press, his serve can become erratic and vulnerable.

MOVEMENT AND BALANCE

Because of his size, Mark must follow a very strict physical fitness program, putting emphasis on movement and balance. Be careful: He loves to eat.

ATTITUDE

For such a young age, Mark is doing very well in this area. He is a very quiet boy with very high morals. He is now accepting the fact that he does have the guns to play with the very best and win. But he still needs to develop a degree of independence. He has to become the leader of a supportive team.

HOW TO BEAT HIM

You have to make him feel that if he can't get that big serve in, he can't win the match. Once he feels that pressure, he becomes vulnerable. The weakest part of his game is his return of service. If you serve well, you can take advantage of his youthful inconsistency.

AUSTRALIAN OPEN: THE SURPRISES

Every year since 1991, the Australian Open singles championships, men's and women's, have been won by a player who lived or trained for weeks, months, or years at the NBTA. Monica Seles, Steffi Graff, and Mary Pierce have divided the women's titles; Boris Becker, Jim Courier, Andre Agassi, and Pete Sampras the men's titles. Melbourne is sort of Bradenton West.

In 1996, Monica, Steffi, Boris, Jim, Andre, and Pete returned to Melbourne, to its blistering temperatures and its wonderfully warm crowds, and so did I for only my second Australian Open, coaching Mary Pierce and Mark Philippoussis. Both of my young students shocked me with their performances.

A few days before the competition began, Nick, Mark, and I sat down in the Regent Hotel and spent a couple of hours talking about the year ahead. I warned Mark that it would be an up-and-down year, that he would not be constantly improving, that there would be setbacks in practice and in matches. I told him that no matter what happened, he shouldn't panic. He should be positive, he should learn from losing. I stressed that he has to carry himself like a professional on and off the court, that every move he makes must be a signal that he knows what he can do, and he wants everyone else to know. "Just be the best you can be," I said. "That's all I ask. That's all your father asks."

Mark drew a qualifier named Kiefer in the first round, an Israeli named Ran in the second round, neither of them ranked among the top one hundred and fifty in the world, neither of them quite capable of threatening Mark. Then, in the third round, once again the two sons of Greek immigrants collided, Sampras and Philippoussis, both of them bearing considerable gifts. I watched the match, and frankly, I didn't believe what I was seeing. "Is this for real?" I asked Mr. Philippoussis.

To the amazement and the applause of thirteen thousand fans, most of them Australians, Mark won the first set, 6–4. He won the second set, 7–6. And he won the third set, 7–6. The match lasted only two hours and thirteen minutes. Mark served twenty-nine aces, clocked at speeds up to one hundred twenty-eight miles an hour. "I didn't have a sniff at getting a serve back," Sampras said.

"Tonight was like nothing I ever felt before," Mark told the media. "I just felt I couldn't do anything wrong on the serve."

No one had beaten Sampras in straight sets in a Grand Slam tournament in three years, not since Edberg crushed him in the semifinals in Australia. No teenager had upset the world's No. 1 player in a Grand Slam tournament in seven years, not since Chang beat Lendl in the finals of the French.

"The thing I learned tonight," Mark said, "was that I could beat anyone in the world."

"He has what it takes to be No. 1 in the next two or three years," Brad Gilbert said. I was stunned that Brad didn't say that if he were coaching Mark, he would be No. 1 within the next two or three months.

Mark's victory was the biggest for an Australian in nine years, since Pat Cash beat Ivan Lendl in straight sets and won the 1987 Wimbledon championship. Cash was twenty-two then; he had reached the semifinals of both Wimbledon and the U.S. Open when he was only a teenager; he rose to No. 4 in the world before his twenty-third birthday. He was Australia's hero, but success in sports is frighteningly precarious. A series of injuries and illnesses shattered Cash's career; his ranking plummeted, and he was off the tour before he reached thirty.

It wasn't easy, but I tried to low-key the victory over Pete. The Australian newspapers, of course, burst into banner headlines, waving both the flag and Mark's nickname, Scud, a tribute to his missilelike serve. *He's still a boy*, I thought. *We have to slow the ship down.*

His next match was against a fellow Australian, the doubles specialist, Mark Woodforde, and the trouble was that his countrymen now expected Philippoussis to win certainly this match and conceivably the whole tournament. *He conquered The Man; he can conquer the world.*

I warned Mark that Woodforde would not be easy, that, at thirty, he was as crafty as any player in the world. He wouldn't overpower you, but he would chip a little, sneak in a little, frustrate you with junk, like a knuckleball pitcher. Woodforde played a lot like Brad Gilbert, which made it doubly frustrating to me when he whipped Philippoussis, 6–2, 6–2, 6–2. "I wasn't pumped up enough," Mark said. "I don't know why."

How did Nick Philippoussis react to the defeat? Remarkably well. He rushed up to Mark and gave him a big hug and a kiss and said, "Son, were proud of you."

I was proud of both Mark and Nick. I admit that I hadn't really expected Mark to beat Sampras. I was startled but not nearly so startled as I was by Mary Pierce's performance in the tournament she had won so convincingly the year before.

10

GOOD-BYE, MARY

GOOD-BYE, MARY

Mary Pierce rose to No. 3 in the world after winning the 1995 Australian Open, and I was confident we were on our way, heading toward the top. I had no inkling that the year was going to turn into a disaster.

In February, two weeks after Melbourne, Mary reached the finals of an indoor tournament in Paris, then lost to Steffi Graf but remained a solid No. 3, behind only Graf and Arantxa Sanchez Vicario, her elders by a few years. Mary was still only twenty years old.

In March, she returned to the academy to train, to prepare herself for the spring season, for the clay-court tournaments leading up to the French Open. Boris Becker had elected to skip the Lipton, so, for a few weeks, I could concentrate my thoughts and energy on Mary.

I was pleased with her progress, both mental and physical, until one day, without any notice, she sat down on the grass, turned to me and Sven Groeneveld and José Rincon, her team, and told us that she had suffered an injury, would be out of action for a while, and would need some kind of surgery.

She said nothing more. What was the injury? To this day, I don't know. I heard reports that Mary had pulled a groin muscle, but she never told me that herself.

Mary missed ten days of practice. Presumably, she underwent surgery. When she returned to the courts, she had a new racquet and a handsome new home. She had switched to Yonex, but she said she planned to take her old Wilson with her on tour. I said, "No, you won't." Mary said, "Why not?" and I told her, "Mary, if you miss more than two balls with your new racquet, you will run to the racquet bag to get your old one. I insist that you stick to the new one— without the option to switch." I didn't want Mary to have any doubts in her mind about her new weapon.

Her new home was not far from the academy, and I sent her a large-screen television set as a present, and then, reluctantly, Leah and I attended the housewarming party. I went only because Mary wanted me there so badly. There were at least a hundred guests, and I don't like being with large groups of people, particularly if I don't know most of them and especially if many of them are drinking. Strangers always seem to approach me and try to impress me with their knowledge of tennis and ask me questions like When will Seles return? or Don't you wish you were back with Agassi now that he's No. 1? Leah and I congratulated Mary on her lovely new home and stayed at the party for no more than ten minutes.

Mary was never the same on or off the court after her mysterious "injury." She had moments, she even won a tournament, but her attitude, her commitment, was radically different. She did, however, recover from her surgery in time to play the French Open for the sixth time and Wimbledon for the first. In Paris, she swept her first three matches in straight sets, then ran into my former student, Iva Majoli, and lost to the seventeen-year-old Croatian, 6–2, 6–3. A few weeks later, in her debut on the grass of Wimbledon, she won her first-round match, beating Sandra Dopfer on court 14, the two hundredth match Mary had won in her brief career. But in the second round, she was eliminated by Nathalie Tauziat, 6–4, 3–6, 6–1.

I was preoccupied, of course, with Boris's march toward Andre and the semifinals, but when I thought of Mary, I had a sick feeling that this engine could put out a lot more steam but was just refusing to do it. I couldn't figure out why. "Nick knows how to push the right buttons in anybody," Mary once said. "He knows how to get you going." She was wrong this time.

In July, Mary was again sidelined by what she said was a kidney infection. Her health and her tennis were suffering, but her social life seemed to be thriving. She was dating a French rugby player and was good friends with Seal, a British pop singer.

At the U.S. Open, she lost both her third-round match and her traveling coach. She lost the match to Amy Frazier and the coach to frustration. Sven Groeneveld resigned, partly because he felt Yannick Pierce, Mary's mother, was interfering with his role and partly because he sensed a lack of dedication on Mary's part. "I felt that my principles were in jeopardy," Sven said. His decision was a major setback to Mary; Sven had played a large role in her success.

Yet soon after the U.S. Open, after a week in Bradenton,

hitting with one of my elite pros, Craig Wildey, Mary went to Tokyo and won the tournament there, whipping Arantxa in the finals, 6–3, 6–3. We thought we were back on track, but it was a false and fleeting impression, nothing more than a last hurrah. The rest of the year was a complete zero.

In October 1995, in Filderstadt, Germany, Mary lost once more to Iva Majoli, who went on to win the tournament and move into the top ten for the first time in her career. The previous year, when I elected to spend my time with Mary, I could have chosen to coach Iva instead. I weighed the possibilities and decided that Mary had the greater potential. I was beginning to suspect that I was wrong.

Craig Wildey and I spent the next two weeks working with Mary in Bradenton, trying to get her ready for the big November tournaments in Philadelphia and New York. Craig was interested in becoming Mary's traveling coach, and I thought he would be a good choice even though Mary's mother took an immediate dislike to him. Mrs. Pierce was not lifting the spirit of the team. Mary wasn't helping too much either. She stole time from training for quick trips to Fort Lauderdale, New York, and even Paris.

The two weeks in the Northeast were horrendous. Mary lost her first match in each tournament and looked terrible in defeat. Zina Garrison Jackson beat her in straight sets in Philadelphia, and Mary spent much of the match staring into space.

Then we went to New York, and in the first round of the WTA Championships, Mary drew her old nemesis, the young German she had finally beaten in Australia, Anke Huber, who was barely a month older than Mary. Mary showed up for the match only physically. She hit her first serve, and Huber put it away. Huber won the first seven points of the match. It was as if she were playing against a ghost. Mary looked lost, like she had a piano on her back, which, in a sense, she did. She was supporting her mother and her brother, playing for everybody but herself. Huber won, 6–2, 6–3, and went on to reach the finals and put up a stirring five-set fight before losing to her countrywoman, Steffi Graf.

It was somehow appropriate that a year that began so gloriously for Pierce with a victory over Huber in Australia should end so miserably with a defeat by Huber in New York.

Mary spent the early part of December playing exhibitions in Europe. José Rincon was traveling with her, and his letters were ominous:

> Mary played one good set in [five matches], but all others she really didn't try after she lost the first set.... When we first arrived in Paris, her boyfriend, or ex-, was there. They had lots of problems.... Yannick is putting a lot of stress on her daughter.... I've had to deviate from the strength and conditioning program due to Mary's health.... I get eighty percent out of her on the miniworkouts we do. She's strong, and her aerobic capacity is decent. Unfortunately, she's carrying about eight pounds extra. I'm afraid that Mary has the tendency to overeat when she's stressed out.... I had one small "confrontation" with Mary. She has the horrible mania of showing her opponent and every single one of

the spectators whatever minor ache, pain, or injury she may have as she plays. This happens especially when you are not around. One day I couldn't take it anymore and I told her to stop.... I am sure you have noticed that Mary has some sort of sleeping disorder. Late at night she "bounces off the walls," and she could easily sleep until early afternoon every single day. Mary's "biological clock" is messed up.... I am afraid she thinks the Australian Open starts on January 15, without realizing that it started several weeks ago. We are running late. We have to catch up fast!!!!

When Mary came home, I could see José's fears were well founded. For the first time in our relationship, I dreaded going on the court with Mary. I dreaded her sulking, her mood shifts. Her mother and I were avoiding each other, barely talking. I forced myself to make the same effort we had made the previous December, when Sven, José, and I had driven Mary to be ready for the Australian Open, but it wasn't easy, it wasn't fun. I missed Sven. Mary griped. She went through the motions. She was at least ten pounds heavier than she'd been the previous year. I stopped one workout and gathered the team at the net and said, "You, young lady, have been on sabbatical for the past nine months, and now you're in pain because José is trying in vain to make up for your leave of absence."

We went back to practice, and after two and a half minutes, I said, "That's it. I'll see you at 3 this afternoon."

Mary didn't show up. The team waited till 5:30. Craig Wildey couldn't take anymore. "I thought I could be a good,

GOOD-BYE, MARY

steadying, calming influence on her," he said, "but I failed. I tried to get to know her, and I failed. She's a sweet girl, but she's got a lot of things on her mind, and not all of them are tennis." He decided he couldn't go to Australia; he couldn't be a member of Mary's team. There were moments when I kind of wished her father were back, when I thought what she needed most was the type of discipline he had demanded.

"Mary," I said, "tell me what you want to do, and I'll tell you whether I want to be part of it."

I certainly wasn't coaching Mary for the money. In 1995, for the full year, for being with her at all the Grand Slams and several other tournaments, for spending six weeks or more focusing on her in Bradenton, for taking time away from Boris and time away from the academy, for counseling her by phone and by mail, I had been paid about $50,000. For the year, Mary had earned $700,000 in prize money alone; her total income certainly exceeded $1 million. She was already suggesting that she couldn't afford my coaching in 1996. I told her fine, just pay me $50,000 for the year and I'll be an advisor, a consultant. But for that price, I won't be a coach, a friend, a second father, and a baby-sitter.

Still, I wasn't quite ready to give up on Mary. I cut short my annual skiing vacation, changed my flights, went to Australia six days earlier than I had planned to work with Mary and Mark. This time I wrote a note to myself, telling me what Mary had to do if she was going to challenge the top players:

1. A total commitment from Mary Pierce that not only does she accept the ability she has, but will do anything to put it to use.

MY ACES, MY FAULTS

2. A total physical and nutritional program on a year-round basis.
3. She must endure pain, she must adjust to the unknown, she must turn her head away from everything when she enters the Battle Zone.
4. She must tell everyone around her what her goal is, and they must accept this and go on their way.
5. She must understand that she is twenty years old, and because she must put all her energy, mind, body, and faith into her goals, her family members cannot all lean on her.
6. She must change her social life, which is off the wall.

The defending champion was wiped out in the second round of the 1996 Australian Open. Mary lost, 6–4, 6–4, to a young woman named Yelena Likhovtseva from Kazakhstan. I had never heard of her. I certainly didn't know how to spell her name or how to pronounce it. I was disgusted with the way Mary played. I was embarrassed. She put more effort into throwing her racquet than she did into her forehand. I was ashamed. One Australian newspaper said she put on "a flat, listless performance," and that was kind.

"I never felt comfortable on the court," Mary said. "I felt like I was moving very, very slowly." Of course she was moving slowly with all the weight she was carrying. She had been No. 4 in the world going into the Australian Open. Now she would drop out of the top ten, all the way down to No. 13. Iva Majoli, who reached the quarterfinals, and Anke Huber, who got to the finals, both rose past Mary. I wasn't confident that she'd ever get back up again. "I'm not going to yell at Mary anymore," I told reporters. "I'm not going to be her baby-sitter."

I don't know whether I was more frustrated or furious. Her lackluster performance contradicted everything I stood for, everything the academy stood for. *The ship is sinking. I'm not going down with the sinking ship. She has to bring the ship up. She has to be the leader of her team. I'll always be her friend, but I won't be a part of her team.*

I called Mary before I left Australia and told her I would no longer be coaching her. "Mary, I'm sure you read the papers," I said, "and I hit you hard, Mary, I hit you hard. You've got to make a commitment to yourself. The academy's your home. You're always welcome there. You bring your coach there. You practice there. I made the same offer to Andre, you know, and he gave me the finger, he said, 'Screw you, Nick, I'll show you how good I am!' He became No. 1. I hope you'll do the same. If you can reach the top, Mary, I'll be the happiest guy in the world, because I'll know I contributed to it."

"Thank you, Nick," Mary said. "Thank you so much. I feel much better knowing I'll be welcome at the academy. Nick, I love you."

Mary's comments to the media in Australia were not quite so affectionate. "I totally disagree with Nick," she said. "I'm playing tennis because I love it, and if I didn't, there's no reason I'd be here today. I had enough pressure and stress and hard times with my dad. I don't have to play. I'm playing because I want to, and my dream is to one day be No. 1.

"Maybe Nick's version of commitment is waking up at 5, running ten miles every day, staying on the court ten hours, eating celery sticks all day, and going to bed at 8. But that's not a life for anybody.

"The last time I went out dancing and stayed out past midnight and had a drink was when I won this tournament last year.

"My dad was very outspoken. Like Nick is. My dad would talk to anyone about anything. Kind of like Nick. And my dad would talk about everything openly and sometimes exaggerate it or blow it up. Kind of like Nick."

I know her dad had his faults. But he wasn't all bad.

A few weeks later, Mary chose her new coach. I was pleased she chose someone who had studied at the academy. I probably would have been even more pleased if it had been someone other than Brad Gilbert. I was beginning to get the feeling that Brad was following me.

I'm certain that Brad will share some great moments with Mary, just as he has with Andre. I'm certain that he'll try his best to turn her around, to get her headed toward the top again. And I'm certain that if he succeeds—and I hope he does, I truly hope Mary becomes No. 1—he will not be bashful about claiming the credit or about discounting the contributions I made to the development of Mary's game.

I am certain of one more thing: that sooner or later, for good reason or bad, Mary will leave Brad, and so will Andre. Or Brad will leave them. Stuff happens. Look at Goran Ivanisevic and Bob Brett. Bob, who had once been Boris's coach, began coaching Goran in 1991, when Goran was nineteen years old, and by the time he was twenty-two had helped him become No. 2 in the world. They stayed together for four and a half years, then separated late in 1995. Goran replaced Brett with a man named Vedran Martic, a Croatian whom Goran had known since childhood. In the first two months of 1996, Goran played the best tennis of his life, reached five finals in six tournaments, and won three of them. "I am happy to play tennis again," Goran said. I would guess that Brett's teachings had something to do with Goran's success in 1996.

I hope Brad enjoys his time with Andre and Mary, and I hope he isn't too disappointed when it ends.

AUSTRALIAN OPEN: THE CHAMPIONS

After Mary Pierce and Mark Philippoussis were eliminated in the 1996 Australian Open, I flew back to the States. I didn't see the semifinals and the finals. I didn't see two of my former pupils win the men's and women's championships.

Monica Seles won the women's title, her ninth Grand Slam championship, her first in three years, since the 1993 Australian Open.

Boris Becker won the men's title, his sixth Grand Slam championship, his first in five years, since the 1991 Australian Open.

Boris had never before won a Grand Slam championship in front of his wife, whom he met in 1993. "She always said, 'Please do it one more time for me,'" Boris said after his victory, "and I told her, 'I'm trying my heart out. It's not that easy.' Now, finally, I have won one for Barbara."

Monica had only one difficult match in her march back to the top of women's tennis. In the semifinals, she lost the first set in a tiebreaker to Chanda Rubin, a nineteen-year-old American, then won the second set convincingly. In the third and decisive set, Rubin went up, 5–2, one game from an incredible upset, but Monica, who never quits, fought back and won the next five games and, eventually, the championship.

At the age of twenty-eight, Boris was the oldest player to win a Grand Slam tournament since Andres Gomez, at thirty, took the French Open in 1990. Boris had to struggle in Melbourne. He trailed by at least a set in three of his first four matches; in the second round, he had to rally from two sets down to defeat a twenty-year-old Swede named Thomas

AUSTRALIAN OPEN: THE CHAMPIONS

Johansson. But Boris got stronger as the tournament went on. He won twelve of his last thirteen sets, and in the final, he had little trouble with Michael Chang, who had, until then, won eighteen sets in a row.

To my astonishment, after he beat Chang and hoisted the championship trophy over his head, Boris Becker said, "Nick gets all the credit."

In the previous seven months, Boris had reached the finals at Wimbledon and the semifinals at the U.S. Open and had won the Australian Open. No one else—not Sampras, not Agassi, not Muster, not Seles, not Graf—had gotten to the semis or further in all three Grand Slam events. Boris told *Sports Illustrated* that I was responsible for helping him find his game ("Everything went better each year ...") and his new coach ("... and at the academy, I found Mike DePalmer").

Boris Becker and I *almost* talked a couple of times before he won the Australian Open, but we never quite did. We saw each other at the Compaq Cup in Munich and again in Melbourne, and we asked about each other's golf game and we said we'd get together, but we didn't. I wanted Boris to tell me exactly what went wrong with our relationship. Had I insulted him? Had I slighted him? Had I misled him?

Instead, in the fall of 1995, we communicated through our representatives, Frank Falkenburg, my personal manager, and James Murphy, the controller of the NBTA, corresponding with Dr. Peter Duvinge, an attorney in the office of Dr. Meyer-Woldan. They were arguing over money, over expenses and bonuses and fees, over invoices that Boris had paid without question in the comeback year of 1994 but now were matters of contention.

In November, Boris played once again in the ATP Tour World Championship in Frankfurt, and this time, with a gutsy straight-set victory over Michael Chang in the final, 7–6, 6–0, 7–6, he thrilled his fans and earned first prize of $1,225,000. In December, Boris reached the semifinals of the Compaq Cup and earned another $431,000. He had won $1,656,000 in two tournaments, and clearly my efforts in the previous two years had helped prepare him for those tournaments, and yet his attorney insisted that I had no claim to any share of Boris's earnings after we "agreed" to split up in August. I felt cheated. Barbara Becker understood. When I saw her at the Compaq Cup, Barbara said, "I hope that Boris never does to me what he did to you. We love him, and you helped him be what he is today. That was wrong, what he did to you, and I hope it doesn't happen to me."

Two weeks after the 1996 Australian Open, I sat down and wrote to Boris, reviewing our whole relationship, explaining my feelings. It was a very long letter, even by my wordy standards.

Dear Boris:

It's February 13, about 4:30 in the morning, and I've been thinking about writing this letter for a long time. I had hoped that I'd have a chance to talk to you at the open or in Munich or Australia, but the opportunity never came. A lot has gone through my mind since then and I just feel that I want to write you and Barbara about everything we have been through together. Boris, you know I can't wage a vendetta against people. I never have and I pray to God that I never will. My purpose here is to relate my thoughts on our relationship and let you know that I have many fond memories of that time and will always accept it as a very special time in my career and my life.

... It all began during ... the French Open of 1993. The question was, What do you see for Boris Becker's future? The general response was that you were too fat, too wealthy, lazy, that your private life was totally screwed up, and that you just did not have the desire to win anymore.

I faxed Mary Carillo and told her ... Why didn't they just ask Boris what he wanted to do with his tennis career. Approximately five months later, I got the opportunity to find out the answer for myself when you and Carlo visited the academy ...

When I went to the Compaq Cup in 1993, I did not know that Axel planned on us being a team. Axel arranged for a meeting at your temporary apartment, and I ... finally got to ask the question I had wanted to ask so many months earlier. "Boris, what do you want to do with your career?" Without hesitation, you blurted out that you loved the game and wanted to win again, that you did not care about all the other things but just wanted to win! With that, I stuck out my hand and said, "You have a coach."

Axel said he would work out the terms of the contract ... and when I went back to the hotel, I was fly-

MY ACES, MY FAULTS

ing to think that I had been selected to be the man to bring you back. We made the selection of the traveling coach, Red Ayme, and we sure knew he was a character, but there was no one better fitted to do all of the daily chores than Red. We decided to begin at the end of December, and you wanted Red and a hitting partner to spend about ten days with you, because you were sort of out of shape. In fact, you were looking like a very healthy Santa Claus.

Each day Red would call me and give me all the details. He reported that you were working very hard, training twice a day, plus another two hours of doing your physical fitness and playing basketball with the guys and your trainer.

I arrived on January 10. We decided that because of the direction that we needed to take to get you to the next step and Barbara having the baby in a couple of weeks you would miss the Australian Open.

You were really something to watch the first week and I really did nothing because, to tell you the truth, I was sort of scared to even open my mouth.

This is what I saw:

1. You took a position about five to seven feet behind the baseline, then hit with all sorts of body motions.
2. Then you came up to the service line and did your famous volley routine: stand on the service line, volley with one step forward and then come back to the same position.

3. Finally your service practice, which starts out with you shaking and moving your entire body, including your rather big fanny, as you were carrying fifteen to twenty pounds of excess baggage.

Slowly but surely, I'd put a word in here and a word in there. I remember that I began by telling you that you were rolling your shoulder and your swings were so big. Then we talked some about your serve return on the deuce with you practicing that inside-out backhand, and then the easy balls would come and you would still hit your inside-out backhand. I was wondering why you didn't run around and hit a big forehand. Then from the other side you would always chip it on the second serve and let the guy off the hook, and I was saying to myself, "My gosh, he's got a great underspin backhand, but he's got to start hitting over the ball so he can have a combination of both." In that fashion, I began to slowly win your confidence and take a more active role in continuing to develop your game. Carlo's work with you and going to the gym began to yield results as well....

Slowly but surely, the timing began to come back. My comments were very few. My mind was anticipating our next moves.

The day then came when Noah became part of your and Barbara's life and our team. You were really smitten that afternoon when we sat at the bar and you said to me, "I hope I don't have to have a kid to get a half-day off all the time with you, Nick." We chuckled and then you asked Red and me if I would stay one more day because you didn't perform too well that day and, what the hell, you had just had baby Noah.

I began to know you a little more as a person, and ... then slowly but surely you and Barbara began to talk to me, and ... we went back to some of the other students that I had, and you already knew a little bit of what happened with the Seleses and the Agassis. *Both you and Barbara assured me that this would never happen again because our relationship was developing into something very special!!*

I went home at the end of January, and then I (with Red) started the tournament circuit in Marseilles and Milan, and ... you began to get back into that winning mood ... everything was moving along beautifully ... the weight began coming off you, you began getting in shape, you had little Noah and your beautiful wife to go home to every night, and everything began to fall in place.

In 1994, there were some good signs, Boris. You would win some, you would lose some, but the signs were there. I do remember very distinctly the embarrassment and the pressure of the first few matches with Andre Agassi, especially the first one at Lipton. I'll always remember that, and I'll always remember the look in your eyes when we left Lipton that time and I know damn well you said right there, "Andre, the time will come when I will beat you."

As the year progressed, you began to know me as a person. All through this period ... there was so much question and doubt in the German press and the Ger-

AUSTRALIAN OPEN: THE CHAMPIONS

man people. Even some of the players and coaches had said, "How in the hell is this going to work, Nick Bollettieri and Boris Becker together?" As time went on, Red did such a great job with you, Boris, I don't know how many people could have gone through that early part of the first year, but Red did it because he loved you and he was the type of guy you needed. . . . He was there, he would get the courts, he would take care of everything. Then we needed a replacement, and ... Mike Jr. was available, and you seemed to like him, he was quiet and laid back, and everything fell into place. . . .

In my mind, things began to go off at the Australian Open of 1995. You had to talk me into going there, but it didn't require too much talking. . . .

But then, when you lost in that first round, that's when I should have been with you and Barbara, to show you that you were my priority, that I had a commitment to you. Instead, I stayed on with Mary Pierce, and she won the Australian Open, and then as the year began to develop, Mary did quite well, and you floundered the first part of the year. You floundered at the French Open. I should have been with you. Now I realize that that's the time you needed me. When you lost, you were ashamed and you were hurt and angry. With your strength of character, you told me, "Stay on with Mary Pierce, give her what she needs, bring her back," but I should have gone with you. I was beginning to tell you things that you should be doing, but I wasn't there to follow those things up.

MY ACES, MY FAULTS

As the year went on, we seemed to turn things around quite a bit, and I wanted to be there at Wimbledon with you ... because it was so important to you. At Wimbledon, I dedicated every ounce of my strength, my faith, and the knowledge that I had gained over my thirty-eight years in tennis.... Please note that I did not go out to play golf. Mike asked me to come play, but I said no. Although I played a couple of times with you, I was on a mission. You told me that Wimbledon was the D-Day tournament for you, that nothing meant more to you.

I went to the courts and I looked at the people you were going to play. I remember the night before the semifinals at the tennis courts where you said to me, "What about tomorrow?" I told you a few things, but I said, "Boris, I want to work on this tonight, I must work on this thing." I went home and got up early in the morning, 5 A.M., and I wrote down all those things. The match with Andre Agassi was one that in my heart and my soul, I never wanted anyone to beat somebody as badly as I wanted you to beat up on Andre Agassi. In the locker room afterward, I said something to you that I think you took out of context. I said, "Boris, I never, never in all my life thought that you could play that way. You played far beyond what I thought." Boris, believe me, that was an expression that meant that you played a fantastic match. It was the most sincere, honest thing I could say to you.

I wasn't with you all those earlier years; I just saw

you on TV. I never saw anyone come back like you did, down 4–1 in the second and turn that around, and that was my way of saying, "Boris, you are far better than I even anticipated you could be."

Then I remember getting in the car and going up the hill and you telling me, "Nick, I told you the big f——ing match would come someday, I told you. This was the f——ing match I told you would come, and we won it." And you put your hand on my leg, and you thanked me for the strategy and the support, and I was the happiest person in the whole world. Then, the next day, with Pete Sampras, Boris, there was no doubt in my mind that you could beat Pete Sampras. But I also knew and felt the exhaustion, the strain, the mental energy that went into the Agassi match.... You said, "Nick, my legs just couldn't go anymore."

Later, you told me, "Nick, I'll pick you up in a few minutes. I want you to go with me somewhere." When you picked me up ... we went down to where Ulli and Val were staying, and you said to me, "Nick, come on inside," and there were maybe two or three dozen reporters, and I had no idea what was going to happen, and you sat me in the middle and you said, "This man is responsible, he gave me the will again, he gave me the motivation, he gave me his eyes. All of these things helped me, and I owe all this to this man."

That was a proud day for me, a proud few minutes when I received that acknowledgment from Boris Becker. As we went home, you told me about the dinner we were going to have that night ... [and] I told you about Michael Stich's phone call. "Boris," I said, "Stich wanted to know if he could come down to the academy to train, and I was stunned, I didn't know what to say to him and I told him I would get back to him." Immediately, you said, "Nick, that's a compliment to you. Go ahead and do it." I said, "Boris, I can't do that, you're my man, and I'm coaching you. I can't give anything to anyone else. I'm helping Mary because she is not one of your competitors."

That night I brought it up to you and Barbara and said that I could never do that, and Barbara just went out of control. I remember her saying, "How could that blankety blank call? Doesn't he know that you're with us, and he's our enemy?" And, Boris, I didn't know what to say, but there was no thought of me ever doing that. After dinner, before I was to go home and you to Munich, you said, "Tell me what we're going to do this summer; write me one of those famous letters of yours." I had Red hand-carry the letter to you because I didn't want you to feel neglected. In the letter, I spoke of

A. How well you served the big points.
B. Monte Carlo, and I said that even though you double-faulted on your first clay-court championship point and the title went out the window when you served one hundred nineteen miles an hour to Muster, you went out like a champion.
C. I told you that that's why I believed you won those titles, that's why you beat Agassi that day:

AUSTRALIAN OPEN: THE CHAMPIONS

You took some chances. I said, "Boris, don't be afraid; keep doing that."

D. I said, "Run around and hit those big forehands."

E. I asked you to take a look at your old serve. You were a step farther inside the service line to hit that first volley, you've got to work on that.

F. I suggested that you work on your lob from your backhand side.

G. I encouraged you to sneak in more. You've got to keep attacking, but you've got to run around from the deuce side and hit those big, big returns.

H. Hit deep crosscourt backhand slices and practice hitting down the line slices short.

... I should have come and spent time with you, Boris. That's my fault, and I apologize for that. You needed me then....

At the end of New Haven, that was the first time that I saw you give a match away. You did none of the things that I told you about in the letter, nothing. In the locker room, you said, "You're telling me things, but you're not around to help me." No, Boris, I'd been telling you those things all along and you were beginning to get them. Where I went wrong was not being there to help you implement them.

Other problem areas surfaced when I got into it with some of the members of your team, the team that depends on you, their life depends on you.... They have nowhere else to go. Boris, you're it, you're their meal ticket, you're their man. Of course they've been dedicated. Why shouldn't they be? They owe you every-thing. And here I come, an outsider.

... Perhaps I was the only one in the whole group that didn't need you as a means of leading a good life. I'm not a millionaire; I don't have millions at all, but I do have me....

Now we come to Axel Meyer-Wolden being caught in a very difficult situation.... "Boris doesn't want you to come to Flushing Meadows." He tried to make it soft.... That was degrading to me, an insult.... Then the statement we issued. Boris, I agreed to that state-ment even though it wasn't absolutely true.... I swal-lowed my tongue because I did not want to take away from your tournament. I could not do that to you....

Michael Stich did come to the academy.... The doors are always open to anybody. But I never pitted Michael Stich against you, Boris, never.... I've never tried to hurt people deliberately, I never can and I never will....

At Flushing Meadows, you passed me by.... I was hoping that I could at least get to chat with you and wish you luck, but it never came about.... Boris, now I want to tell you something. This is going to come out in my book, but I want to write to you and tell you, Boris, that I rooted against you at Flush-ing Meadows.... I wanted you to lose when you played Andre Agassi.... I rooted against you because I now knew how Andre felt when he saw me with you. I rooted against you. Please forgive me for that. I can't control my emotions, and I can't lie to you about this, but try to understand that I believed in you.

Boris, you were very generous with me. You were the only one who was generous with me. You told me all sorts of things: that I would be with you until the end, that I would never have to worry again, and that you felt that I deserved something for all the years that I had put into tennis. I said, "Boris, you don't have to do that. You've been paying me and giving me bonuses." You said, "No, Nick, I'm going to make sure that you're my last coach and you will be taken care of."

Boris, I believed all those things. I believed them heart and soul, and I wanted it to happen that way. You must understand that Barbara is a great lady, and to be with you, Boris, is not easy, man. You lose and you come home and you sit in the garden and you don't talk to anybody, and, Boris, Barbara loves you, man, this is the person you're going to be with for the rest of your life. Barbara and Noah, your son, you can never ... put them in a position that they wonder, *What about me? Is Boris going to say good-bye to me?*

... You know, Axel told Frank [Falkenburg] and me, "Boris is going to pay you right through December 31, and then we can work out a consultantship," and I said, "No, Axel, when it comes to the end of the year, there shouldn't be a consultantship, I won't be doing anything for Boris then. But I feel ... I should be paid

through the end of December." But then we got into ne-
gotiating, which hurt me beyond words. Why did I
have to negotiate? In our twenty-one months, I gave
you everything I could. . . . I didn't care what the academy's needs were; you came first. . . . There's never been a
student that took more out of me mentally than you
did. I had to figure out how to help you, how to react
to you, how to coach you, and all the time I told Mike
DePalmer every single thing to watch for. . . .

. . . the Australian Open. I want to tell you that my
respect for you came back. I said, "Jesus, here's a guy
who was down and out. Tennis needs this man; he's
great for the game. People should watch how he works
the game, how he works the court, how he works the
linesmen, how he works the opponents, how he works
the umpire—this man is a genius. . . ." And I want you
to know that I did want you to win the Australian
Open. I want you to know that . . . I told Mike a long
time ago that you could, and probably would, be No. 1
again. I'm happy for you, I'm happy for Barbara, I'm
happy for little Noah. For Ulli and Val, I couldn't give
a shit less. . . .

My Leah is hurt, Boris. She's hurt inside. She's a
great human being. She didn't know what happened.
She cried. She said, "I can't believe this, Nick." I
used to tell her about the wonderful talks you and I
and Barbara had, and to this day, Leah doesn't understand what happened. But that's life, Boris. I'm proud
of you. I hope you do make No. 1, and in my heart I

certainly hope that you will have some fond memories of the times you spent with me. . . .

Boris, continue on, my boy. I'll be seeing you on
the circuit. I thank you for the comments you made [in
Australia]. They were kind and generous words. . . . I
hope that you don't have anger or disrespect for me. I
felt that I did get sort of shortchanged. . . . I didn't
make you a champion, [but] I helped you become what
you should have become, and I don't think very many
people would have been able to do that.

In closing, Boris, I want to offer a piece of unselfish
advice. Take care of Barbara and Noah. Others will
surely come and go, but Barbara and Noah will be
there for you long after things have become quiet.

Nick

11

NO END IN SIGHT

NO END IN SIGHT

I know I am the best tennis coach in the world. I have no doubts about that. Other people do have doubts. But not as many as I once did.

They used to say that I never taught anyone to play, that I didn't really know the game, that I coached only players who came to me with great ability and good instincts.

There's some truth to those charges. When I first started coaching, I faked it. I pretended to know more than I did. I bullshitted my way through. But I looked and I listened, and slowly but surely, I learned.

Jimmy Arias, Aaron Krickstein, Andre Agassi, Jim Courier, Boris Becker, Mark Philippoussis, Kathleen Horvath, Carling Bassett, Monica Seles, Mary Pierce—all achieved remarkable success as professionals while I was coaching them. Of course each of them came to me with considerable talent, some with more than others.

But hundreds of tennis players with great natural ability never made it on the professional tour, never became champions, never even made a living. Maybe they didn't have someone who pushed them, who cheered for them, who believed in them, who broke his ass to bring out their ability. That's what I did. That's all I did. That's my talent. I help young men and women live up to their ability.

How much longer can I do it? How many more weeks can I spend on the road? How much more pounding can I take? I look at Don Shula, at all he accomplished with the Miami Dolphins, and at the end, they were all over him, the media and the fans. What have you done for me lately? That's all they wanted to know. I look at the president, and every freaking day, he gets pounded. The most powerful man in the world, probably, and he gets criticized every day. How does he maintain focus? How does he keep his energy, his enthusiasm?

I've often said I've never worked a day in my life because I always loved what I was doing. But early in 1996, with Mary Pierce, with Mark Philippoussis, I was working. I had to push myself some days. I had to force myself to be excited sometimes. I still love my golf, my skiing, and my workouts, but I don't know if I love tennis like I used to. As a matter of fact, I know I don't.

Has it all been worth it? I used to say—*insist*—that I had no regrets. I never looked back. I never questioned my impulses or my actions. But now I wonder. Why was I always racing so far in front of the speed limit? Did I mess up the lives of my five wives? Did I hurt my five children? Why didn't I spend more time with them? They're the ones who love me. They're the ones who need me. Why haven't I helped Jimmy open the gallery he's dreamed about? Why couldn't I make Danielle and Angel feel more secure? How can I protect Nicole and Alex from all the dangers children face these days?

And Leah. I don't ever want to lose Leah. She is the ultimate lady. She loves life and she loves people and she loves me. I want to be able to provide for her, for us. I don't have expensive tastes. I've gotten the Mercedes and the Corvettes out of my system. I'm happy with dinner at the Bollettieri Sports Grille, with a turkeyburger and an iced tea and maybe a beer once in a while. I can play golf on public courses. I don't need a country club.

How much more can I do?

I hate to say this, but—a lot. I love being at the academy. That's not work. I love standing with thirty or forty or fifty kids and teaching them and seeing them listening to every word I say. I owe this to the kids who go to the academy. I owe this to their parents who've sacrificed, and not just financially, to send their kids to the man who coached Agassi, Courier, Seles, and Becker. They deserve my attention.

One of the reasons I'll have more time for the academy is that my relationship with Mark Philippoussis has ended. I will continue to root for him, to hope that he develops and flourishes, but I will no longer be involved with his coaching. I ignored the warnings, I thought Nick Philippoussis and I could work together, and I was wrong. After the Australian Open, in the spring of 1996, Mr. Philippoussis decided he didn't like stepping back. He disagreed with my contention that Mark's forehand needed small, but significant adjustments. Nick stepped forward again. He chased Todd Vining, the trainer, away. Then he drove me away. He treated me like the water boy, not like a coach. Whatever I said, he said the opposite. He embarrassed me in front of other players. He embarrassed Mark, too, berated him in the locker room at Monte Carlo. His rivals should be intimidated by Mark; they should not be feeling sorry for him.

I have decided that for the foreseeable future, I am going to concentrate on my youngsters, especially on two players whose games, and personalities, have been nurtured at the academy. Tommy Haas and Anna Kournikova.

Tommy has suddenly come of age. He reached the finals of the Orange Bowl tournament at the end of 1995, and was ranked among the top five or six juniors in the world. Then, playing basketball, he broke his foot, an injury that threatened to set back his plans to play professionally and jeopardize his whole career. His recovery has been astonishing, physically and mentally. Maybe the injury prodded him, woke him up, showed him how easily he could lose everything he had worked so hard for. His game leaped up a level, or more. I now believe Tommy has the potential to be as good as, or better than, any player ever to come out of the academy. And that includes Andre Agassi. I also expect Tommy and Gregg Hill to be a top doubles team very soon.

Anna Kournikova's future is equally bright. I've had her at the academy for five years, since she was nine years old. At the end of 1995, at the age of fourteen, she won the Orange Bowl, the *eighteen*-and-unders, stamped herself the No. 1 junior in the world. A few weeks later she went out and won her first professional tournament, a small tournament in Midlands, Michigan.

I was concerned about Anna for a while. IMG spotted her in the Kremlin Cup when she was only nine, brought her from Russia to the United States, and placed her at the academy. She was a dazzling little girl, bubbling with enthusiasm. When she was ten years old, she hit with Pete Sampras on our red clay court. "I was hitting him always drop shots," she says, "and I remember him yelling and saying, 'You're beating me with drop shots!' I remember that." Anna also hit with Andre. "I felt more comfortable with Sampras," she recalls.

Anna was pampered, placed on a pedestal, hailed as the next Seles, and as she entered her teens, she thought she was Queen Tut. She was rude, conceited; in other words, she was a teenager. I began to suspect that, even though I believed Anna had superior tennis talent, she would be surpassed by Venus Williams or Martina Hingis, both of whom spent some time at the academy, both of whom made their professional debuts at fourteen.

Venus came to the academy with her sister and her father. Martina came with her mother. "The first impression brought me back to my youth in the USSR," Martina's mother wrote to me. "I thought it was huge and perfect, but cold, a sports school. But the next day, when I heard laughter and all the good ambiance, I was very impressed. We came as strangers, and we left as friends."

Right now, if I had to choose among Hingis, Williams, and Anna, I would certainly lean toward Anna. Hingis, it seems to me, has landed on a plateau; she's going to have to improve her weapons, her second serve, for instance, maybe even change some strokes, if she's going to rise to the very top level. She does have the capability to do that. Venus is still very raw, very short of competitive experience. Meanwhile,

Anna, with considerable help from her mother, Alla, has survived a couple of tough years and begun to grow on court and off. Her self-confidence is, to say the least, considerable.

Asked if she was getting too much attention after the Orange Bowl, Anna responded, "I've deserved every bit of it. I earned the attention with my results. And I've worked hard. I certainly haven't gotten the attention that some players we know have. I watched Serena and Venus Williams play and they're not that good. They've been given more attention than me, and they haven't even played tournaments. They don't know how to play points or how to win. I've put myself on the line. It's not easy to be the No. 1 seed every week with everyone trying to beat you. I've absolutely earned it all."

Then she punctuated her remarks. "To play pro tennis and be No. 1 has always been my dream and one I will not let go no matter what," she said.

Charlie Pasarell, my old friend from Puerto Rico, saw Anna and said, "With her looks, her personality, her talent, she could be bigger than Agassi, bigger than Seles." That's big. I'd love to see that. I'd love to be part of it.

> *Sometime's Nick's like a doctor to me. When I'm like sick on the court, when I don't have a good shot, he stays for one minute, watches, then tells me what to do, and I feel like perfect, like I went to the doctor. Unbelievable!*
>
> —Anna Kournikova

I'm delighted with Anna's progress. I'm delighted with Iva Majoli's, too. At seventeen, Iva jumped up among the top five or six women in the world. She came to the academy when she was thirteen, from Croatia, like Monica Seles. Bob Jellen, whose daughter was one of my students, saw Iva playing in Croatia and called me in the middle of the night to urge me to bring her to Bradenton. She's a great kid. I'm so happy for her and for her family. I'm just sorry I wasn't smart enough to realize how good she was going to be. When I first saw her, I thought she'd never be a top-ten player.

Notice something? Philippoussis. Haas. Kournikova. Majoli. Hingis. Williams. Only one of them is an American, only Venus Williams. Only one American is ranked among the top fifteen junior girls in the world. Only one American is ranked among the top thirty junior boys. Right now, at the pinnacle of tennis, we have a wonderful rivalry between Andre and Pete, a pair of Americans, but where are the future Agassis and Samprases, the future Everts and Billie Jean Kings, the McEnroes and the Connors?

I've been criticized for concentrating on non-American players, but Courier, Agassi, Wheaton, Arias, and Krickstein all came out of the academy world-class American players. But these days there don't seem to be many young Americans of that caliber. I place much of the blame on the United States Tennis Association (USTA), the organization that is supposed to promote tennis and produce quality players in the United States.

For thirty years, I've been offering my services to the USTA; for fifteen years, I've been offering the facilities of the NBTA. And for all those years, they've snubbed me. I'm not good enough for them. I remember the old days when the U.S. Open was played at Forest Hills. I never had a prayer of getting into that exclusive clubhouse. I'm not from the right side of the tracks. I don't have the proper manners, the proper grammar, the proper connections. All I do is produce tennis players, lots of them, good tennis players, some great ones. I know how important it is to get as many players as possible, and to get them young, and to teach them to enjoy the game, to love tennis, to take pleasure in playing well.

Year after year, I write to the USTA, I offer to help. I don't want to run their program. I want to support it. I've offered them some of our land. I've offered them our coaches. I hear they're afraid of me. They're afraid I want control, I want to take over. Nothing could be further from the truth. I want to teach. The USTA makes Stan Smith a coach fresh from his playing days. I have tremendous respect for Stan and for what he accomplished as a player. I know his record. He knows my record. Why doesn't he respect me for what I've accomplished as a coach? I'd like to work with Stan. I'd like to work with John McEnroe. Years ago, John belittled my tennis knowledge, but I think he's changed his mind. I think we could work well together. I think we could create excitement and create American tennis players.

I would also like to put together a team of players from the inner city, a sizable squad of minority athletes, give them the coaching and the facilities and the financial support to bring their tennis skills to the highest level. I see African-American athletes dominating football and baseball and basketball, and I want to see them excel in tennis, too.

I don't understand why the USTA, year after year, ignores my letters and my offers to work with them in upgrading American tennis. I've written to almost every USTA president in the last fifteen years, and most of them have pretended I didn't exist. The only exceptions were Randy Gregson, who was the president in the mid-1980s, and David Markin, who was the president in the late 1980s. Gregson really liked the idea of working with the NBTA and, to show good faith, sent us a nonreturnable check for $10,000. But he made one mistake. He had forgotten to consult with his fellow USTA officers. They crucified him. They shot down the idea. We got the check from the USTA but nothing else. Then, when Markin was president, he used me as a consultant, an advisor. I wanted to do more. I wrote to Bob Cookson, who succeeded Markin, saying, "Let me know how I can help you." I wrote to his successor, Bumpy Frazer, "I hope we can work closely together." I never heard a peep out of them. Why couldn't they at least answer and say, "Nick, you're an asshole?" I could understand that. But, instead, they say nothing. They go and waste hundreds of millions of dollars on redesigning and refurbishing the USTA Tennis Center at Flushing Meadows, on making it a little more comfortable for the people who can afford the $10 sandwiches and the $5 beers, and they ought to be putting that money into programs for kids, inner-city kids, country kids, anybody who wants to pick up a racquet, who wants to find out what a great game tennis can be, who is eager to learn all the lessons of life you can learn playing a sport as competitively and as cleanly and as well as you can. I can understand players dumping me, canceling me—they're individuals, subject to all the usual whims and pressures—but I can't understand why the USTA doesn't use me, doesn't take advantage of my experience and my ideas.

I don't give up. I keep writing to them. My latest letter

went out early in 1996 to Lester Snyder, the latest USTA president:

Dear Mr. Snyder:

I am writing to you, the new president of the USTA, as I have written to your predecessors for nearly three decades. I write to you with a sense of hope for the future but also with a sense of confusion and frustration concerning the USTA's nonresponsiveness to the critical problems facing America's youth. I am at a loss for words. No, I'm angered, because I can't understand why my offers of assistance have been routinely rejected by USTA officials over the past decades.

More often than not, this rejection takes the form of nonresponsiveness to my letters. Although my notoriety is based almost entirely on my success at the professional level of tennis, my heart, my energy, and my resources have always been devoted to the less talented, the grass-root players of this wonderful game. Although the media has enjoyed reporting the problems that I've had with some of my students, these altercations are everyday business with all tennis coaches. It happens that my students were Monica Seles, Andre Agassi, Boris Becker, and Mary Pierce. As a result, routine business decisions soon took on monumental proportions.

In July of 1995, I wrote to you, not only to congratulate you on your appointment as president of the USTA, but to describe a low-cost program that I was successfully using to introduce tennis to mass numbers of children. This program utilized a curriculum that enabled the children to enjoy learning to master the spatial skills required to become proficient at tennis. The program was entertaining and amusing, and at each and every test clinic, the children displayed uncontrollable enthusiasm. I offered to share this concept with you so that we could increase the number of children playing tennis in America. That was more than six months ago, and I have yet to receive a response.

I am perfectly willing to accept the fact that the past is the past, that my personal involvement was unwanted, yet my students, the products of my labor, carried the United States to countless Davis Cup victories; the products of my labor convinced America and the world that the USTA efforts to produce quality tennis players had been successful. I am willing to overlook the past because we have a much larger problem to deal with, and if we don't act decisively, the losses to our nation will overshadow any concerns that we may have about tennis.

In a recent report issued by the Carnegie Foundation, the headline read: "America's Worst Fears for the Future of Its Children Are Being Realized." The article went on to state that an alarming number of children are becoming victims of a unique type of neglect. This neglect is neglect of nurturing; the relationship that bonds mother/father and child at the earliest stages of life. This neglect is producing a generation of babies that display symptoms of violence and destructiveness at the age of three months. Without intervention, without an attempt to restore the self-esteem of these children

in the earliest, most formative years of their lives, this
generation of children will destroy America. Another
study, published in *Pediatrics* magazine, indicates that one
in every four children suffers from some kind of abuse.
This study showed that the most vulnerable children are
Hispanics and blacks. Northern Kentucky University
conducted a study in 1993 that showed that forty-nine
percent of all elementary schoolchildren in the United
States lack the fundamental skills needed to participate
in sports activity. Finally, a recent study by the National Center for Health Statistics and the President's
Council on Physical Fitness and Sports shows large numbers of adults participating in fitness programs but more
children overweight and underexercised. How can those
of us in positions of strength sit idly by while America's youth deteriorates under our noses?

Although these statistics are daunting and the voices
of America's social conscience are getting louder and
more terrified, this situation is not new. Long before
the USTA's Minority Participation Initiative [MPI] was
established to include minorities in all segments of the
tennis community, Arthur Ashe and I developed the
Ashe-Bollettieri "Cities" Tennis Program. Our program
has been addressing these social problems for nearly
eight years now, but keep in mind that Arthur and I
wanted to administer this program *with* the USTA. We
offered our hand in unity back in 1987 and we were rebuffed. Back in the late 1980s, we raised and spent
more than the USTA now commits to its entire MPI
program. We understood that the USTA might not

want to join hands in a prototype program that was
being operated by another group, so Arthur and I pro-
ceeded on our own. We went into the inner cities and
developed a successful formula that we were anxious to
share with the rest of America. We again offered our
hand to the USTA in unity. Again, we were rebuffed.

Instead of devoting resources to the real problems
facing America, a new stadium is being constructed (at
Flushing Meadows) at a cost of more than $200 mil-
lion. I realize that Bud Collins and I share a degree of
confusion as to the wisdom of this expenditure, and
many will say that it will generate more money to help
expand the sport. This may be true, but there are three
other realities to be considered:

1. The problems facing America are tearing at the
   very fabric of life in this country and a new stadium only permits twice as many affluent people
   to view the U.S. Open.
2. Historically, the USTA resources are not used to
   address the issues of inclusion, but that these resources are used to generate more money and to
   create greater exclusivity.
3. The interest alone on the $200 million price tag
   could easily address the more important issues
   facing the tennis industry, namely, the children.

In conclusion, I want it to be clear that I want *only*
to make the sport of tennis as beneficial to all as it has
been to the few. You are the president of the governing

body of tennis in America, and I want to encourage
you and support your efforts to improve the game. If
you accept my help, then I will not only help you to establish a moral paradigm that the other youth-serving
agencies should follow, but I'll help you raise American
tennis to a level never achieved before. In addition, I'll
help generate the sponsors to underwrite the effort. If,
however, you don't want my help, please take the time
to call or write so that I may understand why my offers
of assistance have been consistently declined.

Sincerely,

Nick Bollettieri

President and Founder

Bollettieri Tennis and Sports Academy

I still haven't heard from Mr. Snyder, but a few days after
I wrote the letter, I went to a junior tournament in the
south of France. I saw a thirteen-year-old girl there who was
unbelievable. She played like she was from another planet.
She was from Croatia, just like Monica and Iva. Her name
was Jelana Pandzic. I invited her to live and train at the
academy.

You know, with the right coaching, I think she can be
a champion.

ACKNOWLEDGMENTS

Nick Bollettieri and Dick Schaap would like to thank all of the players, coaches, officials, friends, relatives, and reporters who, in person, in letters, and on the telephone, offered up their thoughts about Nick—his aces and his faults.

We owe a special debt to Mary Carillo and Bud Collins, two of the most articulate and knowledgeable of tennis reporters, both of whom read the manuscript and spotted and corrected errors of fact and emphasis. The errors that remain are, of course, our own.

We both are grateful to our families, especially to Jimmy Bollettieri, whose magnificent photographs brighten these pages; Danielle Bollettieri, who checked countless names and dates; Joanna Schaap, who transcribed tapes of Nick's recollections; and Jeremy Schaap, who, besides transcribing tapes, gathered pertinent magazine articles, newspaper clippings, and reference books.

Tennis Week, Gene Scott's handsome periodical, provided invaluable background; so did *International Tennis Weekly,* the official newsletter of the ATP Tour. Peter Alfano, the ATP's vice president for communications, was unfailingly helpful.

Lou Aronica, our publisher, was patient and encouraging at all times, and David Black, our agent, who brought us together with Avon Books, offered wise and constructive counsel. Thanks, too, to Ted Meekma, who reviewed the manuscript as a lawyer and as a friend.

Nick would also like to acknowledge the great support of his NBTA sponsors—including Adidas, which keeps him in clothes and shoes; Penn, which provides him with tennis balls; Oakley, which keeps his eyes shaded; Head, which gives him racquets to wield; Sarasota Ford, which keeps him in wheels; Life Fitness, Body Masters, and Hammer Strength, which keep him in shape; and Swiss Army Watches, which keep him punctual—and of his friends and associates, so many of whom are quoted and mentioned in the text of the book. If Nick had his way, he would also have quoted, mentioned, and praised Gabe Jaramillo, Steve Owens, Steve Shulla, Richie Schutzman, Don Engel, Jack Schneider, Bernie Schmidt, and Terry Kennedy. If he missed anyone, which he probably did, Nick apologizes and says, please remember, he has always been lousy with names.

INDEX

INDEX

INDEX

INDEX

INDEX

INDEX

INDEX

INDEX

INDEX